Women in Asia Publication Series

A WORLD OF DIFFERENCE

A WORLD OF DIFFERENCE

Islam and Gender Hierarchy in Turkey

Julie Marcus

London and New Jersey

First published in 1992
Allen & Unwin Pty Ltd

Published in the rest of the world outside of Australia, New Zealand,
Southeast Asia and South Asia in 1992 by Zed Books Ltd,
57 Caledonian Road, London N1 9BU, UK and 165 First Avenue,
Atlantic Highlands, New Jersey 07716, USA.

ISBN 1 85649 185 4.
ISBN 1 85649 186 2 (pbk.).

A catalogue record for this book is available from the British Library.
US CIP is available from the Library of Congress.

Set in 10/11pt Times by Graphicraft Typesetters Ltd, Hong Kong
Printed by Kim Hup Lee Printing, Singapore

Contents

Preface

The illusion that by getting ever closer to our data we will somehow know and understand more, and that knowing more is knowing better, is crucial to the structuring assumptions of anthropology. It is an illusion convincingly disposed of by both Einsteinian theories of general relativity concerning space/time and the uncertainty principle of an opposing quantum mechanics which shows that the more accurately you try to measure position, the less accurately you can measure speed, and vice versa (Hawking 1988). The commonsense assumptions of the nature of the natural world, that time and space are fixed entities and that its physical properties can be accurately known, are embedded in cultural models of both nature and culture. They therefore constitute barriers to understanding the world in the ways we have previously considered suitable. The aim of this book is to show how one element of those familiar commonsense natural worlds is constructed around racism and sexism, and to show how difficult it is to work beyond them. I hope to make clear the ways in which an ethnography is the product of a particular politics and a particular time; how the interests and experience of the researcher constitute a narrative and textual politics; and how this individually deployed politics is necessarily part of the myriad ways in which the relations of power of dominating economies are reproduced through their representations of other's cultures. Despite the critical intent of the analysis, it is my intention to offer some hope as well as showing the difficulty of the task facing those who would always know more and better. That hope comes, of course, from an illusion, but it is hope nonetheless.

While it may be clear that all knowledge is uncertain, unstable, constructed and imposed through relations of power, it is here that hope lies. There is no need to abandon the search for a more adequate approximation, or the desire for a more just and equitable society, simply because exactitude and certainty are denied and the shifting

vii

nature of truth exposed. For in the knowledge of the constructed nature of truths lies the possibility of reconstructing knowledges. What is needed is the determination to accept the inevitability of power and the individual and social responsibility for altering it that such inevitability implies. But in order to approximate better and to reconstruct, the politics of knowledge and the ways in which particular constellations of truths are enforced must be laid bare.

I shall be arguing that religious beliefs have a much greater significance in a supposedly secularised world than is sometimes recognised, and that this is the case for both nominally Muslim and nominally Christian regions of the Mediterranean. I shall also argue that the shifting of certain of the narratives of western knowledge from domains perceived as religious to those perceived as anti-religious, has little impact on the popularity and pervasiveness of important aspects of the ways in which we inhabit constructed and imposed worlds of similarity and difference. The central questions of difference which occupy so much scholarly and political space today cannot be resolved outside those of gender. In other words, within western knowledge today there is only one real question: that of gender.

The refusal of so many of the recognised and respected social and cultural theorists of our time to reflect upon or reframe their work within the parameters laid out by the variety of feminist critiques is the source of the failure to be found within much mainstream western social thought today. Whereas women writing from a variety of feminist theoretical positions routinely scrutinise malestream theory for its value, limitations and applicability, male scholars of critical importance like Eco, Barthes, Habermas, Foucault or Derrida rarely reflect upon the implications of feminist critiques for their own projects, rarely grant feminist theorists the formal consideration and textual space that their male colleagues receive. Foucault, for example, manages to write a history of sexuality without mentioning women, while his volume on homosexuality in ancient Greece gives one line to lesbianism. In this context, the rise of the field known as the 'new masculinity' within the humanistic disciplines indicates both the threat of feminist theory and the direction taken by men who purport to engage with it. In the 'new' masculinism, the liberationary thrust of feminist theory is perverted into a reinscription of 'liberated' men at the newly formed, feminised centre, with the question of women and their oppression by men once more marginalised. Similarly, what we often see today in a supposedly post-colonial, critical or 'new' anthropology is a strength built upon reaction, a strength built upon the obliteration of feminist discourse, its interests and its challenges to men from anthropological theory. Today, the major arguments within the discipline of anthropology remain arguments among men and about men, arguments about the matters men consider important; those matters remain those of the past—relations between men. As a result, the solutions they propose fail to address the essential gendered politics of their problems, and their project of writing the author into the 'new' texts fails through the inability to reconceive the author as gendered without lapsing into sexual self-indulgence. Their solutions are effete.

My work here is a description of the engendered structuralist approach to Turkish society that I worked out during the late seventies, together with an account of how that approach emerged from a personal and narrative politics. As that project developed, its focus shifted away from the original attempt to describe the lives of Turkish women, toward the questions surrounding the construction of a hierarchy of genders. As a result, this book does not canvass the scope of Turkish women's experiences, but seeks out those overarching elements of religious practice which refer to the placing of women and men in a hierarchical relationship. It is intended to explore one possible path and to point to both its limitations and its possibilities. It is also an account of the politics of knowledge which produced that approach and the ways in which the focus on gender led me to consider problems of comparison (of determining the parameters of similarity and difference) as both central and political. As I said above, I see my work as offering hope rather than despair, and as pointing to several areas and methods for a future anthropology. In reworking my doctoral dissertation into a manuscript for publication, I have tried to show the ways in which the author is implicated in the text, and to do so in ways which do not rely on obfuscating terminology. How successful I have been can only be determined by the reader. In my commitment to exposing the politics of knowledge lie the critiques of both my research and my politics. This is as it should be.

The final revision of this manuscript began on January 15, 1991, a day on which the world waited to hear whether yet another frightful war was to begin. The familiar tropes of orientalism were replayed in each day's press and television news reporting with all the force and cohesiveness that state propaganda machines could muster. Once again, the racialised stereotypes of orientalism were expressed, and once again, the difficulty found by so many well-educated, liberal and well-informed citizens in speaking outside them, became apparent. As George Bush labelled Saddam Hussein the 'rapist' of Kuwait, as the people and policies of Iraq appeared in American media reporting as effeminised, 'black' and irrational, the essential gendered nature of these categories was laid bare. The creation of representations, the fabrication of difference through violence, the structural deployment of gender and sexualities, lie at the heart of dominating, international understandings of the nature of the world. Work aiming to provide a critique of the interactions of gender and sexuality with orientalist racism therefore takes on a greater urgency.

Many have contributed to making this book possible and here I mention only a few. I should like to thank Ian Smith for his valuable logistical support during fieldwork in Turkey, for accepting such a disruptive project into his life, and for providing many of the photographs. Of the European residents who helped settle me into Izmir and opened their homes and minds to me, I should like to thank Evelyn Kalças, Ruth Pope and Yvonne Winterhalter for their very special kind of friendship. Of my Turkish friends, Vedat and Güldan Toga offered consistent help and interest far beyond the call of either duty or hospitality, and for this I am very grateful. Although this is not the book they will be expecting, nevertheless it could never have been written without them. I should like to thank, too, those at Bogaziçi University, Istanbul, the Middle East Technical University, Ankara, and particularly all at the Aegean University in Izmir who helped me find my way through the tribulations of the early days of fieldwork.

I also thank Kate North for working so hard on turning an oblique, discursive shambles into something more readable. I know the effort cost her dearly and remain indebted to her for it. Lenore Manderson's thoughtful comments on the text have been consistently valuable and greatly appreciated. I am grateful for the support and discussion provided by Shirley Ardener and Helen Callaway at the Centre for Cross-Cultural Research on Women, Oxford, and to all the women participating in the seminars and conferences organised there for the scholarly and helpful environment they created; and to Renée Hirschon of the Aegean University and Oxford Polytechnic for her unstinting encouragement and friendship. I wish to thank all those who harassed me into completing a text so long overdue that it risked never being born at all; Anna Yeatman, Margaret Jolly, Nicholas Thomas and Andrew Lattas for helpful discussion; and Andrea Malone for making it possible. Funding for this project was provided by Macquarie University, Sydney, and I am grateful for the freedom and stimulation offered by my supervisors, Chandra Jayawardena and Ian Bedford and for the helpful and constructive comments provided by my examiners; to Shirley Dean who saw me through it all; and to Annette Hamilton for continuing and timely encouragement. The editorial assistance of Susan Blackburn, editor of this series, has been consistently constructive and unfailingly helpful.

And finally, I wish to dedicate this book to my parents, Annette Western Marcus and Alexander Marcus, in recognition of the opportunities they provided which allowed their six unruly offspring the latitude necessary to develop into independent and critical adults.

1 Travelling to the Orient

While still at school I came across a copy of *The Wilder Shores of Love* (1954) by Lesley Blanch. Her vivid descriptions of courageous and flamboyant women who, despite hardship and privation, gave their all for love and adventure in the east, awakened an interest that has lasted a lifetime. Blanch told of the magnificent Jane Digby el Mezrab, who set out to buy Arab bloodstock in Syria, of Aimée Dubucq de Rivery, captured by pirates and sold to the Ottoman Sultan, and of dissolute and desperate Isabelle Eberhardt, dressing as a man but enjoying clandestine sexual relations with an Algerian soldier. Her description of the fateful meeting between Isabel Burton and her reckless husband-to-be, Richard Burton of the magnificent black eyes, led me first to Burton's own account of his dangerous mission to Mecca, and later to the gold-embossed leather-bound volumes on my father's bookshelf, *The Inner Life of Syria* (1876) by Isabel Burton herself.

Isabel's account of her wild gallops across the Syrian plain, her visits to harems, her accounts of her neighbours, both European and Syrian, and her encounters with the fascinating world of the orient, created within me a desire to do as she had done, to follow in the footsteps of these bold, and sometimes bad, women. She had wanted to step out of the cold, hard world of Europe into a romantic and colourful orient in which she might be free, but my early desire to lose myself in the romance and hardships of the east had first to be met vicariously.

I came to read travel books of all kinds and my mind roved freely across the globe. Those I loved most were the tales of daring and endurance produced by travellers who had been to the Middle East: Lawrence of Arabia, Arminius Vambéry, Richard Burton, and many others less well known. With them came the letters, diaries and reminiscences of government officials, governesses and engineers, many of the most distinguished of diarists being, of course, women. I read the letters from Turkey of Lady Mary Wortley Montagu, quite failing

1

to understand the personal tragedy which lay behind them, and I read of Gertrude Bell, her exploits, her service to a fading empire and her death in Iraq. Theirs was the world I sought.

When, much later, my travels took me from Australia to Europe and then to teach English to a French family in Morocco, I was delighted. Morocco was wonderful. The colours of the countryside, the picture-book mountains, a climate that was invigorating, fabulous wildflowers, colourful local dress, a variety of tribes and bazaars— everything was just as I had expected. The names of the towns alone were enough to cause a frisson of excitement. In Marrakesh, the latticed shadows of the markets fell upon woodturners, metal beaters, engravers, perfumiers and dyers as they worked at traditional trades. There was the scent of cedar, of musk, rosewater and hashish. There were beggars wearing the scars of congenital syphilis, watersellers in shady hats carrying goatskins of cool drinking water. In the great square of the city, storytellers entranced their audiences, dervishes danced and a metal-collared monkey performed amazing, if reluctant, tricks. We wandered through goats, chickens and children in Berber villages plastered neatly onto terrifyingly steep hillsides, and saw the fabled blue men on their camels, transitory desert raiders, come in to the Atlas towns. In Fez, intricate city of narrow streets and oriental buildings, the white-robed men were often of an elegance unparalleled in Europe. The King's brilliantly dressed black guards were constantly on parade in Rabat; on the great Islamic feast days alms were cast from the tower of the King's palace to a seething crowd below in a riveting scene that I experienced as medieval. One day, as I walked towards the town, a solitary man in long and flowing robes sitting sidesaddle on his loaded donkey trotted briskly along the path beside the red mud, castellated walls of the old Chellah. For a moment I felt as if I were in Palestine at the time of Christ, and that He would shortly come around the corner. The timeless oriental illusion was complete.

As I left for the airport after six months working and living among the expatriate French and British of Rabat, I was painfully aware that I had not one Moroccan friend, spoke not a single word of Arabic and knew nothing whatsoever about either Islam or the daily lives of the Moroccans among whom I had lived. The first longed-for journey out to the east had failed. I had intended to be friendly and had very much wanted to get to know as many Moroccans as possible. Instead, I had been a spectator at a brilliant pageant but never even approached the possibility of entering into the scene myself. I had lived comfortably among people remarkably like me, and whatever I learnt of Moroccans, those people had taught me. I had learned a great deal about the conservative and disciplined French bourgeoisie, a little about the French army and its work in Indochina and Algeria, and a little, too, about the French colonists of north Africa, the *pieds noirs*. The Moroccans I had met were domestic workers, shopkeepers and policemen. I had not said two words to a local woman.

By the time I came to do anthropological fieldwork in Turkey I was better prepared. I had spent three months in London learning the rudiments of Turkish grammar and syntax, and over some years of reading had developed a knowledge of at least the parameters of Ottoman history, the ethnic composition of the country, its geography and its political economy; and had learnt, too, of the fierce desire of Turks to secularise, modernise and take their independent place on the world stage. I had read through the scholarly debates on the nature of Islamic cities, the arguments concerning the differences between European and Islamic empires which explained why capitalism arose in feudal Europe rather than in urban, technologically superior Turkey, and the varying accounts of the ways in which Islam affected the lives of Turks and, particularly, Turkish women. I was fascinated by the idea of the traditional markets I had read of in the medieval period and thought that I had seen in Marrakesh, and was convinced from my reading that the banned craft guilds which traced their ancestry back to the Ottoman era and beyond were almost certainly still alive and active in Turkey. And more than that, I wanted to see the Mevlevi dervishes in action and to discover what remained of the other important dervish orders of the past. It was the aspects of modern Turkish life that were submerged and hidden from the casual eye that proved so fascinating. I had also read the great travel books, searched through them to try to piece together an ethnography of earlier years; I had been captivated by the drama and colour of the oriental lives portrayed within them. How could present day Turkey be understood without taking this great and romantic past into account?

At that time, it seemed to me that any study of contemporary Turkish social life must take Ottoman history into account. This was particularly the case because of the long urban tradition to be found in Turkey and the eastern Mediterranean region. At a time when Europe consisted of little more than muddy villages separated by vast expanses of almost trackless forest, Persia, Anatolia and Syria had been glorious seats of learning and mercantile activity, sites of an urban prosperity, culture and dominance which was not lost until recently. And because of Turkey's urban past, its urban 'nature' almost, it seemed essential to study urban rather than village or tribal life. Paul Stirling's *Turkish Village* seemed to me to epitomise the limitations of traditional ethnography applied in countries like Turkey. It was not that the detail of certain aspects of village life provided by Stirling was itself uninteresting or unrepresentative, but that the village appeared as a tiny isolated cosmos, cut off from the ferment and activity of the rest of the nation. To me, village social relationships seemed as much the product of their poverty as anything distinctively or 'traditionally' Turkish. Because of their poverty and Stirling's avoidance of anything to do with religion, villagers appeared as a people without culture, and as living somehow outside history.

Some of these defects could have been remedied by locating the village in an economic, geographical and historical context. After all, the villages Stirling studied were not far from Kayseri, a town noted for its canny businessmen and crafty dealers with an urban history going back at least to the days of the Romans. And no matter how isolated by muddy tracks and winter snows, Stirling's villagers were of necessity welded into that greater economic and administrative network within which they had to live. By ignoring all this, the villagers and Turkey itself appeared oddly disconnected from time and place so that they became less comprehensible and, of course, less relevant. Stirling's book was probably the last of this long and venerable line of ethnographies, exemplary but dated even as it appeared. Later village studies focused precisely on the interaction of local and national variables and succeeded in situating their villagers and small townsmen within a more recognisable world. Still, Turkish culture sometimes seemed of limited relevance to these works too, and the Turkishness, or specificity, of the lives they described through studies of economic relations, industrialisation, geographical relationships and trade were far from clear. Despite my own interest in markets, petty commodity production and trade, it was through the culture of markets that I hoped to comprehend their economics rather than the other way around. So I sought some form of 'traditional' market to study, one more closely related to my oriental reading and my travels in Morocco, one in which a 'real' market *culture* with its dense web of social relations might reasonably be found. The big factories, the cement, fertiliser and car industries, these were international in origin and structure and had little about them that seemed to me distinctively Turkish.

I began to read systematically about the medieval markets and their industries: the fabulous brocaded silks of Bursa, produced by slaves as well as free labour; the leather industries renowned for their supple product; the goldsmiths and jewellers. These early Ottoman industries were structured and organised through the guilds and through religious affiliation. Mosques and their schools were located near them. As I wandered through the markets of Izmir and Bursa, by casting my mind back to Marrakesh and Fez, I could visualise the activities of the bustling medieval merchants who had preceded me. For information on the period just before Atatürk's secular republic (created in 1923) I went to the first-hand narrative accounts provided by the nineteenth century travellers, not only of those who had been through Turkey, but also the orientalist classics describing other regions, other climes. These works included Edward William Lane's *Manners and Customs of the Modern Egyptians* (1836), *Hajji Baba of Ispahan* in which the English author (Morier 1895) cloaks himself in Persian guise in order to write about European culture, and Goitein's (1979) detailed scholarly work on Jewish life in medieval Cairo.

As I read, it seemed to me that Izmir, the Smyrna of the Greeks, might be the city I was looking for. Izmir's genealogy was impeccable on any timescale—because of its place in the great trading empires, it had often had an important role as a port city of some wealth and culture. There had been a town on the site, on and off, for millennia. Polyglot and cosmopolitan for centuries, this most literary of merchant cities shared the romantic ambience of Lawrence Durrell's Alexandria.[1] The Hittites had passed close to Izmir, Greeks (pagan and Christian), Romans, Crusaders and Seljuks in their turn. Then came the Ottoman Turks and the Levantine Greeks again. To the Greeks, Smyrna had been the apple of their Aegean eye, their tragic gateway to resurgent Hellenism in Asia Minor. But for me, Izmir was a city providing the backdrop upon which the last great struggle between the European powers and the crippled Ottoman caliph, the West and its Orient, could be read. Nineteenth century Izmir contained all the elements essential to the conflagration to come, and on its ruins the new and purified republican Turkey would rise. In the troubles of Izmir lay the troubles of Europe as well as those of the Turks, distilled and clear for those who would see.

So I set out for Izmir.

Learning of the past

On my first visit to Izmir's market I bought a small copper coin bearing the mark of ancient Smyrna, the double-headed axe of the Amazon women. The Greek name of Smyrna is preserved in its Turkish etymology, Izmir. The sense of immediacy caused by three thousand years of western history was very strong: the history of a city, the history of a world long gone. I had sought out a city with history but how to write it and why? What illumination of Turkish life is to be found in history that cannot be known from the present? Or, should not the pasts of the Turks be sought elsewhere than in ancient Greece—in the Turkic lands of central Asia, in their religion from Arabia, and in the glories of the Seljuk and Ottoman Empires?

But even standing in that clamorous city, in which the fumes of traffic obliterated the scent of orange groves and almond orchards, it seemed incredible somehow that the Turkish city of today should be severed entirely from the 1500 Greek years of its recorded past. Even a cursory glance at Izmir's recent history shows how deeply the Greeks are embedded within it. It was from Izmir that the Greeks launched their ill-fated attempt to regain their ancient Asian provinces (the eastern shore of their Mediterranean) and it was at Izmir that the Turks finally pushed the Greeks back into the sea and declared their new republic. That last Greek invasion of Izmir can be understood as a clear example of the themes and fantasies of *ancient* histories being played out in the present, and the disastrous consequences flowing from their unrestrained and unreflective realisation. Within it can be found again the crusading zeal that comes from pitting a 'west' against an 'east', 'Christian' against 'Muslim', European 'civilisation' against Oriental 'barbarism'. An understanding of the invasion must therefore be set within the histories which produced its possibility, as well as within the context of British machinations and schemings, and Greek fantasies of their classic greatness.

Izmir has two very different genealogies, two separate trajectories through time. One follows its place in the history of the steady movement of Turks from central Asia towards Europe and Japan which led eventually to the glories, achievements and efficiencies of four centuries of Ottoman rule. The other is embedded within the history of western knowledge and leads along a path moving from the east through ancient Greece to the modern west. These two currents flowed into opposition in the eighteenth and nineteenth centuries, when the European nations sought to expand their economic and political influence, or to prevent others expanding, across the Anatolian plateau towards India and into the 'far' east. Until recently, those conflicting histories were often written in the crudest and most chauvinist of forms. The history of the Ottoman Empire has been written in terms of rise and fall, the fall being attributed to an internal moral corruption gnawing away at the empire's vital parts. The history of European capital expansion and political thrust across western Asia, however, has been written in terms of the endless rise of a competitive and superior moral and political order. In these histories, the long struggle of European capitalists to infiltrate the Ottoman Empire has been transcribed into an archetypical struggle between East and West. The question here is not one therefore, of how to make sense of the present through writing the past into it, but rather one of how European historical knowledge is constructed and of the place of Izmir within those constructions.

I came to know Izmir's European past from two separate but related sources. The ancient past I knew through the vast collections of antiquities in European and Australian museums. Those collections made the Greek myths and the ancient history which I read at school more tangible, so that when I arrived in Izmir I knew something of the great events of the ancient world which had involved the city. In this chapter I take up the problems created by the place of Izmir's past in western narratives of the east, particularly the ways in which western ideas about its origins are mapped onto an Aegean landscape known to us through our histories of the ancient Greeks. My intention to incorporate history into an anthropological study of Izmir encouraged the exploration of the ancient Greek past of Turkey, and I began a series of visits to the fabulous archaeological sites nearby. I also visited the great museums of Turkey and was prompted to read Homer, Pliny the Younger, other Greek and Roman writers, and accounts of the social life of the ancient period. Naturally the sense of the past in the present became very strong, bolstering the sense of continuity contained within much of the literature on Turkey's past. The road leading from the Anatolian plateau down to Izmir's harbour, for example, runs beside the grey and white slabs of marble that Alexander laid, and shoppers at the Sunday market on Eshref Pasha walk along that Alexandrian road as they jostle to buy the luxuriant fruit and vegetables for which the city has been justly famous. That road seems an intrusion of the lost Alexandrian world into the present, one which demands recognition, and value. Yet it is only those reared upon a diet of their 'classical heritage' and driven by the desire to prove the truth of their record of their past, who can truly value such slabs of marble. Without their place in western historical narratives of conquest and civilisation those slabs are nothing; they cannot be recognised and carry only the utilitarian value attributed to them by shoppers. My naturalising sense of the presence of the past in the present was itself one of the illusions which western histories create, an example of the constitutive power of history over individual consciousness. It is also one of the ways of maintaining the subordination of the Turks within those essentially western histories.

The more recent past I first knew mainly through the eyes of travellers rather than those of scholarly historians. I read the delightful vignette of the colonial atmosphere in the town during the springtime of the last days of the Ottoman Empire provided by Tugay, one of the few Turkish writers to publish in English, who went to Izmir in 1910:

> We arrived to find spring at its most lovely in Izmir. White and yellow climbing roses framed every doorway and formed canopies over the narrow streets, growing along wires stretched from one side to the other. Carpets of wild red anemones with dark purple hearts grew on the hills, under the olive groves. The scent of jasmine and syringas perfumed the suburbs of Buca and Bornova, where a large colony of Whittalls and families connected with them by marriage owned palatial houses built of pink, green or yellow stone, quarried nearby. (Tugay 1963: 275)

I read also of the camel caravans travelling along roads unsuited to wheeled traffic:

> Strings of camels ... continually passing, each comprising about forty-five, and headed by a man upon an ass who leads the first, the others being mostly connected by slight cords. It is a beautiful sight to see the perfect training and docility of these animals ... I have just watched a string of them stopping on an open plain: a child twitched the cord suspended from the head of the first; a loud gurgling growl indicated the pleasure of the camel as it awkwardly knelt down, and the child, who could just reach its back, unlinked the hooks which suspended from either side of the bales of cotton; another child came with a bowl of water and sponge,

and was welcomed by a louder roar of pleasure as it washed the mouth and nostrils of the animal. On a given signal in the afternoon, at about three o'clock, every camel resumed its own place, and knelt between its bales, which were again attached ... I am not surprised at finding the strong attachment of these animals to the children; for I have often seen three or four of them, when young, lying with their heads inside a tent in the midst of the sleeping children, while their long bodies remained outside. (Fellows 1852: 220)

It was this Izmir, the city of scented docks, camel trains, raisins, colourful robes and lilac hedges, that I came in search of. A British archaeologist travelling through Izmir in 1840 had described the bustle I sought:

The variety of trades, the novelty of the articles for sale, the busy scene among the camels and porters, contrasted with the composure of the shopkeeper, who, with his luxurious pipe in his hand, awaits patiently on his cushioned couch the call of a chance customer ... the harmonious cries of the traders, and the sonorous bells of the passing camels ... The shops for the sale of eatables are very numerous, and mostly for dried fruits and sweetmeats. There are also many for the favourite food of the Turks, which is principally composed from the produce of the dairy ... The total absence of shops for the sale of stimulants, of spirituous or fermented liquors, still continues a striking feature ... (Fellows 1852: 232–3)

The composed shopkeeper was easily found, even if the 'luxurious pipe', the *nargileh*, was now most readily seen in the tea shops along the waterfront.

These processes of searching for and locating the 'real', the 'authentic' and the interesting, replicate a past into the future through deeply felt personal experience; they illustrate the ways in which the narrative past becomes an integral part of any individual's present. The present thereby comes to be known through the prism of a particular past— and that past is essentially textual and narrative. This is why it is important to show how the process of writing itself works to produce a new text; and why the past is so politically important and must be written into an account of a present which seeks to disentangle itself, even if only to a small degree, from the shackles of its predecessors.

There are other reasons for giving some thought to the past, of course. The amount of interest shown by national governments of all political persuasions in determining and exploring their pasts should signal its political role in justifying particular claims to land, culture, legitimacy and identity. But these points go without saying, and are not the ones I take up here. My intention is to illustrate the ways in which the processes of writing the western past, particularly those of the travelling and mapping through which it becomes known, become an impediment to observation, shaping careful observation into recognisable and familiar narratives that are part of European, rather than Turkish, history.

My Izmir was essentially a creation of the literature I had read and the knowledge accumulated from the museums and galleries I had visited. I had come to know the city, just as I had come to know Turkey, through the European texts and monuments I had consumed. My journey to Turkey not only replicated those which had preceded me but was, in a very real sense, the product of those earlier journeys. Because of this, an ever-increasing store of facts about Izmir's past could not address the problems posed by the politics of the underlying narrative structures of history-writing. Indeed, the more I sought the 'truth' of Izmir's past in the accumulation of detailed facts, the more immersed I became in the European preconceptions and fantasies about the orient.

When I arrived in Turkey, the hotel to which I was recommended was the Pera Palas where, from the palatial rooms and spacious baths of an earlier time, one looked out over the romantic Golden Horn. This is the hotel which perhaps best epitomises the European view of what the Orient really is. Built by Thomas Cook as the eastern terminus to the vast rail network along which the Orient Express travelled, it makes manifest the European dream of oriental splendour and projects it back upon the tourists journeying out in search of it. It was to Thomas Cook's tiled arabesques of the Pera Palas that Agatha Christie went to get some 'authentic' local colour for the murder mystery, *The Orient Express*, and many others have done the same. Its creaking birdcage lift, the conveniently placed spittoons, the delightful ceilings and tiles and, in 1978, its atmosphere of genteel decay—here was comfort *and* authenticity. The Pera Palas becomes a monument of real eastern-ness, an expression of the essential difference between an 'east' and its 'west', one through which we know the nature of the imaginary orient. It is within the nostalgia for that well-designed and controlled European orient that travellers now find their comfort, and it is through this comforting form of familiar and well-travelled orientalised 'difference' that they come to know the Turks. For me, as for so many others, the Pera Palas became both a comforting and an ironically appropriate place for the beginning of my journey into a Turkey which I knew largely through travellers' tales.

Travel narratives pose problems for the way in which western histories of the orient are experienced. They utilise familiar distinctions between traditional and modern, east and west, active and passive, black and white, primitive and civilised, female and male, in order to create a safe world of difference in which the oriental, the Middle Easterner, Middle Eastern religions, cultures and societies will always appear as unchangeable essences which, no matter how sympathetically described, are somehow always *less* than those of the Western European to which they stand opposed. The processes of European mapping were particularly important in the imperial eighteenth and nineteenth centuries of discovery, but although I shall concentrate on these centuries here, the forces motivating these mappings are by no means limited to them. Constantly recreated through tourism, pilgrimage and the re-reading of nineteenth century travel narratives that tell how it 'really' was in the uncontaminated past, and thus how we should see it now, mappings are as creatively active today as ever.[2] Through the history of Izmir, processes which I discuss as fantasies, dreams and mappings have a gruesome reality of their own which, I believe, cannot be understood only as economics. But how do fantasy and economy feed upon each other to produce such unsavoury offspring?

2   Izmir, the 'Infidel City'

It is common for people who know Turkey well to say that Izmir is not *really* a Turkish city—it is too 'westernised' and therefore cannot be authentically Turkish. Izmir is too Greek, they said when I arrived there; it is *still* the 'Infidel City' of the Turks, a city always Greek. So often was this said to me before arriving in Izmir that I was relieved to find that Izmir's people *did* speak Turkish, were Muslims, and considered themselves Turks of the very best kind. Despite its Turkish populace, the opinion that Izmir is somehow 'still' a Greek city is widespread and rests upon both the notion of some kind of folk memory able to transmit the ancient primordial essences of a past otherwise invisible, and that the real Turkey is not 'western' as the Greeks were western, but 'oriental'. In other words, Izmir's correct narrative geography (its place in western mappings of the world), and essential nature are contested.

Between Greek Smyrna and Turkish Izmir lies a turning point within the history of the Ottomans, one which Turks understand well and have thoroughly evaluated. To reach an understanding of the present, the significance of the gradually widening gap between the Byzantine past of Izmir and the Ottoman city which it later became must be grasped. The arrival of the Turks on the Aegean mainland coast provides a real rupture in European narratives of the uninterrupted Greekness which triumphed first over its eastern and 'Asiatic' predecessors, Hellenised the conquering Romans and later, Christianity; a Greekness represented as continuous and encompassing, no matter what the swings of local fortune, standing in contrast to (if not always resisting) the seduction and the threat of the forces of the 'orient'. Yet the changes wrought by the slow conquests of the Turks were assimilated into western historical narratives as an eclipse rather than a total rupture, in which the essential Greekness of western 'civilisation', like the sun, remains in place, later to shine out as strongly as before.

11

The failure to recognise the nature and significance of this particular rupture in the European narrative is not without consequence. In Izmir, the fantasy of a continuing Greek presence in the 'Asiatic' Aegean provinces had the very serious repercussions that I referred to earlier in this chapter. It led directly to the British-backed Greek invasion of Izmir in 1919. When people today refer to 'Infidel Izmir', and speak of the Turkish dislike of the Greeks, they are using an epithet which originated in the battles between those earliest Christian European travellers to 'their' sacred land, the Crusaders, and the nomad, colonising Turks, moving steadily westwards, whom they encountered.

From the tenth century onwards, waves of central Asian Turks and Mongols fought and migrated their way across Anatolia. As they succeeded, they built roads and bridges, hostelries and mosques, and established their dynasties and states as permanently as they could. But until the Ottomans managed to subdue their own competing kin as well as the Greeks, much of Anatolia was of the nature of a vacillating frontier. The long period of conquest, reconquest and settlement produced both the destruction resulting from centuries of war and the processes of assimilation that a long period of negotiation implies. While the Aegean coast was more likely to be devastated by Europeans than Turks, from 1344 until 1402 Izmir was a divided city. The upper, Alexandrian, city nestling around the castle on the hill was held by Turks and known by them as 'Muslim Izmir'. The lower city, huddled around the harbour, was held by Crusaders; this was the 'Infidel Izmir' (Ülker 1974:16) of the Turks. With all the major trading cities of Byzantium falling to the Ottomans by the fourteenth century (Inalcik 1973), tiny Izmir was finally taken in 1424. The Turkish conquest took close on three centuries of continuous strife, with most Christian Greeks killed, deported or converted (Vryonis 1971). By then, Anatolia was largely Muslim (Inalcik 1970[b]: 306), with trade and commerce entirely in Ottoman hands.

With the rupture with the ancient Asian landscape of Greece brought about by the decisive Ottoman presence, the mapping of those lands by European travellers took on a new significance. The familiarities of Greek Asia became the strangeness and opulence of the European orient, the land became foreign, and the location of the originary past of Europe had to be re-established through the processes of exploration, discovery and language. The European Renaissance, the rediscovery of Europe's true secular past, origins and sacralised landscape, coincided with the pinnacle of Ottoman glory, the era of the greatest Ottoman spread into the European peninsula of Asia.[3] That era saw English drama, for example, set within legend or history rather than the present, and favouring exotic locations over the local (Williams 1989: 83). The cultural ground was laid for the political 'liberation' of those originary Greek lands which later cloaked British economic expansion into Asia.

Trade and the traffic of the present in the past

Each of the European states traded with the Ottomans. The glittering court at Istanbul received delegations from Europe, Russia and elsewhere. What Izmir shows so well is both the pattern of trade and the demographic aftermath which created the neo-colonialism leading to the recreation of 'Infidel Izmir', the Greek Smyrna of the racist orientalising fancies of an emergent west creating its decaying, effeminised, fascinating 'other'. The conflict for this emerging and expansionist 'west', lay in the parallel location and development of the east as the source of trade and of sacred biblical knowledge. The overlaying of the sacred east with a secular (near) orient of desire, gave sacralised knowledges and the sexualised and engendered moralities of domination a peculiar thrust not found in quite the same way in the imperialising texts of Africa or the 'far' east. In the processes of working through the conflicts of those fictions, it was not the Ottomans alone who were racialised, but Jews and Armenians too. Feeding into the resurgent European anti-Semitism of the nineteenth century and the often virulent hostilities between eastern and western Christianities, an imperialising, purifying and nationalising 'west' paved the way towards the extermination of inconvenient others in both Europe and its 'orient'. Izmir became a microcosm, both exemplary and causal, in processes not yet played out.

The English government, so deeply implicated in 'near' eastern politics, had a consul in Izmir from about 1611. The Dutch, Venetians and French were hard on their heels (Hasluck 1918–19: 142). Although still half-ruined from the destruction and reorientation of conquest, by about 1620 Izmir was growing (Steensgaard 1973: 187). Quite rapidly it became the most celebrated town in the Levant, a comfortable and picturesque depot for travellers, officials and scholars on their ways 'east'. Silt made the city's small inner harbour (used intermittently since antiquity) inaccessible to the European trading ships, so instead, they tied up at the renowned Frank Street, Frank or Frenk being the local term for Europeans. European merchants built their houses on the landward side of Frank Street so that goods could be unloaded directly through their back doors, sometimes avoiding customs duties (Ülker 1974). The port traffic connected with the terminus of the main overland caravan routes to Iran and the south (Mantran 1970) with long camel trains, sometimes of as many as 600 beasts, carrying goods in both directions (Ülker 1974: 75). Trade was such that by the last half of the seventeenth century Izmir had about 10 300 houses grouped into ten Muslim quarters, ten 'Frank' and Jewish quarters, two Armenian quarters and one Gypsy quarter (Ülker 1974: 35). Already, trade had created the cosmopolitan populace of a bustling port which was to characterise the city into the twentieth century. Increasing prosperity permitted the amenities that a city required—mosques and medresses (seats of scholarship), public buildings and the customs house which, despite widespread tax avoidance, collected so much in export dues. The taxing of exports indicates both the direction of flow of goods through the port and the strength of the internal economy. In addition to trade, Izmir also began to manufacture soap, printed cloth and dyed goods (Ülker 1974: 36) and prosperity grew.

Then, in 1688, an earthquake, fire and plague destroyed most of the city, the merchants' documents and their money and, it is said, fifteen or sixteen thousand lives. Despite the disaster, Izmir remained the preferred outlet for the transcontinental trade, retained its reputation as a better port than its alternative, Aleppo, and was slowly rebuilt. While the population fell, Izmir remained the largest export port (Ülker 1974: 71–2). In those years, Turks were the largest group in the city, with foreign merchants a tiny minority. But non-Muslim Ottomans were already a large presence. By 1699 Greeks were the second largest component of Ottoman Izmir, many of them traders and interpreters.[4] Much of the important silk trade, including the transportation of raw silk, was in the hands of Ottoman Armenians (Ülker 1974: 230–2). Bilingual Ladino Jews, too, originally from Spain, appeared as wholesalers and financiers, acting as economic and cultural brokers between the foreign merchants and Turks. In these years, smoking grew in popularity in Europe, stimulating Anatolian tobacco cultivation (Issawi 1966: 60); later, the opium trade began to develop.

Important aspects of this trade were still in Ottoman hands, but the processes by which foreigners came to control trade, commerce and the important public services like railways and ports were already under way. In the coming century, taxes and capitulations demanded by the Europeans would ensure that Turks who wished to trade were penalised and prevented from doing so. Economic development was to become a European business. The role of mercantile and cultural brokers between the Muslim Ottomans and Christian Europeans thereby became increasingly significant. From the eighteenth century many of the Ottoman Christians constituted an urban middle class of brokers with close connections to the European, Christian, trading nations, with the Armenians employed extensively within the Ottoman bureaucracy.

By 1740 travellers again described the city as beautiful, with solid houses, public buildings and a growing population (Pococke 1772 [vol. 5]: 17). The local countryside was fertile and relatively stable, producing the excellent and varied fruit and vegetables for which it was renowned (Chandler 1764: 62). In 1780, Izmir was easily the most important market in Anatolia, despite incidents like that of 1783 in which a rebel army under Saribeyoglu surrounded the city until a large ransom could be collected and assault thus avoided (Hasluck 1929).

It was this era of Ottoman prosperity that enticed so many Greeks from the neighbouring Aegean islands into emigrating to the mainland

Turkish coast. Some came as traders (Vryonis 1971), others as trades-men, servants and labourers. These migrants, already Ottoman subjects, formed the majority of the eighteenth century Greek population of Izmir and its hinterland.[5]

As local industries declined during the nineteenth century, poverty in the Aegean Islands and the Morea (mainland modern Greece) increased, so that from about 1850, Greek migration to Anatolia in-creased, swelling further the Greek communities of Izmir, Istanbul and the surrounding countryside. Izmir's population was 198 937 in about 1894 when the first modern census was undertaken. Those figures show that by then the Ottoman Turks had become a minority in the city and that the number of non-Muslims, both Ottoman and foreign, had grown enormously.[6]

The beginning of the twentieth century saw Izmir prosperous, bust-ling, but bitterly divided along religious and ethnic lines. Ottoman administrative structures formed around religious affiliation (the *millet* structures) were developed, expanded and hardened through Euro-pean demands and interference. Contacts between the foreign mer-chant community and Ottoman Turks were limited both by the failure of Europeans to learn Turkish and to accept local social customs based on cleanliness and gender segregation. With time, increasingly enforced religious barriers to mixed marriages widened the gap. The wealth of those foreign merchant families (many of whom were not Greek) can be seen today in the surviving country houses set in large and shady gardens in the outlying mercantile villages of Bornova and Buca. They retain the air of their colonial days, conjuring up the balls, afternoon teas, picnics and shooting parties of their past. The European-built trains ran from Buca and Bornova to the city centre, timed to carry the foreigners to work and then home again for lunch. On the whole, Turks did not board those trains (Kiray 1975).

There were districts of nineteenth century Izmir that looked very like a European town with European-style shops. A French company built the splendid new quay in the European quarter which, to Geary's (1878: 299) marvelling eyes, appeared as 'a sort of marine Champs Elysées'. Foreigners and Greeks gathered there in the cool of each summer evening to promenade and nibble the local nuts and snacks. Few of the local Turks participated in this life and Europeans of the time often spoke disparagingly of them. This was when the old title of Izmir was resurrected. To the Ottomans, Izmir had again become Giaour Izmir, 'Infidel Izmir'.

The epithet refers to all Christians of course, but particularly to the foreign merchants and Greeks. These were not those of ancient times nor even those of Byzantium, but those who had migrated later and turned their hearts, minds and purses to Europe rather than to Istan-bul. It expresses the bitterness of a situation in which the Ottomans had lost control of their economy and understood that the cause of their political troubles often lay in Europe. This was also the time of increasing missionary effort, with American missionaries particularly active (though with little success among Muslims) throughout the Near East. Although Turkey was never a colony, its economy was effectively in the hands of Europeans. More thoroughly than if any one of them had been overtly in control, the competition between European powers for economic and political advantage wrecked Ottoman efforts to reform their bureaucracy, educate, industrialise and exploit their own resources. Worsening economic conditions and the continuing extension of European privileges to non-Muslim Ottoman subjects sowed the seeds of serious inter-communal economic divisions that grew steadily deeper and more bitter. Questions concerning the difference between Europeans and 'orientals', always important in European explanations of the causes of what they saw as Ottoman decline, attained a revived prominence in a crude nineteenth century, anthropologised racism.

The chauvinism of David Hogarth (distinguished English gentleman, archaeologist, spy, and patron of T.E. Lawrence), who visited Izmir on his way to dig at Ephesus, is not at all exceptional and indicates the ready acceptance of such views. 'In energy and intelligence', he wrote,

> [the Turk] takes rank a grade below his dog, who shares his profound and not altogether causeless suspicion of strangers, but attacks more vivaciously and is reconciled more frankly. Ask an Anatolian if any single thing, the commonest in all the economy of nature, is to be found in his village, and he will say 'No!' before he has had time to grasp your question. (Hogarth 1925: 44)

Later, Hogarth would admit that the Turks had some redeeming features, but the contrast with his approach to the peasants of Crete, where he also dug for many years, is very great. In Crete he had close and friendly associations with his peasant labourers and performed many services for the nearby villagers. Hasluck (1929: 61, note 2) claims that Hogarth ended up deified by the grateful Cretans, who seem to have identified him with a local saint. The difference in his approach to Turks and Cretans should not be overlooked, for it exemplifies the attitudes and narrative assumptions of scholarly producers of knowledge of his time. On the one hand, he saw romantic Cretan peasants as directly descended from the magical mysteries of the western past he was busily uncovering. On the other, he saw a benighted Turkish peasantry sunk in the decay of eons of oriental irrationality, exemplars of nothing but innate incapacity. As Herzfeld's recent work shows, Cretan peasants have continued to hold their sway over the western anthropological imagination (Herzfeld 1985). Turkish peasants have been less well served.

The steady growth of such chauvinism and its relations to the ram-

pant European racism of the time can be seen in an account of a visit
to Izmir fifty years before Hogarth's. Noting the repugnance of his
friends for the local Turks, Senior asked a doctor why this was. The
doctor said, according to Senior,

> 'I do not believe', he answered, 'that we *can* sympathise with them. I
> scarcely think that we belong to the same species. The head of a Turk,
> unless it be the head of a Turk born of a Circassian mother, has much
> less brain than that of a European, especially as respects the organs of
> the nobler faculties. His forehead is low . . . He cannot reason, there is
> no logical sequence to his ideas . . .' (Senior 1859: 225)

Circassians from central Asia were, of course, held to be European
rather than Asian, with the women renowned for their fairness and
beauty. Circassian slaves were held to be the most beautiful and therefore the most valuable. Orientalist paintings of the nineteenth century
make much play on the Circassian/African distinction among Ottoman slaves. They exploit the hierarchy of sexuality in which female
slavery forms an important element and in which fear of white enslavement is juxtaposed against white racial superiority. Of the Turkish life of Izmir, however, Europeans like Senior and Hogarth knew
very little, particularly the domestic life of women and slavery. This
accounts not only for many of their dishonesties in writing about Turks,
but also for the insulation from challenge of their cherished racialist
and orientalist preconceptions. They sometimes talked of the Turks as
a dying race, a piece of wishful thinking that allowed them to believe
that Izmir might one day turn Greek of its own accord.

There is no doubt, however, that while 'Infidel Izmir' prospered, the
stresses of the colonising and extractive economic order and the series
of debilitating Ottoman wars fought during the nineteenth century left
large areas of Turkey depopulated and poverty stricken, and the
surviving villagers very isolated. At the end of the nineteenth century
many villages contained no coinage at all and struggled to subsist
(Ramsay 1897: 42). Following the Allied defeat of Turkey in the first
of the world wars, there was an unprincipled scramble among the
victors to grab the Ottoman lands. Among other things, Lloyd George
proposed that the Greeks should return to their ancient land and occupy
Smyrna once more. Proposing to protect the Greeks from further
Turkish maltreatment, mistaking the myth for reality, he succumbed
to the fantasy of the western origin myth. Accompanied by a British
destroyer, Greek ships appeared in Izmir's harbour on 5 May 1919,
inaugurating more than two years of carnage. This misguided invasion
by Greek soldiers, expecting to be welcomed as liberators, culminated
in the slaughter of the Ottoman Greeks and Armenians who had fled
to Izmir in search of the protection so freely offered by Britain, but
which could not be provided. The Turks re-entered 'Infidel Izmir' in
1922 and the city burned to the ground. The only areas spared the

flames were the markets around the ancient harbour and the Turkish houses on the hill above it. The European shops, the warehouses and banks, the Armenian and Orthodox cathedrals, the Christian churches, the saints' shrines which Izmirli women of all faiths had shared to the last—all were razed. Once more the city was in ruins.

The devastation of Izmir and the slaughter of the Greeks can be seen as the direct result of those European fantasies in which an imaginary west is understood as being in opposition to an imaginary orient, worked out in a series of fantastic ideas revolving around race, gender, sexuality and progress. When Byron went to help liberate the Greeks from their Turkish oppressors, he was living out the dream. When the European powers established the fledgling Greek state, complete with imported royalty, they were not just fostering their own dream but helping the Greeks make it come true for them. When, on a wave of romantic philhellenism, the English Prime Minister promised support to a Greek liberation of the ancient homeland, he fed the ambitions and fantasies of Greek politicians like Venizilos as well, so that they became part of a deadly real life drama.

This is not to deny either the significance of politico-economics in shaping the circumstances of war, or the individual variation and intentions of those caught up in their dreams, but there are times when it is useful to invert our usual perceptions. It is useful to stop and ask whether there might be something gained by looking at history writing as a literary practice which constructs the spaces and provides the opportunities for imperial capitalism to create the specific forms of reality which governed nineteenth century Europeans' understandings of themselves as westerners.

While I have sketched only some of the elements of the economic expansion of western capital which underpinned those fantasies, the potency of the ancient origin narratives which I have been discussing (particularly in their increasingly racialised nineteenth century forms), their emphasis on purity and whiteness and integrity, and the continuing attempts by Europeans to reinscribe them onto the sacred territory of the mythical past, must not be underestimated. The assumptions of superiority built into these views of western history—the desire to pillage the wealth of an 'oriental' empire conveniently deemed corrupt and rotting from within, and the moralising imperative to improve and progress through the increasing deployment of rational, western, knowledge—are those which justified the movement of capital and the encompassing of subordinated economies and populations. How they worked and why they were so effective can be illustrated by scrutinising the historical narrative which places the Greeks, and Izmir, in such a formative position.

Because the Aegean coast of Asia Minor is inserted into western genealogies as such a significant originary site in western narratives of knowledge and culture, its histories must be read with care.

The mapping of the ancient past

Europeans like to believe that, in a perhaps unsteady line, the great and distinctive heritage of 'the west' came from the Greeks. That heritage guarantees the success and supremacy of 'the west', its political democracy, rational knowledge and eventually, the religion which completed the desacralisation of the magical world through which the gulf between humanity and nature became entrenched.[7] Izmir has an important place in this trajectory from magical, undifferentiated paganism to rationality and Christianity, and many of the names still familiar from the truncated versions of Greek mythology and ancient history known to schoolchildren are linked to ancient Smyrna.

The primordial, tribal Greeks, for example, are said to have first colonised the Aegean coast in about 1100 B.C. They named their city for Smyrna, the Amazon who, after conquering Ephesus, marched northwards to found a new city (Strabo 1928: 201–3). Amazon Smyrna was a little to the north of the present one, a neat stone and marble grid of streets set beside a safe harbour (Cadoux 1938: 55 & 60). Those brave women lost their city in what might be thought of as an appropriately female way. The city was taken from them by the Ionian Greeks whom the hospitable Amazons had received and honoured as their guests. Those men, protected by the duty of hospitality and a code of behaviour guaranteeing the integrity of the stranger and the honourable actions of the women, penetrated to the heart of the Amazon domain. Once inside the walls, the Ionian men turned against the Smyrnaean women, leaving them forever outside their city which was to be, then and for all time, resolutely male. As Herodotus (1954: 102) tells the story, the Ionians waited until their hosts walked in procession to the fields outside the walls to celebrate the festival of Dionysus. Left alone within the city, they closed and barred the gates against the Smyrnaeans. Ever pragmatic (for this is how our historians see this nation of female warriors recast into an inferior trading mentality), the Smyrnaeans negotiated, and were able to retrieve their movable property. They took their jewels and clothing, perhaps, but could not have been permitted their arms. And so the city, and much more, was lost to them, and to us, forever.

The treacherous Ionian men of the Amazon myth are those who, in western histories, brought about the enlightenment of a Greek Dark Age sunk in oriental chaos. They are the beings allocated a generative role in a superior 'western' culture, creating the luminous flame of civilisation which was never again, we like to think, entirely extinguished. With the coming of these Ionians, women vanish from history and the city-state and rational thought arrive simultaneously. From that time the distinctively Greek knowledge and culture which we claim as ours flourished. Vernant, for example, one the most distinguished of France's *mythologues*, writes of this crucial moment of generation:

If we wish to document the birth of this Greek rationality, to follow the path by which it managed to divest itself of a religious mentality, to indicate what it owed to myth and how far it went beyond it, we must compare and contrast with its Mycenaean background that turning point, from the eighth to the seventh century, where Greece made a new start and began to explore paths that were peculiarly its own: a period of decisive mutation that laid the foundations for the government of the *polis* at the very moment when the Orientalising style was triumphant, and which ensured the advent of philosophy by secularising political thought. (Vernant 1982: 11)

In the story of the old Amazon ancestry of Izmir, the potent mixture of myth and history, the archaeological knowledge of city foundations, inscriptions, dates and places, and the mythical tales of warring women and treacherous men, are combined into a foundation stone for one of the great narratives of western knowledge. In both histories the Ionians play the same role. They are the bringers of a new order of secularised knowledge (rational thought) and the founders of a new political order (democracy). Thenceforward the land bears *their* name and *their* land is the kernel from which so much else will grow. Clearly evident within both the Amazon myth and Ionian history are the structuring elements of that grand narrative of time through which westerners imagine the lineages of their superior selves: female and male, east and west, the civilisation of the city, and secularising rationality. The white-ness of the Ionians and their monuments is a critical element not only in western racialisms but also in our sexualities. They provide the whiteness of the contrast exploited in orientalist harem paintings against which the blackness of the slave is so important. The Ionians occupy precisely the same role in myth and history and in both guises form a pivotal point in an endless history of western thought continuously verified through archaeology, ancient history, philology, orientalism and anthropology.

These same structuring elements and oppositions are reinscribed into the histories of later eras. This is very noticeable in accounts of Byzantium, the world of a gorgeous 'eastern' Christianity incorporating many features of the luxuriant, sexualised orient in which it lies embedded. One of the most important of English Byzantine scholars uses just this framework to structure his history. 'Already in the Third Century', he writes,

architecture had begun to breathe a new splendour that was Oriental and spontaneous. The East was to triumph against Classical tradition not so much by its conceptions of majesty as by its more purely spiritual ideas. A disillusioned age turns to religion, as an escape from the uncertainties of the world. But the old religions, the pagan joy in life of the Greeks, the State-worship of Rome, failed when life was full of dread and the State in obvious decay . . .

That Christianity should be the triumphant faith was not surprising. Its message had far wider appeal than any other. The Oriental with his apparent patience is in truth highly impatient. Unable to bear pain and sorrow he at once takes refuge in communion with higher things and escapes from the sphere of earthly sensation. The Westerner kicks against the pricks because they hurt. His comfort lies in hope and in faith that it will not be for ever. The Hellenistic Greek was midway between. Behind his nature-worship lurked mysticism, and a love of symbolism was innate in him. All these yearnings could be satisfied in Christianity. Christianity encouraged mysticism, it preached an eschatology of hope, it was rich in symbols and had a noble ritual . . . The second great strength of Christianity lay in the influence that from its earliest years it had allowed Greek philosophy to exercise over it. (Runciman 1975: 17–19)

There is no need now to consult Runciman on this era. There are more recent, less self-conscious scholars working the field (Brown 1971 and Patlagean 1987, for example). Nevertheless, Runciman's work is frequently republished and widely circulated, and the distinctions he draws are replicated within lesser or more popular scholarship (Stoneman 1987; Merlin 1984: 219). Western histories of the Ottoman era following the conquest of the Byzantine state are structured in precisely the same way. Said (1978) and many others (Djaît 1985; Malek 1963; Daniel 1962) have already had a great deal to say on the structuring of orientalist knowledge so I shall not repeat their analyses. Izmir's place in historical narratives of the evolution of western supremacy allows us to grasp the point that in these self-aggrandising and congratulatory histories of *ourselves*, Greece is the primordial source of the rationality and philosophy which was to provide a counterweight to the 'oriental' mysticism that eventually gave birth to the 'triumphant faith' of which Runciman speaks. Byzantine Izmir was, on the whole, eclipsed by Ephesus, but in ancient Greece, Izmir occupied an important place within the sacred originary landscape from which sprang the philosophy which led to Christianity. It is because of Izmir's place in western dreams of itself, not because of its place in history, that an account of the ancient history of Izmir offers the possibility of re-examining some of the certainties of popular histories of east and west.

The role of the European traveller in Turkey has been to take these textual modes of constructing differences within histories, and through their own texts to inscribe them upon the landscapes they explored. It is their work which sustains the illusions of history by establishing their truth.

It is still possible, I suppose, to discuss Izmir's past in terms of its truth. Some facts are known independently of the texts written about them, perhaps, but those facts do not really address the issues that concerned me when I was living and working in Izmir. At first I thought they would—that by learning more detail of the past, I should better understand the continuities of the past with the present and the genuine cultural differences that distinguished the Turks from, say, their European or Asian neighbours. But the answers were not so easily located and the more I read the more difficult it became to overthrow the narrative structures of that reading. The more I sought the answers in the facts of the matter, the worse the problem of difference became. So much of interest to our ancient history can be found in and about Izmir that over and again scholars return there to explore the beginnings, the development and the guises which classical knowledges and writings offer. Foucault's second volume concerning sexuality (Foucault 1986) is only one recent example of these processes at work, while the role of tourism in recreating these pasts, their essentialising differences, racisms and sexualities, is another.

Mapping the modern past

When the modernising European traders, officials, missionaries and travellers began their journeys along the coasts of the eastern Mediterranean and across the Anatolian plateau during the eighteenth and nineteenth centuries, they were part of the massive mapping process which located with precision the 'east', its divisions into near and far, and, later, India. It did so in order to construct a bridge between the tribal domain of Africa's dangerous blackness and Asia's intermediary step towards civilisation. This crawling all over the face of the landscape had as its dynamic the verification of the classical and biblical texts and the creation of knowledge of its detail. The amount of effort put into locating the ancient sites was phenomenal and the difficulties of getting to them sometimes very great. The real hazards of some of these journeys—the pestilence, brigands, official disapproval, absence of roads and shortage of supplies—indicate their significance. The reward of writing the travel books was glory, and that of mapping, membership of a learned society or perhaps imperial honours; yet neither really explains the impulse to explore, map, and tame that these journeys 'out' towards the authentic and originating landscape represent. Travellers went to locate, inspect and record the sites of the classical and biblical texts. Public interest in these endeavours was intense and accounts of travellers' discoveries and their observations of quaint and barbaric customs were widely read. The search for the site of Troy is a good example of the high level of scholarly and general interest taken in these matters. Not only was Schliemann's quest declared successful and the location and secret removal of 'Priam's treasure' vividly described, but the discoverer has been inscribed into history through numerous biographies and commentary.[8] His Troy, like so many other sites, is now a museum, with the Trojan Horse roughly reconstructed outside it to entertain the numerous Turkish and foreign tourists.

But it was in Christianity that the classical philosophy of the ancient

Greeks was able, it is held, to flower, modifying the basically eastern religious traditions from which it originated to produce the rational set of monotheistic beliefs that were essential to European and western thought. In the passages from Runciman and Vernant quoted earlier, this transformation is made perfectly explicit—ideas like theirs have long been both widespread and widely assumed.

The western search for origins has therefore always been two-pronged. It includes on the one hand, the classical pagan heritage and its philosophy that marked the break from a sacralised primordiality; on the other, the biblical heritage and the religious knowledge which originated in the fertility of the east but which is transformed through the encounter with rationalising philosophy. The archaeological discoveries of the Christian past provoked great excitement; in times of prosperity, Christians sought to travel again the roads of the apostles, to stand where they had stood and somehow to see how the past had been. While Palestine was the focal point of this sacred cartography, much biblical and classical history also lies within Turkey. According to the Christian texts, the apostles travelled extensively across Asia, Africa and Europe and the Gospels provide endless opportunities for recreating those sacred journeys. Travellers in Turkey sought their dual origin, the early Christian sites as well as those of pagan antiquity. They were pilgrims as well as tourists and merchants, and sought Nicaea, Caesarea and Tarsus. H.V. Morton's much later accounts of his journeys, *In the Footsteps of St. Paul* and *In the Footsteps of the Master*, first published in the 1930s, have gone through a series of editions and today are again popular and reprinted. Armed with Morton, one travels the dusty Roman roads, sees the Tarsus of St Paul, and reads again of the conversion of the virtuous but almost forgotten St Thecla of Iconium.[9] The world of Paul and Jesus is very different from the reality of the Turkish world of the Ottomans (or of the later Republic) through which the traveller must pass in order to get to it.

On the whole, the language of European mapping was Latinised Greek (and its variations), for those were the names which appeared in the New Testament and its associated texts. Izmir was known as Smyrna, for example, and is written into more recent texts in this form; T.S. Eliot speaks of the Smyrniote merchant in *The Waste Land*, and so on. It is through this language, these names, and this originary trajectory that European readers came to know the lands of the Ottoman eastern Mediterranean.

Chandler's delightful account of his travels along the Turkish coast illustrates these processes at work. He describes his party's approach to Ephesus:

Mount Pactyas here retires with a circular sweep, while Gallesus preserves its direction to the sea ... The Cayster met us near the

entrance of it; and we passed over an ordinary bridge, a little below
which are pieces of veined marble, polished, the remnants of a structure
... (Chandler 1764: 74)

The exploration of the visible ruins of Ephesus was, quite naturally,
described in the correct Latin terminology: 'The temple was *in antis*,
and had four columns between the *antae*. We found their capitals, and
also one of a pilaster...' (Chandler 1764: 82).[10] The internationally
accepted language of archaeological description is derived from the
ancient texts and it is through this process of inscription that Latin and
Greek remain active linguistic factors, ever open to rediscovery and
reactivation. After his account of the ruins of the ancient world, the
specifically Christian associations are inscribed upon it:

> In the records of our religion it [Ephesus] is ennobled as the burying-
> place of St. Timothy, the companion of St. Paul, and the first bishop of
> Ephesus, whose body was afterwards translated to Constantinople by the
> founder of that city, or his son Constantius, and placed with St. Luke
> and St. Andrew in the church of the apostles. The story of St. John was
> deformed in an early age with gross fiction; he also was interred at
> Ephesus, and as appears from one narration, in this mountain.[11]
> (Chandler 1764: 84)

Lacking an antique name, resort was made to those of Byzantium, for
example, Aiasoluck for the village near old Ephesus, and so on. Those
settlements recorded by their Turkish names are those without a known
classical or Christian provenance.

Chandler went to Asia Minor on behalf of the Society of Dilettanti,
commissioned to map and record all that he saw. His attitudes were
those of his time, and a record of a conversation with him shows how
influential were the familiar oppositions between ignorance and
knowledge, Greek and Turk, in forming the backdrop to his apprecia-
tion of his classical past.

> ... Churton describes how when Chandler [in old age] 'adverted
> occasionally to the classical scenes, which he had visited in his travels, it
> was truly delightful, I had almost said enchanting, to my younger ears, to
> hear him tell, his bright eyes beaming with peculiar lustre, how, after a
> long lapse of ages of ignorance and barbarism, and under the cruel hand
> of Turkish tyranny and oppression, the lyre, though not now in the
> hands of a Tyrtaeus or Simonides, was still, however, cherished on the
> banks of the Ilissus'. (Clay 1971: xv)

Chandler worked within a genre already well established and is perhaps the most accomplished of his century's wave of travel writers.
Those who came after him not only retraced his steps but followed his
practice. There are better and poorer writers, of course; there are
more and less observant travellers; and there is great variation in their
degree of interest in the present inhabitants of the biblical lands.
However, his views on Turkish tyranny and barbarism, dating from

around 1760, are markedly more racialised and denunciatory than those
of Lady Mary Wortley Montagu, who was in Istanbul forty or so years
earlier. Throughout the eighteenth and nineteenth centuries, the work
of mapping, collecting and writing the orient into the western, Christian past, went on very steadily and it was done in order to incorporate
that landscape of the Muslim Turks of the present, shifting as it does
into the mythical past of the Christian Europeans, and it was part of
the processes by which western views of the Turks (and others) were
verified through first-hand experience and then disseminated to a ʷide
and, one might say, wide-eyed, reading public.

Recreating the past

As I noted in connection with Chandler's journey, the travellers who
came to Turkey during these years usually used the Greek names for
the cities and regions they saw. Izmir was referred to as Smyrna, Istanbul as Constantinople, Freya Stark wrote of 'Ionia: A Quest' (1954)
and Sybille Haynes (1974) of the 'Land of the Chimaera' rather than
of the coastal region south of Izmir or the district of Milas. And so it
went, a classical world reconstructed. Indeed, it was through the imposition of an ancient cartography upon the Ottoman landscape
within this literature that I learned my first words of Greek and was
induced to remember the outlines of an abbreviated classical mythology
learned in childhood. I, too, came to Turkey via the Greek past.

As they journeyed through their classical past, the travellers sought
to reconstruct the ancient architecture and people it with classical
dignitaries, the better to hear their voices across time. The rude punc-
turing of the dream by the occasional intrusion of reality, of Ottoman
officialdom or the impoverished Turkish peasantry, provoked the
peppery, unreasoned assessments and racism which many of these
travellers so freely dispensed when racial hierarchies and the right to
control were challenged. For as they listened to the classical voices in
the land where once they had lived, it was hard to accept that of all
that imagined splendour so little remained. The classical past lay buried
under tons of earth, the visible marble conveniently mined for local
housing or delivered to the lime kilns for burning. Indeed, the Venus
de Milo (Aphrodite of Melos) was retrieved from the lime kiln just in
time.

But there is a second aspect to the mapping of the past, an aspect
crucial to the search for origins which is generally known as ethnography. For the travellers often received hospitality from Greeks among
the villages they passed through, and among them sought to discover
the remnants of their classical past. Had these Greeks remembered
anything at all of those long gone glorious days? Impoverished as
many of them were, it was widely held that the Ottoman Greeks were

survivors of the classical city democracies and their Christianised continuation, Byzantium. The field was wide open, and folklore flourished. At this time customs were collected, rites described and religious practices observed at a rapid rate. Frazer's *Golden Bough* brought this method of study to its glittering pinnacle. In Turkey, Lucy M.J. Garnett made detailed contributions, particularly in the field of women's lore, and with J.S. Stuart-Glennie prepared *The Women of Turkey and Their Folk-Lore* (1891), Turkey, of course, still containing much of Greece. But there were many others dedicated to the task of restoring the ancient past, and one of the conceptions underlying their work was that of the 'folk memory'.

A particularly long reach of memory was attributed to the uneducated 'folk' of the villages. Lodged somewhere beyond the reach of the great civilisation to which the uneducated villagers were marginal, the folk memory contained, of necessity, the remnants of all that had gone before. Allied to this belief was another. This was that among the folk, the peasants and perhaps the urban masses, religious beliefs were pretty much what they always had been. In this view, there had always been a folk religion that existed despite clerical interference, no matter whether this was a folk-Christianity or a folk-Islam. In this genealogy, the remnants of the polytheism and the iconolatry of the classical Greeks persisted relatively unchanged through time; only the names were different. In the 'great traditions' of Judaism, Islam and Christianity upheld by clerics and their supporting states, monotheism could be enforced and idols and images contained if not eradicated. In their theologies vast differences arose and these, too, were enforced. But for the villager, with local healing spring and lucky tree, state theology made little impression. Local religious beliefs and practices were perceived as primordial, remaining intact from the earlier polytheistic Greek age.

Fortunately, when foreign travellers arrived, the villagers, Turk and Greek alike, were often helpful. After much thought, it was sometimes possible for villagers to lead the way to a sacred spring that they still thought of as peopled with fates or demons. Once located, transcribed into history through the travelogue, the site was mapped onto that sacred topography that future travellers would, in their own time, recreate. This process ensured the continuity of the folk memory and with time led to the recreation of the classical sites. The Rock of Niobe on the hill behind Manisa (ancient Greek Magnesia) is an example of these processes at work. My tourist's guidebook to Turkey first directed me to Niobe and provided a brief outline of the Niobe legend. Her archaeological and literary genealogy is given in more detail in Bean's (1966) more comprehensive archaeological guide, with Bean himself a good and typical example of the last generation of gentleman archaeological travellers. In search of ancient sites, he covered a great deal of Turkey on foot. In his guidebook he retells the

Niobe legend, provides its verification from Pausanias (who was actually born [*c.* 150 AD] nearby and was the leading travel writer of his time); and from the Smyrnaean poet, Quintus (*c.* 400 A.D.). Bean then refers to Cadoux (1938), author of a more recent book on the history of Izmir and traveller in his own right, and to the discovery of the 'true' Niobe Rock by Bossert. In his guide-book, therefore, the genealogy of the site is clear: first the classical mythical origins, then the modern predecessors, and then the Rock herself, petrified Niobe, still shedding tears if one is there at the right moment.

As I walked through the outlying suburbs of Manisa and approached the foot of Manisa Dagi (Mt Sipylus) I saw a small *türbe*, a Turkish mausoleum. Its name was Yedi Kizlar (Seven Daughters). Niobe, in Ovid's account, had seven daughters and seven sons. Her mythical profusion of offspring led her to boast that, because of her fecundity, she was superior to Leto, who had only two. In fury, Leto sent her own two offspring (Artemis and Apollo) to kill all Niobe's children, and her husband too. Niobe's grief at the slaughter was ended only when, after nine days of weeping, she was turned into the stone which still weeps on Mt Sipylus. Niobe's Rock, so confidently identified by Bean, was just a little further up the road from the Yedi Kizlar Türbe, still dripping tears if there had been enough rain. If you look at it from the right direction, he says, the cragginess becomes a human profile. Well, it could be seen that way, I suppose. But the Yedi Kizlar Türbe nearby ... was this then, the link between classical Greek myth and present Turkish folk knowledge that folklorists had always sought? And had the seven sons been obliterated through the force of the Aegean matriarchal traditions?

I spoke to a visitor at the *türbe*. Who were they, the Seven Daughters, I asked? It was not very clear, but they were pious women, daughters of a *seyh* (Arabic: sheikh). The holy Islamic man seemed to have replaced Niobe in one of the transformations so typical of the region, in which women keep losing out to men. Yet the reality of a folk memory is an illusion, a result of the western search for the reality of a mythical and disconnected past and the recurrence of need among the poor to take action to control their fate. There is no mention of the seven sons because the whole legend has long been lost. What has happened, I suspect, is that a series of scholarly travellers, each in search of Niobe's Rock, has introduced anew the saint with seven daughters. As travellers arrived over the years and were shepherded to the rock by guides, so local knowledge of the myth expanded. Now, people living in the area, as hospitable as ever, are reasonably well informed of the classical Greek tragedy. While my first informant was unspecific and hesitant in her identification, the Greek story was known to the man who held the key to the mausoleum. He did not believe it, but he certainly knew where to direct those who sought the Rock of Niobe. There are several Yedi Kizlar shrines in and around Izmir, each with a different story to legitimate the site, and there is no need to locate the origins of this one in a remote and Hellenistic past. Shrines pop up out of the landscape constantly, eruptions of holiness which breach the boundaries of time and space, of past with present and secular with sacred. The break between the classical world and Byzantium may not have been so great, but the break between Byzantium and the eighteenth and nineteenth centuries is unbridgeable. Between them stood at least four hundred years and an entirely new, efficient, state and its religion. While the collapse of state control may well permit the rise of polytheism, these are not resurgences of the ancient, but the recreations of the new claiming the legitimacy of antiquity within the structures of the present.

Europe's myths of origin

I have suggested that the specific trajectory of the evolution of western modern knowledge is established through a powerful origin myth which locates the western emergence from Indo-European tribalism in the development of the ancient Greek city-states (Vernant 1982). It goes on to describe a middle period following the collapse of the ancient empires which was characterised by loss of knowledge; and then the rebirth of a truly 'modern' form of western civilisation in Europe, one based upon the rational knowledge and political culture of the ancient Greeks, that led to the later conquest of most of the world. One version of this lineage is described by Detienne (1981: 124) as 'a lettered tradition from the Hellenistic age to the eighteenth century by way of Boccaccio and Noel Conti in the Renaissance'. One might add Shakespeare and reflect upon the significance of the recent revival in his fortunes, a cult figure over whom debate still boils and for whom the external characteristics of his characters can never be settled. His anti-Semitism, for example, has recently been discussed in the popular press. How is it, we must ask, that a Jewish actor's desire to play Shakespeare, can *only* be satisfied by an offer of the role of Shylock and the reproduction of medieval stereotypes on English stages at a time of rising anti-Semitism? [12]

In this epic saga, Christianity occupies a syncretic position, synthesising the essentially Greek rationalising spirit and forms of knowledge to what were originally eastern and anti-rational cults, in order to produce a religious formation proper to a universal civilisation, valid for all time and places. It is asserted that it is through Christianity that the desacralisation of this world is completed, the gulf between the gods and humans entrenched and the separate responsibility of men to the state sanctified through the teachings of Paul. The method of dating the past and the present in relation to the birth of Christ indicates the role of Christianity in the rise of western knowledge and the ways in which the interruption of the time scale is important in establishing the hierarchies which such fragmentations of time permit. The sanctifying of the calendar and its periodisation through Christ signal the political importance of the control of time in its secular guises.

We cannot, therefore, even begin to know the histories of Izmir's people without disengaging them from the history of the west into which they have been assimilated and which acts as a prism. The ancient history of Izmir is relevant to the city today, not because of an archaeological coincidence which places mosques upon the sites of temples, but because we cannot recognise the present without first trying to strip away the assumptions of the western histories through which we have come to know the Turks. Western histories of the Ottomans, their cities and the cultures of the peoples within them fragment the time scales, organise and select the data to create an 'east' as part of that grand narrative through which rational thought is first made the exclusive property of a white, heterosexual 'west' so that, in the end, rationality can triumph. This way of construing each history as part of the narrative of western history extends beyond the boundaries of those histories directly known in this way, the histories of Ottomans, Arabs, Iranians and Palestinians, and into histories of our selves. It has been used to structure knowledge of the Byzantine empire, the Greek speaking, eastern branch of the Roman Empire, and it has been used to structure western narratives of the Ottomans.

But how can we know a past without falling back onto commonsense certainties that utilise notions of an eternal difference between east and west to assimilate all histories into a grand Manichaean struggle between two elements of itself? When posed in this way, however, the question can be only *partly* answered. This is because it is posed purely as a problem of knowing the difference, of how it might be possible to know the 'truth' about Turkish life and culture without first using and presuming the nature of the differences between Europe and its orient before arriving at them. This is a critical issue, but there is another aspect which must also be taken into account—the matter of gender. It is no longer possible to discuss history and the differences between cultures without coming to grips with the serious challenge posed by recent feminist critiques of knowledge that have demonstrated once and for all time that gender is a hidden factor which *always* counts. In the histories and narratives of western knowledge which I have discussed here, women have been almost totally absent. Where they do appear, it is as final repositories for the timeless essence of the folk memory, as exemplars of the set of universal, holistic and primitive values attributed to them by men, or as founding ancestors who long ago lost their power. Yet that absence is the key to the maskings and substitutions essential to constructing both a racialised east and a sexualised, eroticised orient.

3   Cannibalising the Orient

> Therefore the Lord God sent him forth from the garden of Eden, to till the ground from whence he was taken. So he drove out the man; and he placed at the *east* of the garden of Eden Cherubims, and a flaming sword which turned every way, to keep the way of the tree of life. (Author's emphasis)
>
> *Genesis* 3: 23–4

It is no simple matter to disentangle Turkish women from the misapprehensions that are written into their pasts, particularly when those pasts pose interesting historiographical problems. Nor is it possible to assume that a history, a narrative of any past, can be adequately understood without explicitly coming to grips with the place of gender, both in history and in history-writing. The writing of history is itself a gendered activity and history-writers produce knowledge about a past which is necessarily gendered. It cannot be otherwise. There are two reasons for this.

On the one hand, women are largely omitted from the written past. The past becomes known as a neutral, universal past but is, of course, a masculine past that *claims* to be universal despite, and sometimes because of, the absence of women from it. The absence of women produces images of a past that are necessarily false rather than simply partial. The inclusion of women would produce totally different histories, especially in areas where gender is held to make no difference—in international politics, for example (cf. Enloe 1989). On the other hand, and this has been pointed to repeatedly, pasts are written within the framework provided by particular narrative conventions. These conventions are such that writers of Middle Eastern histories use gender to feminise their images of their east and its inhabitants. The process by which a place and the people living in it become gendered in this way is called *metonymy*, the process of substitution. Therefore there are at least two separable engendering processes which work together within the writing of pasts and the conventions by which they are scrutinised and verified. One concerns the erasure of women as key actors from the events of history, the other the rendering of dominated groups as feminine.

Pasts are not only constructed through official or academic histories. Indeed such texts are known only to a restricted, if powerful, band of specialised scholars. Many of the most influential accounts of the orient take the form of novels, travelogues, memoirs and diaries of the travellers I referred to in the last chapter. They are read by a wide public and they bridge the gap between the reading worlds of scholars and a literate reading public. They offer first-hand accounts of daily life based on the direct observations which constitute their authority. They became important in just this way, providing historical background, when I was preparing for fieldwork. In seeking a historical dimension to my work, there were no ethnographies describing nineteenth century Turkish life to consult. There was a plentiful supply of histories but these omitted daily life, domestic life and culture. Instead, there were large numbers of travel books, from which I constructed a picture of the era which preceded my own. It may be clear that the histories and ideas reproduced from these sources are sometimes incorrect and often prejudiced, but this does not alter either the way in which a wide general audience comes to know a particular place and its past, or the way in which these books can become a resource for scholars. Because the travelogue, novel or diary deals with daily life, individuals, domestic details and personal encounters, it is a powerful way of presenting the reality, and thus the truth, of the scenes being described. This is particularly the case with ideas concerning the real *nature* of the local population, their 'true' characteristics and peculiarities, and their view of the strangers come among them. And that obsession with defining and explaining the nature of 'human nature' in its Muslim form, must constantly refer to the hidden, unseen women. Even a cursory reading of the popular literature on the countries of the Muslim Mediterrean reveals the European obsession with oriental sexuality, with the hidden woman, the harem, and with the homosexuality of women and men that is so often held to be rampant in the east. As I noted earlier, it was precisely these books that led to my first interest in the Middle East, my first failed journey of discovery to Morocco, and my later desire to overcome that failure by carrying out proper scientific research there.

While orientalist knowledge has both a scholarly and a popular face, the two are closely related. Scholarly orientalist knowledge of the Near East goes hand in hand with the writings of the travellers and diarists, with novels set in the exotic 'east', with political and educational journalism (and film), and with the writings of missionaries. The degree of coincidence between them and their precise relationship has varied in differing historical, political and economic contexts, but it is never absent. In each a discourse on women and sexuality plays a crucial role in the symbolic subordination of 'east' to 'west'. The western traveller is usually male, rational, intrepid, conquering and in the end, sexual. This is also the case with the anthropologist (cf. Rabinow 1977). Within the travel narrative there is therefore also a metaphorical structure which is the reverse of these characteristics, a sexed being or place which will be governed by the non-rational and by sensuality which can be objectified and conquered, a 'seduced' who will eventually yield, only to be rejected. In women's narratives the deployment of these tropes shifts, but as I shall shortly demonstrate, it usually shifts in such a way as to retain the relations of power of the masculinist form.

One of the features of these books is their ability to convey information concerning the element missing from scholarly tomes—women. Indeed, the hidden women of the various Muslim countries are the focus of a degree of interest that comes partly from the fact that they are secluded, and thus beyond the enquiring and dominating gaze of the male traveller; and partly from their metonymical relationship to the structuring of the European dream of its 'orient'. The metonymical conflation of an 'east' with 'woman' produces one of the most powerful, enduring and fundamental structurings of western knowledge. This metonymical identification or collapsing of categories utilises two of the most fundamental divisions of European knowledges—gender and the east—to produce a ramifying order of western knowledge of particular potency.

Ever since the Fall, Jews and Christians have longed to find the east and thus the way to the Garden of Eden and eternal life. The east has a mythical potency for Christians that comes not only from the tales of paradise lost, but also from its salience in the origin myths of the Star of Bethlehem and the Three Wise Men which point to the fecundity of the east, to its fertility and generative power. Although the significance of the east in cosmology and as a structuring principle predates Christianity and (until the fall of Byzantium in the fifteenth century) had interesting ramifications for the Eastern and Western Roman Empires, it is the later, post-Byzantine, European Christian world that has most relevance for this study of Turkish women.

For the Europeans of the sixteenth century, the symbolic east and all that it implied coincided with both the geographical location of the sacred landscape of Christianity, and the challenging politico-economic and religious boundary of the Ottoman Empire. For many centuries 'the orient' therefore lay very close to home, and while popular thought polarised and separated east from west, in reality contacts were many and interest great. The Ottomans were well schooled in the conventions of Byzantine Greek culture, and the story is often told that Mehmet the Conqueror, the Ottoman who finally wrested Constantinople from the Byzantines, described his victory as revenge for the Greek sack of ancient Troy.

For practical European purposes, 'the east' was not far away, but near; it lay not only in the eastern Mediterranean but over much of central Europe, and that frightening closeness is reflected in the division of the east into Near and Far. The precise location of the boundary has varied greatly; at times Persia took on this role, at others Greece and the Aegean fell firmly into the eastern zone. The Greek descendants of the Eastern Roman Empire moved west only in the nineteenth century, even though Renaissance Europeans had long before encompassed the ancient Hellenes within the European ambit.

Like all boundaries, that shifting line between east and west is contested. Women have a crucial role to play in these contests, for it was the liberation of the secluded and downtrodden Muslim women that provided a potent moral justification for the destruction of the Ottoman social fabric caused by the political incursions of Christian Europeans.

Women therefore operate within the narratives of the past in two very important ways. Because of the metonymical identification of the generative power of the east with 'woman', the journey to that east becomes a male and sexualised one, a journey of penetration which results in the domination of the culture which has been penetrated and then described. And because of the role of the hidden woman in producing the moral inferiority of Islam, Muslim women have a critical political valency within the narratives in which they appear. Because male travellers are unable to know these hidden women, a great deal of effort goes into discovering them and the reality of their lives. The writings of women travellers become enormously important at this point.

If, as Kabbani (1986: 1) suggests, travel is the moving eye of empire, then travellers demand an analysis which takes into account the power relations of domination that structure the field in which they move. In addition, the language of European travel narratives suggests the relevance of gender as a factor embedded within the power of travel, particularly in the widespread use of metaphors of penetration and the collapse of resistance related to masculinist views of alternative sexualities, seduction and the pleasure of rape.[13] Pierre Loti's novel *Les Désenchantées* provides some wonderful examples of the ways in which 'oriental' women and men finally yield to the conquering, penetrating, male traveller (I. Szyliowicz 1988). In these and many other travellers' tales, the secret and withheld 'truth' of the east is unveiled through penetration. It was this familiar intention to reach behind the facade to reveal the cultural traditions hidden there, to penetrate, which motivated my own anthropological journey to Turkey. I was, I believed, in search of 'scientific' information and was intending to gather data for a travelogue. Once embarked upon such a journey, it is not easy to escape the constitutive powers of the travel narrative. One sees the constraints more clearly by considering not so much the eye of the traveller that Kabbani referred to, or the texts that my predecessors produced, but by looking instead at an aspect of travel previously considered of minor importance—that is, the wearing of native garb by certain orientalist travellers and not by others.

Because of the important relations between travel writers and anthropologists, and because of the different positions occupied by women and men within the travel literature, their contributions to western knowledge differ. Indeed they differ in such important ways that it is necessary to analyse in detail the workings of gender within the narrative and practices of travelogues before attempting to overcome the limitations they impose. Because the processes of erasure and metonymy are complex, I deal with them separately and in sufficient detail to show how they work together to produce the problems of difference and gender addressed in later chapters. Far from being an insignificant detail or a personal idiosyncrasy, the traveller's choice of clothing signifies a great deal about the relations of power at work through the act of travel, the texts which travellers produce, and the significance of gender within European societies.

The detail of authenticity

In order to bring out these crucial relationships of culturalised power, I employ a particular notion of power to explore the relations between an orientalist aesthetic, western fantasies about its true nature, and the individual's search for an identity which lies beyond the constraints of western society. In some cases the traveller's search for identity leads to the symbolic, but effective, consumption of the essential identity of the other. I shall show how the relations between the consumption of identities through adopting local dress are governed by those of gender, and how these relations become particularly visible. Some of the examples are taken from paintings produced by the 'orientalist' school, but, texts in their own right, they are, of course, intimately related to the travel narratives which accompany and parallel them.[14]

Rodinson (1974), a leading Marxist orientalist, makes an immediate connection between an imperialising politico-economic system and particular aesthetic forms. The representation of a separate *exotic* world, he suggests, is absolutely fundamental to orientalist painting and the *exoticism* which, breaking into art in the seventeenth century, enveloped it completely during the eighteenth. The aesthetic exoticism that Rodinson refers to concerns the ways in which the spectator's eye escapes into the 'other' world *without ever leaving its own* (Rodinson 1974: 38 & 39), and this characteristic, prominent in the work of the school of orientalist painters including Gérome, Ingres and many others, renders these paintings essentially voyeuristic, alerting us to their important sexual and racial implications. The way in which the eye stays safely inside its own world is a matter I shall come back to, for it has implications for anthropologists too. But exoticism in art, as in life, contains within it the premise of a *real* world, and it is this which should alert us to the significance of these exotic images for the western worlds to which they stand in contrast.

The world from which the spectator's eye escapes is the world of the real which the nineteenth century was so anxious to describe through the telling and finely drawn detail which would somehow reveal the essential truth of the whole.[15] The detailism evident in painting the protruding and lumpy veins on the back of an old woman's slightly discoloured hand as it rests upon the arm of her chair, for example, is held to tell something essential and encompassing about the whole of the woman, her woman's life and the whole of the painting. This telling detail of the real made possible (or perhaps even necessary) a flight from it into another world, one which escaped the vice-like grip of the rational and imperialising western taste for ever more detail. But the exotic world, once subjected to the rational eye of the western artist, was also represented in the detail so that it, too, could be known intimately and realistically as an exotic, fictional, narrative space. In this context, photography can be seen as offering the ultimate mode of detailing the reality of truth. Nineteenth century photography brought into play a new detailism and a transformed realism that both influenced discussions of aesthetics and made possible the ethnographic postcard.[16] The postcard, and its claims to truth, perhaps shows most immediately the ways in which a particular aesthetics interpreted, and then represented, the racist and sexist politics of the exotic world of the nineteenth century orient to a wider audience.

It was during the nineteenth century that the social institutions guaranteeing the deployment of detail as an instrument of knowledge and power—the prisons, police forces, asylums and clinics—were set up (Shor 1987: 110). It was also during this time that European interest in philology (Said 1983: 47 & 48), the history of religions and geography emerged, and that travellers set out in some haste to complete the naming and mapping of the exotic but rapidly reducing world that resulted from the imperial colonising of the unknown. The mapping of the 'orient' brought its farthest reaches ever closer to Europe, just as did the incorporation of the lands of the Near and Middle East into the expanding European economies. The parallel colonising expansions of knowledge and economy that took place during these centuries constituted the orient ever more firmly as a simultaneously feared and desired world through which Europeans could come to define and know themselves.

As the mapping was carried out, the collection of the ancient past continued at an incredible rate. Lord Elgin's removal of the Parthenon's marbles was only a drop in a vast ocean of marble and stone, clay and coinage that was freighted homewards to grace the private collections of antiquarians and curio collectors. Not only were the more obviously removable pieces gathered up, but in the desire to capture and re-install the mysterious orient within the confines of the reality of the known European world, whole city walls were disman-tled, carted north and reassembled in careful detail to come within the awed gaze of Europe. The magnificent blue tiles of the walls of Babylon stand in Berlin today, a museum memorial to the western determination to appropriate and impose its own universalising taxonomies. Within this desire to capture the essence of the marvels of the orient and to bring ever more of them safely home lies a subterranean concern with the origins and legitimation of European 'civilisation' and a move to incorporate the past of others into the linear and teleological history of the Eurocentric economic world that was so rapidly expanding and which was sketched out in the previous chapter.

The expanding European economy, its necessary politics of domin-ation and the aesthetic use of detail in producing the realism of painting, writing and museums, are connected. Together they have been used to structure and people an exotic other-world of a European 'orient' which the travellers set out to map and detail. In other words, there is a connection between imperial politics, emerging knowledges and the aesthetic forms through which worlds were represented both in art and through the authenticity of the museum and collectors' worlds. Travel was the practice which made it possible and anthropology provided the scholarly face to legitimate it.

Playing the part

As the significance of the exotic orient increased and was transformed during the eighteenth and nineteenth centuries, and as the discovery of increasingly vast remains of ancient worlds was reported, the vogue for paintings and photographs of the oriental traveller in native dress became more pronounced (Jullian 1977; Llewellyn and Newton 1985; Verrier 1979). The merchant adventurer Sir Robert Sherley, like many of the enthusiastic antiquarians of his age, was painted in Persian garb by Van Dyck (around 1622) (Searight 1969: 40–1). David Wilkie, who toured the Levant in the 1840s, insisted on his European subjects wearing oriental dress. A series of charming portraits, like that of Mrs Moore in Beirut (Searight 1969: 16), for example, resulted from his policy and there were many more. Yet his delight in oriental dress was not simply a personal idiosyncrasy but part of a much broader orientalist vogue, and a good many travellers were painted in this way. Among the well-known travellers of their time, Belzoni (1778–1823), William Bankes (1786–1855), Richard Burton (1821–90), J.L. Burckhardt (1784–1817), James Silk Buckingham (1786–1855), Edward William Lane (1801–76) were all painted in oriental dress, and there were many more.[17] Wilfred Scawen Blunt (1840–1922), for example, wore Arab dress not only on his estate near Cairo where Arab food was served, but at his English country house, Crabbet, as well (Tidrick 1981: 125). Other returned travellers created oriental or Egyptian rooms and the vast collections of antiquities which I have already referred to were rapidly assembled.[18]

Many travellers, however, did not assume native garb simply to gratify the artistic tastes of their painter and their European audiences, but to travel in. One of the earliest to do so was Laurent d'Arvieu, who travelled through Palestine in 1664 (Tidrick 1981). The list of those travelling in native dress is long, and includes Carsten Niebuhr on his journey through Iran in 1765–66 (Tidrick 1981: 14 & 15); J.L. Burckhardt, Richard Burton, William Gifford Palgrave, C.M. Doughty, T.E. Lawrence (Graves 1976; Tabachnick & Matheson 1988), Bertram Thomas and, in central Asia, Arminius Vambéry (Vambéry 1865).[19] Some government officials assumed local titles (Glubb Pasha, for example), while others took a local name.[20]

Harold Dickson (1949) is perhaps a special case. In addition to wearing the dress and the title of the people he administered, he went so far as to have a bedouin camp permanently set up for himself, one which moved about with the families concerned. In this way, whenever the Dicksons felt the need of some free and easy nomadic life, they simply rode out to 'their' authentic bedouin camp. Seldom has the dream of the nomad orient been so realistically lived, seldom in such detail, and with never the need to leave the safe haven of the known European world within which they 'really' lived.[21]

While I do not question the undoubtedly genuine identification of Dickson with his Kuwaiti subjects, underlying it is an act of voyeurism which his emotional identification with the 'other' life and world covers up. Victorian voyeurism is perhaps more familiar in the context of the sexual predilections of certain privileged men for servant girls, big red hands covered in the boot blacking of the master and knotty legs encased in rude stockings.[22] There the bodily detail of subordination is linked to aspects of fetishism, service and slavery. In both situations, however, the emphasis on the descriptive detail as a way of determining the truth is contained within a desire to dominate. The focus on what Naomi Shor calls the 'dermal detail' of the warts and all picture that is provided is very marked.

The essential voyeurism, and the 'warts and all' detail of Dickson's classic description of his life in Kuwait, is achieved partly through a massive ethnographic description of 'their' bedouin life and partly through the legitimacy of a peculiar intimacy.[23] It is no accident that the first chapters of his book detail not only his milk relationship to the Arab race and his youth among them, but also the ways in which his special relationship with members of 'his' camp allowed him commerce with the women of their family.[24] His genealogy thus authorises what is certainly a unique European account of women in a bedouin tribe, by placing him from birth as the inside outsider. In fact, it was Violet Dickson who most certainly provided a great deal of the ethnographic information on women.[25] But in the opening passages of his text, it is Harold who uses both the knowledge of bedouin women obtained through his wife, his ownership of a bedouin camp and his purchased role of sheikh within it, to legitimate his claims to authenticity. He invites the reader to follow him inside the bedouin family to look at and come to understand the hidden women as he has done. Through this device the reader steps inside the imperial fantasy and learns to look at these people not as servants of the colonising state but as exemplars of the free bedouin, the pure Arab race, untainted by the civilisation which is, in the person of Dickson, literally buying and selling them and their labour.[26] In his inclusion of the women Dickson has penetrated to the centre of the European fantasy of the exotic orient, he has lifted the veil of secrecy which protected the harem, and he has brought the last site of resistance within 'the orient' into the essentially male gaze of European power.

Unlike the psychoanalytic model exemplified by the 'peeping Tom' in which the voyeur remains hidden, Dickson followed his eye in, but he did not thereby transcend voyeurism. While he sought to become an insider, he was forced to remain a spectator within 'his' camp, the eternal outsider familiar to anthropologists but, due to his imperial status, in a more powerful form than usual. Voyeurism is here the personal act of penetrating the inner world of a subordinated other through the gaze, a gaze which constitutes and objectifies while remaining partially hidden but still outside.[27] Dickson's position of outsider is masked by his adoption of local dress and modes of address and by the collaboration enforced through his position. 'His' authentic bedouin were forced to perform their lives in front of their spectator. It is his journey to the inside world of the bedouin that Dickson graphically details for his audience.

As I noted earlier, voyeurism is particularly marked in orientalist paintings. It is represented in scenes containing nude women, many of whom are slaves or captives.[28] Gérome's scene titled *The Slave Market* exemplifies this form. Harem scenes, with their implications of captivity, are also openly voyeuristic.[29] The men within such scenes occupy a voyeuristic position, whether as lord of the scene or as shadowy, partly hidden, onlooker.[30] In the absence of the represented voyeur, the spectator is positioned in this way too. The eye looks into scenes of intimacy and watches from an invisible position outside. Ingres' picture, *The Turkish Bath*, painted in 1862, is an example of this positioning, while Gérome's *The Great Bath at Bursa* of *c.* 1885 (Croutier 1989: 87) utilises the blackness of slavery to represent the enticing juxtaposition of race, gender and sexuality so crucial to western power relations. Voyeurism is, as Kuhn puts it, 'a kind of "lawless seeing"' in which the object of the look is outside and distanced from the subject (Kuhn 1982: 58). Essential to this form of pleasure/desire is its relation of power. There is no interaction between spectator and observed, no return of the look and no possible punishment. Whereas in cinematic texts, the positioning of the spectator may vary, even within the voyeuristic mode, with single image painted texts, this is less open to variation. In orientalist paintings in particular, the spectator tends to occupy the position of the source of the look and in this way is positioned as a constituting and thus objectifying force (Kuhn 1982: 59).

It is important to understand that the power relations involved in creating the spectator as voyeur also produce and position the spectator as male. Female voyeurism is rare. It appears to occur only under very specific circumstances, and its rarity cannot be explained entirely by invoking arguments concerning either the politics of socialisation (women learn not to look) or those of female invisibility (there would be more of them if we looked harder). The masculinity of the voyeuristic spectator leads to the suggestion that in their relations to 'their' bedouin camp, Harold and Violet Dickson are positioned differently. Like all female travellers in the orient, Violet Dickson can be seen to occupy a male position, but because of her gender she can neither occupy nor realise it in precisely the same manner as a man. The gendering of the exotic orient and the importance of gender and sexualities in organising difference in both the occident and its orient is explicit in European narratives and texts, but rarely more so than in the travelogues.

> The attraction, the spell of Arabia, as it is so frequently called, is a sickness of the imagination. It was not until I had left Arabia and *her* doors were closed to me that, while tasting the bitter-sweets of memor, I began to muse unhappily on how such a barren *mistress*, as that country is, can enslave the heart and mind with so deep an intermingling of yearning and abomination. He is comfortless indeed who has opened the windows of his spirit to *her* parching breath. And it is true that those who have fully known *her* wish never to return. (The Master of Belhaven, cited in Tidrick, 1981: vi. Emphasis added.)

This passage identifies the land itself as female, but it is not the femaleness of the motherland with which Europeans were more familiar but the femaleness of the mistress, the unfettered sexuality that is seen as sick and as barren; that in European eyes is dissociated from love and the female servitude of marriage, and leaves no progeny for the male line.[31] The link between gender and sexuality is critical, for it brings gender into conjunction with morality, and it is European moral superiority which is the constant justification of colonialism. In such a context, the warts and all detail of Dickson's foray into authentic bedouin life and foibles bolsters the moral superiority of the rational, controlled and controlling justice of domination. The presence of the women is of critical importance to the moral judgments implied.

If the gender of the land—the land as unpredictable, parching mistress—is fundamental to the tale of colonial conquest by the European man, it also signals the place of sexuality within the conquest, the place of sexuality in power relations, and the place of occidental sexuality within the imaginary exotic world of the oriental sensuality. The orient provides a fictive space into which the uncontrolled sexuality of Europe, the fears, the longings and forbidden imaginings, can be projected, described and narrated. Rich's (1977) view that a conquered or colonised people is defined as feminine and that the feminine becomes an inevitable and essential feature of the power relations between the two populations is, I think, correct.[32]

I am suggesting that there are at least three areas in which gender operates to structure occidental knowledge and representations of its orient. First, the land itself is gendered female, but in a wild rather than a domesticated rendering of the female. Second, the descriptive detail through which those eastern lands were represented through nineteenth century travellers' tales and their aesthetics is itself feminising. And then, the positioning of the occidental spectator within and without the text is masculine. Within this set of narrative relations, both women's sexuality (always hidden) and that of the feminised, universalised 'oriental' subject, hold a crucial, subordinated, position.

In his book *Orientalism*, Said (1978) documents the European obsessesion with women and oriental sexuality, but he does so incidentally, as part of the process by which the oriental was constructed as an objectified other, unable to speak as an individual and known only through the European writer. He is concerned with how the east and its inhabitants lost the right to speak for themselves, and there is a parallel here with feminist concerns with the effects of subordination on women's voices and subjectivity. The important role of women and sexuality in the structuring of western discourse on the east is a matter he does not dwell upon and, despite his discussions of sexuality, the index to his book does not contain an entry for either women or sexuality.[33] Perhaps because of his concern with textuality, he has missed the sociological significance of this element of his material. Indeed, once having pointed to it, he then seems to go out of his way to minimise its significance. For example, he treats the sexual obsessions of de Nerval and Flaubert as personal qualities rather than as elements of a western discourse on the east.[34] He argues (Said 1978: 181) that although each makes extensive and repeated use of oriental material and themes, neither was actually involved in dominating the east but only used it as an imaginative setting or locale.[35] Intentionality is not, of course, a feature of discourse, so it is strange to see Said try to write it into his concept of domination at this point. One wonders why. The distinctions he attempts obscure the ways in which the orient is represented to a western audience. They also obscure the centrality of women and sexuality to the totality of orientalist knowledge.

Said himself admits to being mystified by the way 'the Orient seems *still* to suggest not just fecundity but sexual promise (and threat), untiring sensuality, unlimited desire, deep generative energies'. He does not see it as germane to his task to unravel the mystery of the combination of fecundity with uncontrolled sexuality, yet part of the answer can be found in the material he provides in his own analyses (Said 1978: 188). The clue lies in his observation that Arab society is represented as passive, both as object to be ravished and through literary metaphor. For example Said notes that the comment of Flaubert's Queen of Sheba, 'Je ne suis pas une femme, je suis un monde', could equally well have been said by the prostitute with whom Flaubert spent an evening (cited by Said, 1978: 342 n. 9). But he does not draw out the implications of the identification of woman and world. A little earlier in his text, he noted the way in which de Nerval wandered through the east's riches and its cultural (and principally feminine) ambience, locating in Egypt especially that maternal 'centre, at once mysterious and accessible from which all wisdom derives' (Said 1978: 182).

Here, the western male is both ravisher and seeker of wisdom, while the wisdom is both gendered female *and* sexed—dangerous indeed. These formulations, attitudes and ideas about the orient are not idiosyncratic but occur throughout the popular travel literature. The explicit metaphorical connection between woman and the world, and the accessible centre of that world as female/maternal, seem to me to suggest that the western 'orient' is indeed a gendered, female orient. It is also a sexed orient, as Said remarked in his comment on the western reduction of the person to a sexed being (Said 1978: 311). This is the relation of domination, the getting of wisdom through penetration, the appropriation of an east by a west through sexuality.[36] Within masculinist knowledges and practices, whether that sexuality is heterosexual or homosexual is largely irrelevant, both in life and in literature, as young woman and boy are assigned equivalent characteristics. Both are soft-skinned, limpid-eyed, prone to tears, and are often grateful to their western overlord (although Flaubert's prostitute [much to his surprise] is refreshingly free from such sentiments). Each yields to the conquering, penetrating, European male of which Pierre Loti's *Les Désenchantées* is a wonderful illustration.[37]

In the nineteenth century, then, several overlapping mappings of a particular form of the world took place. The first was the passion for topography that resulted in the detailed maps of the imperial travellers which was discussed briefly in the previous chapter; the second was the appropriation of the detail of those newly located places through collections of antiquities and the histories that went with them and that now fill museums. Third came the cultural mapping of the unknown world, the detailed ethnology, anthropology and genealogies found in travel tales and ethnographies. Each of these contributed to aesthetic modes using the *detail* which Foucault, Shor and others argue characterised nineteenth century modalities of power and its representations. It is this detail which Shor argues is essentially feminine and perhaps feminising. Each of these mappings overlapped, and each was concerned, in the circum-Mediterreanean at least, with mapping out a feminised, Islamic, near orient through which not only were male sexual fantasies realised, but through which the traveller's imperialising gaze extended ever outwards but also evermore towards the sacred centre of that fantasised space. Burton's visit to Mecca in 1853 perfectly exemplifies this search and the ways in which, as Kabbani notes, the reality of a pedestrian exploration was brought into line with the imagination through disguise, the adoption of an Arab name and metaphors of conquest (Kabbani 1986). Burton was not, after all, the first European to visit Mecca (Ralli 1909) and the Meccans, even though suspicious of British foreign policy, did not murder all foreigners who went there.

But the importance of gender, the femininity of the detail which was often considered inessential to the sublime or ideal which realism presented, must not be overlooked. For if the detail is of the feminine of the nineteenth century, the guise of foreign garb is the detail which is similarly the feminine and essential part of that same world and its conflicts and powers as realised through the marking of boundaries through exploration and travel. The assumption of native garb by the penetrating male traveller, therefore, makes visible the male eye into the feminised oriental domain and appropriates it into its bosom simultaneously. In the process, the authenticity of the feminised other is consumed and reproduced as a lie and a fantasy which the subordinated must accept as genuine. This masterly deception is found in all relations of racism. The European interest in the Semitic races as possible originary Christians was all-pervading in the nineteenth century, and racial conflict continues to be the major focus of colonising 'Indo-Europeans'. The archaeological mythologies of the period and their involvement in theories of racial classification are now being challenged (Bernal 1987).[38] However, it is characteristic that subordinated races are forced to permit certain individuals of the dominating race to enter into their intimate culture and life and to become as 'good' as they are—as black, Indian, Aboriginal Australian or whatever.

In these journeys out to the margins of empire, in their living out of the oriental dream, costume had an important place. It cloaked the dream in the detail of reality and gulled the observer, always present, into accepting the authenticity of the narratives being constructed and portrayed. Many other travellers did not cloak their journeys or their selves in this way. They sought to preserve their dominant status through the maintenance of what they saw as European standards, and their elaborate travelling canteens and trunks and writing desks were only the most obvious part of this approach—the silver and linen alone required that each traveller be supported by a lengthy caravan. Gertrude Bell would never have worn anything other than English clothing, Isabel Burton and Agatha Christie likewise. Yet some of the best known travellers utilised local dress.

T.E. Lawrence, for example, claims that Feisal asked him to wear Arab clothes in camp as they would be more comfortable and make him less conspicuous (Graves 1976: 32). Other travellers had other justifications. Searight suggests that Turkish dress was worn by Europeans within Ottoman lands in order to 'distract ... attention from their alien religion and customs, although by the eighteenth century this was sometimes incongruously accompanied by a European wig or cloak' (Searight 1969: 33). A good many travellers claimed to adopt it for safety's sake and tried to pass as a variant of 'native'—Richard Burton claimed to be an Indian, Arminius Vambéry an Afghan. Doughty wrote that he adopted local dress in order to appear less conspicuous, but far from trying to pass himself off as a Muslim he was doggedly and openly Christian, proselytising throughout his journey and revelling in the discomfort it produced. Comfort is another matter, of course, and many travellers (the Blunts, for example) liked the freedom permitted by the flowing Arab robes or the easy volume of the Ottoman trouser. Yet the number of travellers not assuming local dress, no matter how comfortable, indicates that comfort cannot be taken at face value either. The reason for adopting local dress is not to be found or explained simply through a need for foreign clothing, whatever that need may be. Indeed, the apparent transparency of the reasons for adopting local costume disguises its emotional and symbolic aspects.

More perceptively, T.E. Lawrence later says that 'Of course the mere wishing to be an Arabian betrays the roots of a quirk' (Thomas 1938). Here he acknowledges his desire to *be* an Arab, the desire of the disciplined, rational male to become his other, to relax into the seductions *she* offers, a desire he felt on his first journey out to the orient.[39] It is through the assumption of native dress that certain of the travellers became, in their own eyes, their other, without for a moment leaving the certainties and superiorities of their own world. Perhaps it could be seen as a quirk, but to do so is to allow the idiosyncrasies of the individual to mask the politics of the action and the place of the individual act being played out within much wider narrative and discursive structures. It is here that the romanticism of travel and the individual's reproduction of its images, fantasies and lies are critical in covering up the power which it reproduces.

In the assumption of native garb by travellers in the orient, the real native is, in European eyes, duped into accepting a replica as authentic and betraying the secrets of the hidden cultural world from which the stranger would have been excluded; while the secret foreigner exchanges falseness for the authenticity of the other, receiving good coin for debased. The captured authenticity and reality is then reproduced for the European voyeur and brought into the empire of what might indeed be called the gaze, and exchanged for personal glory. The authenticity of the other is captured through costume, re-presented and taken over to such a degree that ingestion, the gobbling up of reality and power, its incorporation into the body of society and its reproduction through the vitalised and empowered self, comes to seem the appropriate name for this fantasy.

But while the metaphors of imperial travel narratives and their tropes are predominantly those of penetration and unveiling, those of ingestion and incorporation are curiously absent. Their absence is curious because in one sense they are the two sides of the one coin of occidental identity and authority. Within western cosmologies, one can attain power from the sacred centre either through penetrating to the centre of the symbolic and corporeal body or, more directly through consuming the body of the other and thereby incorporating its powers, as in the twin processes of Christianity, pilgrimage and communion. Both these processes are familiar to anthropology and cannibalism has long been a point of fascination in the landscape of other cultural worlds. Lévi-Strauss, for example, proposed a relation between cannibalism and ritual transvestism, and argued that cannibalism is an unstable and changeable form of an underlying schema of behaviour in which identification with the other plays a part (Lévi-Strauss 1987).

Given the abhorrence of cannibalism within Europe, its use as a marker of barbarity and inhumanity, and its association with madness, it is not surprising to find it obliterated from the orientalising texts, tropes and metaphors through which it represents itself. Its absence in the orient and presence in Africa reflects both the evolutionary hierarchy underlying so much of western knowledge, and the way in which it gives priority to one element of 'man's' ascent from nature, with the effeminising of the intermediary stages of the long journey out of cannibalistic barbarity into supposedly failed attempts at civilisation. The assumption of local dress by imperial males, in its attempt to appropriate the life force, the spiritual essence of the feminised other and the freedom of those living outside the restraint of rationality, is not only to consume their identity and to re-present it through the body of the self, just as some forms of cannibalism do, but is also an act of trickery and treachery. The act of ingestion is presented as an act of identification with, rather than the consumption of, the subordinated but admired identity. It is this that is dishonest.

The power of clothing and costume, like the power of masking, is well documented in the anthropological literature. The way in which clothing becomes contagious, for both the passage of strength and of pollution, is equally well known. In the case of the orientalist traveller, the disguise or the costume serves to transfer the power those costumes embody to the body of those who assume them. That power is ingested through the reproduction of the other that the robing involves. But these aspects and powers are all male, a point which Lévi-Strauss emphasises:

> The relation underlying ritual transvestism is always established between men . . . As represented in ritual, cannibalism translates the way men think of women, or rather in which men think of masculinity across and over (*à travers*) women. Conversely, ritual clowning translates the way men think of themselves as women, or try to assimilate femininity to their own humanity. (Lévi-Strauss 1987: 117)

In his brief paper Lévi-Strauss is referring largely to material from the Americas, and his argument is grounded on differences between matrilineal and patrilineal societies and theories of culture which refer to women purely as objects of exchange. Nevertheless, his analysis offers interesting possibilities when generalised to European ritual transvestites in their feminised and subordinated orient. Certainly he highlights the masculinity of it all, and indicates a clear need to incorporate gender into any discussion of cannibalism, whichever form it should take.

4   Women and the Orient

But what of the women travellers who also assumed native dress? Lady Mary Wortley Montagu (1689–1762), for example, is well known to her readers through her portraits in Turkish guise (Melville 1925: 136; Pick 1988; Adams 1878); Lady Hester Stanhope (1776–1839) wore Arab dress in her later years; Jane Digby el Mesrab (1807–81) adopted it (Allen 1980: 94) and so did Emily, Shareefa of Wazan (Wazan 1911). Were these women simply pawns in men's colonial games of conquest, or are these powers and others constituted and refracted differently according to gender? As I noted earlier, a good many other women travellers of the orient would never have dreamed of abandoning their European dress and the femininity that went with it. When Freya Stark made her last journey, aged eighty, through the Himalayan mountains, it took a caravan of ninety donkeys and their keepers to get her to her destination. Gertrude Bell, wherever she went, carried with her a quintessential Englishness, one which she recreated as she went along. When Vita Sackville-West met Gertrude Bell in Teheran in 1926, she wrote:

> ... a door in the blank wall, a jerky stop, a creaking of hinges, a broadly smiling servant, a rush of dogs, a vista of garden-path edged with carnations in pots, a little verandah and a little low house at the end of the path, an English voice—Gertrude Bell ... The garden was small, but cool and friendly; her spaniel wagged not only his tail but his whole little body; the pony looked over the loose-box door and whinnied gently; a tame partridge hopped about the verandah; some native babies who were playing in a corner stopped playing to stare and grin ... wouldn't I like my bath? ... she ... would be back for luncheon ... and so, still talking, still laughing, she pinned on a hat without looking in the glass, and took her departure.[40]

Not only do those women who most fit the heroic mould of traveller, explorer, recorder (that of Burckhardt, Burton, Doughty and their line), not assume local dress, but those who do, do so under rather different conditions to those of their male counterparts.

The role of heroic conqueror of the feminised oriental other was not fully open to women, even to those who sought to appropriate it. Both Gertrude Bell and Freya Stark (who went to the Middle East a generation after her) were exceptional. They were also both single women, as was Mary Kingsley (Kingsley 1897 & 1899; Frank 1986), who travelled and recorded her travels in West Africa just as a man might have done. What these women sought was access to the world of men from which they were excluded at home, and they sought to gain that access through moving outside the feminine world which they found constraining and humiliating. Consequently the dynamic of their travel, as well as their position within a gendered society, no matter how financially privileged they were, was quite different to those of the men of their day. They sought access to male power in their own male world. In such a situation one would predict that women who altered their dress would assume that of European men. It is clear that Bell and Stark (and indeed Kingsley in Africa) feared that their access to the male world and their success in carrying out men's work would mean the loss of their femininity and identity as women. Many of the successful women explorers were vocal anti-suffragists who put a great deal of effort into confirming both their femininity and their sexuality—for a woman who worked and walked 'like a man', wore trousers, rode astride, a woman who is outside male control, risked then (and still does) being labelled as a lesbian and rendered thus unnatural, denatured and non-woman.[41] Thus the pictures of Gertrude Bell surrounded by local children, her hats, the fripperies and changes of clothes with which she and Freya Stark travelled—the images of their femininity. And thus too, Gertrude Bell's despair when her servants refused to break camp on a morning so cold that the tents were frozen stiff, and she wished she were a man so that she could horsewhip them into obedience. Because she lacked the physical strength and the maleness of presence of even a small man, and because in reality she had no experience in whipping servants or anyone else, she had to find other ways of dealing with recalcitrance and rebellion. Sometimes, of course, she had to accept humiliation, simply because she was a woman.

Most women who travelled, however, could not so readily slip into the imperial heroic mould of the men. They travelled as wives or as servants of some kind. Isabel Burton (1876) travelled in just this way, and the narrative of her travels with the Captain Burton who is rather better known than his wife is altogether different from his, though she was far from retiring or incompetent. Her dramatic rides across the desert, her exhaustion and anxieties, were most frequently caused by the wild captain rather than the wild natives surrounding her. Most of her book is taken up with her good works, her piety and her efforts on behalf of her lord and master. Indeed, her sufferings were so long and plentiful that I have a great sympathy for her when, in a final act of revenge upon him, she consigned his erotic and pornographic orientalia to the fire.[42] One cannot help but wonder if her devotion to presenting herself as model wife and pious Victorian Catholic was not partly a response to her desire to be as free and as adventurous as her husband. Certainly she seemed devastated by their sudden and unpredicted removal from Syria and the life she so loved there.

Married men who were explorers and travellers, men like Burton, were hardly touched by their marital or domestic responsibilities. Mary Kingsley's explorer father, for example, was rarely in the house at all, and Richard Burton spent as little time at home as possible. Wilfred Scawen Blunt and Anne (Blunt 1879 & 1881) were exceptional in that, on the major journey into Iraq, Lady Blunt not only accompanied the expedition, but wrote it up for publication.[43] Because she travelled with her husband, Lady Anne Blunt was wedded into her journey not as solitary hero traversing a primordial landscape, naming and noting its features, but as a structural accompaniment. This is very clear in her diaries, where she defers constantly to her husband, although her knowledge of horseflesh was unparalleled and it was the search for pure Arab breeding mares that inspired their journeying.

Similarly, Lady Mary Wortley Montagu, an accomplished letterist of the eighteenth century, travelled to Istanbul in the company of her husband. While at times she certainly wore local dress and is often portrayed in it, she did not assume it as disguise in order to travel incognito. Her wearing of the dress of Turkey was precisely what it claimed to be, the temporary assumption of a costume for purposes which were in themselves restricted in time and space. She disguised herself in Turkish dress for a visit to Edirne's market place and found the Janissaries most respectful of her; but on her visit to the mosque of Sultan Selim realised that she would be recognised, no matter what she wore. Later, she would conform to Turkish dress requirements and wear the veil in order to move freely about Istanbul (Pick 1988: 133, 136, 179 & 188), not as a Turk, but as a conforming visitor.

She did not disguise her 'self' from the local people, nor was her costuming part of an attempt to get inside the identity of the other and consume it in order to establish her own power and the legitimacy and truth of her text. In the famous letter on the Turkish bath, her authenticity rests first upon her gender (it is gender which gets her inside the *hamam*), and then upon the curiosity of Turkish women concerning Lady Mary's terrible stays and the truth-giving which this reflection of the other's view of Europe confers. Within women's travel narratives, the theme of local curiosity concerning European bodies is pronounced. She refused to disrobe completely in the baths and would not gratify their curiosity as to the nature of her naked body.[44]

From this point of view, too, ritual transvestism for women travellers in the 'orient' would have to involve the appropriation not of the local woman's dress of the feminised other of which the imaginary orient consists, but that of the European, occidental male, and this indeed proves to be the case. Women travellers in the 'orient' frequently adopted male dress and rode astride rather than sidesaddle. At the same time this option, because of the hierarchical nature of occidental gender relations, could also become a disempowering one rather than a cannibalising one. European women are deprived of the power of the ritual transvestism proposed by Lévi-Strauss, deprived of the power to incorporate the power of the other through cannibalising it. They must remain forever locked into a position where they are forced to receive power à *travers les hommes*, wife-takers forever, as Lévi-Strauss would have it, with their dress reflecting their position with the fields of discourse within which they must move.

Because of the ways in which women travellers in the orient interact with the gendered and sexualised field through which the orient is represented, biographies of such women readily fall into orientalist modes of interpretation. Whigam Price's (1985) account of the lives of the distinguished twin sisters Agnes Lewis and Margaret Gibson, and Ursula Kingsmill Hart's (1987) rendering of Isabelle Eberhardt's life, exemplify the stereotyped interpretations operating within the genre. In the absence of more sympathetic and complete data, the often fragmentary information about the lives of women travellers in the orient must therefore be handled with care and nowhere more so than where costuming is concerned. Here I discuss three women travellers who are known to have travelled extensively in local dress—Lady Hester Stanhope, Jane Digby (Lady Ellenborough) and Isabelle Eberhardt. Each chose to wear men's clothing, though for differing reasons. None returned to Europe from the oriental world they so wholeheartedly entered into.

When Lady Hester Stanhope took to male dress, she was delighted with it. She writes:

Hamar, 22 January 1813: You have heard, I suppose, that I am dressed as a man; sometimes as Chief of Albanians, sometimes as a Syrian soldier, sometimes as a Bedouin Arab (the famous robbers in the desert), and at other times like the son of a Pacha (Massingham & Massingham 1962: 177)

There are no portraits of Lady Hester painted from life. Her familiar picture, seated cross-legged on her divan, smoking the long Turkish pipe and receiving oriental visitors, was done from the imagination. Yet she was, from all accounts, a strikingly beautiful woman. She was also a superb horsewoman and a competent organiser. Her affair with Bruce, a man somewhat younger than she and said to be of an effeminate style (Sim 1969: 126), left her alone in Syria, there to end her days (Bruce 1951). Like T.E. Lawrence, she created her own legend; just as he created himself as 'king' of the Arabs (Tidrick 1981: 218), Lady

Hester created herself Queen of Palmyra, a queen of the desert, indeed, the new Zenobia.[45] The difference between Lawrence and Stanhope, however, is that Lawrence never left his world, a world in which he occupied a secure position. His eye remained outside the other, and he came back. No matter how much he wanted to be an Arab, no matter how much he incorporated their identity into his, he never left his own unhappy world and the punishments and degradation which seem to have constituted it. Despite her social status, Stanhope was left in poverty by the series of males associated with her and ended her days an imperious recluse on a Syrian mountain, her fine costumes, her appropriated maleness and her effeminised and subordinated lover all long gone. The life she lived on her mountain was far from the exotic fantasy of the orient lived by the Blunts. It was real.

Of Jane Digby (Blanch 1954), however, there are portraits painted from life which show the spirit and intellect which made her marital adventures possible. She appears to be the only woman travelling in the orient of her time for whom domestic life was not a constraint. Her children, legitimate or not, were with their fathers, stayed with them, and had little contact with her. Like Lady Hester's, Jane Digby's venture into the world of the orient was one from which she did not return. She took as her fourth husband Sheikh Abdul Medjuel el Mesrab; she died (1881) in the bosom of his family. But whichever world Jane Digby entered, she entered into it wholeheartedly. When at the age of 46 she ran off to the mountains with an Albanian brigand, she put on the costume of an Albanian woman, dressing, sleeping and eating rough as they did, and galloped over the hills with her lover (Allen 1980: 84) in what was a decidedly un-Albanian way.[46] Her horsemanship was legendary, and it was the search for new Arabian bloodstock for her European stables that first took her to Syria. When she married el Mesrab in Damascus, she did so under Islamic law, donned local dress, lived partly according to local custom and entered as fully as was possible into the world in which she lived. She did not live precisely as a local woman of her status and means would have, but she set out to conform and to live in her tempestuous way within its confines. It is here that the freedoms of the maleness of her other come into play. She maintained her interest in horses and rode them consistently. Unlike the other women of 'her' tribe, she accompanied her husband on his raids and expeditions and is said to have fought alongside him, bought guns for tribal skirmishes, and bled tourists dry through operating protection rackets. At the same time, her Damascus house had both European and Syrian sections, together with the magnificent English garden for which she became famous. She too was known as queen of her tribe. But perhaps one of the most striking aspects of her character, in so far as it is possible to know it from the sources available, is the way in which the people she met were all dealt with as individuals and as independent, adult persons. She was free of much of the superiority which led to the stereotyping and culturalising of individuals within the fantasised orient. She exercises considerable restraint in her descriptions, she frames and interprets rather than relying on the telling detail, the dermal dislocation which culturises and demeans.

Unlike the prominent male travellers among the Syrian and Arabian tribes, Jane Digby was not mapping and naming the orient as she went, not recording it for the Geographical Society or for posterity. She entered into that strange other-land to buy an item which could be bought nowhere else—Arab horses. Her journeyings (she too went to Palmyra) were certainly to see, but they were in the nature of joyful jaunts on horseback, journeys similar to those she had made throughout Europe and Greece. Her entry into the world of the other was a movement in which the wearing of local dress was simply the icing on the cake of acceptance, rather than a subterfuge or disguise. It indicated her intent to cross the boundary of another world completely; a strategic intention and action far from the temporary ritual transvestism of the male visitor in the fantastic orient.

Unlike Lady Hester Stanhope and Jane Digby, Isabelle Eberhardt, perhaps the most spectacular of those women who sought their release in a mysterious and liberating orient, is known more for her transvestism than for her travels. Yet while this emphasis is, I believe, a mistake, it indicates the difficulties faced by women who searched for an other-world outside the domain of the feminine but which still lay within the male tropes of exploration, the desert and the orient. The ways in which her life has been represented also signals the difficulties and challenges posed by her search for otherness and the ways in which a woman's active sexuality becomes a mode of relentlessly reproduced domination for those who transgress.

During her childhood in Switzerland (Kobak 1988), Eberhardt's father insisted that she dress as a boy. This mode of dressing continued through her youth; she assumed a variety of male names, and when she first went to Algeria adopted Arab male dress at once. I have been pointing to the ways in which differing engendered positions produce differing responses to the journey out to the orient. Eberhardt's most recent biographer notes precisely this difference:

> Disguise for her was not just a way of tricking herself into a different society, not just a scholarly nosiness. It also represented an identity she genuinely wanted to assume. Her whole background had predisposed her to want to *become* 'the Other'—not as an amusing ploy, but because she found it deeply seductive. Other more or less contemporary travellers— Kinglake, Doughty, Bell, Bird, Kingsley, North and even Burton—were at heart very much in the colonial mould, with a strong sense of their own national identity, and usually superiority, which prevented them ever wanting to become 'the Other'. (Kobak 1988: 90)

It is the ability to become the other which is absent in ritual transvestism and its associated cannibalism, a transvestism which can only ever
be temporary and which always aims at power.

Kobak offers a very useful account of Eberhardt's family life, Rus-
sian emigré politics, erudition and anarchism to explain her penchant
both for crossdressing and for low life. In accounts of women cross-
dressers in Europe, their association with labouring and manual work
and the mimicry of a tough masculinity, sometimes accompanied by
visits to brothels and workers' bars, raises the possibility of female
voyeurism (Wheelwright 1989; Dekker & van de Pol 1989). Eberhardt's
voyeurism (*her* visits to brothels, dancer/prostitutes, and her pleasure
in the dock areas of town) should be seen in this context and contrasted with the direction of the gaze of Europe toward oriental domestic life. It points to the way in which transvestism offered her a
way out of male control together with a freedom of movement otherwise closed off to young women. Eberhardt's life shows, too, the ways
in which her way out of a gendered occident became totally immersed
in that journey out to the orient, to the emptiness of the desert and the
journeying associated with crossing it. Her difficulties with living as a
man in Europe, her fascination and skill with oriental languages and
her immersion in the scholarship of orientalism, meant that her other
was located first in a rough masculinity and the manual labour that lay
outside the social niceties of her class, and later in the pursuit of that
masculinity's other in its orient.

There is then no precise equivalent to the male traveller in the
heroic mould of ritual transvestism that I have yet been able to locate
among European women travelling in the orient, despite the seduct-
ive fantasies of desert freedom, Arab purity and oriental sexuality
which had their impact on all of them. In her sexuality, Eberhardt
appears to have sought out men whom she could dominate, men who
were undisturbed by her male dress.[47] However, her attempt to take a
masculine role and to explore the sexualities of the orient in a male way
is perhaps as close as any woman could go to emulating the male
model. But in such an approximation, the strength and quality of the
move is such that the identification with the other, the search for it,
becomes consuming. Eberhardt converted to Islam, was taken seriously
by religious scholars, unsuccessfully dabbled in pro-Algerian politics,
utilised alcohol and drugs in an ever more consuming obliteration of
the previous self. Again, it was very clear that for her, there was no
going back. She was swept away to her death in a flash flood in the
desert. It seems a consistent end to twenty-seven intensive years of life.

The journey home

Let me now return briefly to the aesthetics of travel narratives, the
realism which they sought and the rise of detail in the nineteenth

century which coincided with the full flourishing of the heroic travel narrative. I do so by referring to Doughty's extraordinary work, *Travels in Arabia Deserta*. First published in 1888, this book covers travels undertaken in 1876–88. It exemplifies the connections between the journey out, the narrative text through which it is reproduced, and the wider aesthetics within which that narrative can be located. Doughty's most recent biographer, Tabachnick (1981: 40), sets the narrative of *Arabia Deserta* beside the works of William Morris, Holman Hunt and Edward Burne-Jones and points to the links between Doughty and the pre-Raphaelites. These connections can also be seen in the Morris tapestries favoured by Wilfred Blunt in his Sussex home. Underlying the concerns and politics of the pre-Raphaelite painters lay a common enthusiasm for the medieval and biblical worlds and an attempt to reinscribe those earlier languages directly into the present. With this enthusiasm came a concern with precise factual description and a pleasure in what Tabachnick (1981: 41) refers to as the 'indiscriminate detail' through which they tried to make the medieval and biblical pasts real and tangible.

Read in this way, Doughty's idiosyncratic language is no longer anomalous but can be seen as the product of precise political and economic factors and a common aesthetic. Doughty's journey through the biblical lands of the Old Testament can be seen both as the imperialising gaze and as the realisation of the occidental fantasy in its nineteenth century detailistic form. He set out to map and locate the reality of the ancient biblical past, and he also set out, according to Tabachnick, to recast himself as the archetypical biblical Christian. He never at any stage contemplated staying in the world he was so humbly reinscribing for himself, and a bedouin offer of marriage was rejected precisely because its acceptance would have amounted to selling out. His separation from his own world must not result in entry into the other (Tabachnick 1981: 89) that would have resulted in the loss of power and his reinscription as the 'native' rather than as 'hero' or 'prophet'. Doughty's journey, his assumption of local dress and a new name (Khalil), his text and its detailistic narrative forms, thus coincide precisely with the empowering, voyeuristic entry of the nineteenth century male eye into the territory of the other and the cannibalising of the authenticity and legitimacy of that oriental other. In his detail, the warts of reality are part of the way in which Khalil is transformed. Whatever is meted out to him, he accepts. Indeed, he feeds upon the orient with such success that his text becomes the masterpiece. Once that feeding is gone, his poetry and prose are worthless. Surely there is no better example of the power of the orient for the occidental imaginings of itself.

The women who journeyed out towards the dream of desert purity and languid otherness did so in a male world and sought to occupy a male position within it. A feminised other could offer them nothing but more of what was already theirs. When they abandoned occidental dress, it was not the eternal feminine they sought, but freedom from it. What they found was that freedom from feminine constraints was not readily available to occidental women, and that it was difficult to step in and out of one's culture. Those dressed in male Arab dress seem never to have gone home. Those who generally maintained their usual form of dress, like Gertrude Bell, sometimes found so little on offer to them on their return that they chose not to accept it. Bell died of an overdose in Iraq, aged fifty-seven (Winstone 1978: 259), marginalised and unhappy with the prominence of Lawrence and his supporters in drawing up the boundaries of Iraq. Others, like Freya Stark, were luckier.

Stanhope, Digby, Eberhardt, Bell and Stark—these were the women who were most influential in my early longings to travel in the orient and it was their lives I saw as providing ways of living my own. When the main journey came, I sought to step out of their preconceptions and to use my anthropology to overcome the constraints they worked within. It is essential to say that nothing in my preparation for Turkey equipped me for this task. The more I read, the more natural their ideas felt and the easier it was to follow along the path already so well trodden. In my anthropological ambitions and desire to get inside the truth there was little to distinguish me from the travel writers I sought to supersede. On setting out for Turkey, my interest lay not in women but in the male world of markets. As an anthropologist I sought a holistic approach, one which would naturally contain data on domestic life, but with the focus lying elsewhere. My dream was to penetrate the male domain of trade and commerce, and to write an account of it, just as a male anthropologist would have done. As I came to see the centrality of women to the writing of ethnography, that ambition was replaced. But in replacing it I went straight back to the travel literature for more information about women and their lives in the nineteenth century. In showing how travellers and travel writers are part of a larger economic enterprise—and I accept Kabbani's (1986) argument that travel itself is an artefact of empire—I place my work as an anthropologist within the political framework that both Kabbani and I have criticised. In trying to escape those political limitations I turned again to women's writings.

Women's images of the orient

Until recently there were relatively few autobiographies or memoirs written by Muslim women available to English-speaking readers which might have challenged European views of their lives, so the role of European women's writing within orientalist literature is an interest-

ing one.[48] The continuing popularity of Lady Mary Wortley Montagu's
letter describing her visit to a Turkish bath indicates a European interest in domestic life which was absent from the sociology, history
and ethnography of the west, where such subjects were often derided.
Anthropologists writing about women were generally marginalised
within their profession and the glory went to those working on the
structuring of male lives, male culture and male social life. That emphasis was necessarily stronger in those ethnographies dealing with
gender-segregated societies. It was his penetration of the hidden world
of women which made Harold Dickson's account of Kuwaiti domestic
life unique. In general, narrative accounts of the lives of Near Eastern
women were produced by European women. These carry greatest
weight when they originate from inside the hidden world of Muslim
women from which foreign men are usually excluded. Women writers
have therefore been particularly important in providing material for
the moral criticism that accompanies economic penetration of the
Muslim Mediterranean and which focuses on the status of women.
Because of the superior truth claims of women's accounts of Muslim
women's lives, they play a crucial role in popular discourse on the
nature of the orient and are therefore deeply implicated in the structuring of the comparisons through which an orient and its women
become placed within some of the fundamental narratives of western
knowledge. The comparison with the western, Christian woman and
the moral condemnation of her status within Islamic society may be
unspoken, but it is always there, running like a subterranean stream
beneath the engendered cultural landscapes of European descriptions
of Muslim women.

To nineteenth century middle-class western observers, women and
men alike, it seemed self-evident that Muslim women were oppressed
and that their oppression was the result of a harsh religious code that
reduced them to the status of chattels. Their view of the determining
role of the religious law of Islam retains its currency in some recent
scholarship (Keddie & Beck 1978: 27). Indeed, despite the ways in
which other religions have enjoined some very unpleasant practices
upon women (Confucian foot-binding and Hindu widow-burning, for
example), Islam is consistently represented as one of the religions
most oppressive to women. Earlier writers certainly assumed that it
was, and although that unspoken comparison was fundamental to their
descriptions, they set out to describe the objective dimensions of that
oppression without addressing the issues which an already established
comparison raises. When they attempted to describe the lives of women,
their western beliefs about Near Eastern social life readily led to the
misunderstanding or misinterpretation of observations in such a way
as to confirm previous beliefs. In the male imperial literature, observation rarely disturbed such dearly held preconceptions. David Hogarth
wrote:

> I have seen a mother pass and repass a rapid rocky stream, carrying in
> succession a husband and two grown sons; and on the bare stones of the
> Taurus all the women of a migrating horde trailed their bleeding feet
> after the camels, horses and asses which bore their fathers, husbands,
> and brothers. (Hogarth 1925: 45)

Although Turkish women today must often labour under harsh conditions and undoubtedly did so in the past, this description is unlikely
to be complete. If indeed he ever saw the incidents he reports, Hogarth
probably had little idea of precisely what he was seeing. He may well
have seen *old* men riding, and fit and healthy women walking; the
young men could well have preceded the group. It illustrates, however, the easy fitting of observation into preconceived ideas. As for
bleeding feet, peasant life was extremely harsh at this time and one
cannot help but wonder if the cause was poverty.

While it would be unreasonable to expect women writers to transcend their historical and political conditions, women observers have,
sometimes, been less ready to see women in Near Eastern societies as
totally under the sway of men. Of the clearly wealthy and privileged
women already turning toward the west for intellectual support whom
she met, the headmistress of a mission school in Isfahan (Iran) wrote
that:

> the veil has got its uses as well as abuses . . . the Persian woman has no
> inferiority complex . . . when things get too strained and life is intolerable
> in her own quarters, the lady puts away her beautiful silken veil, replaces
> it with an old common one, and goes into the streets . . . She has a day
> on her own quite free. No-one can speak to her . . . This ability to throw
> off all constraint . . . seems to me one of the things that has preserved
> woman's equilibrium. (Aidin 1931)

And in Damascus at the end of the nineteenth century Isabel Burton
records that women there told her:

> If our husband is too severe . . . we dress in *izar* and *mendil*; we go down
> to the Suk [market] and buy, and we visit all the other harims of our
> acquaintance. We might even stay on a visit to them for a fortnight if we
> liked.[49] (I. Burton 1876: [1]160)

These women suggested that seclusion might have advantages; that
the anonymity conferred by an enveloping outer garment may defeat
the purpose for which it is assumed to be intended, and that separate
women's quarters can be used to provide a haven for dissatisfied or
unhappy women from other households. To admit such advantages is
neither to recommend seclusion nor to apologise for it.

Because of the framework of comparison underpinning European
observations about Muslim life and women, women travellers were
sometimes confused by the contradiction between what they expected
and what they actually found. Jenkins, for example, witnessed the
intensive political involvement of Turkish women in the Young Turk

Revolution of 1928. She knew from her own experience that Turkish women could be deeply concerned with politics and heroic in political action but, despite her practical knowledge, she considered that Turkish women lacked physical and moral self-control, and were not sufficiently intelligent to be truthful (Jenkins n.d.: 212). The notion of truthfulness as a quality of European intelligence relates to the moralising evolutionary ideas of her time and background, so that Jenkins is in the uncomfortable position of proposing two opposing views of Turkish women. On the one hand, she *believes* Muslim women in Turkey are oppressed and hopeless creatures—because of their religion; and on the other, the women she meets are actually pragmatic political activists with a remarkable and unexpected degree of personal autonomy. She resolves her conflict by pointing to some assumed underlying moral failings of Turkish women in general, allowing herself to regard the intelligent women she actually knows as exceptions. In her work there is therefore a deeply-rooted contradiction between her observations and the assumptions derived from a Christian politics loaded with moral criticism.

Much earlier, Lady Mary Wortley Montagu formed an opinion of Turkish women which indicated that European assumptions were in need of review. 'Upon the whole', she wrote, 'I look upon the Turkish women as the only free people in the [Ottoman] empire' (Melville, n.d.). She described how husbands supported their wives yet were unable to touch their wives' property—an important contrast with English law—and how secluded women of the elite led extraordinarily sociable and independent lives. Rodinson (1974: 39–41) suggests that her view of elite Ottoman women's lives coincided with a generally more favourable opinion of Ottoman life that derived from the philosophical and theological attitudes of Enlightenment Europe. Yet her view of these women—as freer than the men—although very widely known, was later ignored rather than discussed; it simply did not fit in with the expectations of people about the status and lives of Muslim women. Europeans *knew* that Near Eastern women were oppressed and they *knew* that Islam was the cause of this oppression.

Women's writings about Turkish life do little to disrupt the narrative structures of difference and subjugation characterising travel writing. Their difficulties have many sources, but first among them is the place of the harem and its women within western imaginings of its orientalised other. The harem of the western imagination is filled with women competing ruthlessly for the sexual (and thus political) favours of just one man, of women filled with necessarily unfulfilled lust (there is, after all, only one man) that turns inwards (inverts) onto themselves. At a time when homosexuality was increasingly defined and penalised in England, an era in which love between women was unrecognised in law and totally excluded from discourse, the images of the harem moved constantly toward lesbianism.

These women's worlds, deeply sexualised and surrounded by a boundary of black desexualised eunuchs, were at the heart of nineteenth century explanations of the failure of the Ottoman empire. In an amazing twist of fate, Ottoman sultans—lords of the harem—were declared incompetent and soft because they had been raised by those same secluded women, away from the influence of men. These notions should not be seen as unrelated to other areas of nineteenth and twentieth century knowledges. They developed parallel to an emerging western psychology increasingly centred on individual sexuality as the core of normalcy and maturity, which came to locate homosexuality in undue attachment to the mother, and later placed mothers at the centre of the successful psychosocial development of the child.

The drama and romance through which I came to know the east and first came to read of Izmir and its histories provided an enormous barrier to understanding Turkish society and culture as I was to experience it. Those romanticised travellers' tales, the earlier economic reports and accounts of village lives, and my nostalgia for nineteenth century Izmir, had etched steady traces upon the mind which acted as a filter and taxonomic key against which I automatically organised my experiences and observations. I was well equipped with historical knowledge, but my immersion in what were essentially the mythical structures of western fantasies of an orient which never existed acted to block my ability to know the Turks, understand their motivations and desires so as to arrive at an explanation for the cultural differences I perceived. I wanted to enter into Turkish life and live it as they did, so that I could know its truth. My desire was precisely that of those who had preceded me. I too was following in their footsteps, working within the familiar literary forms of the travel literature.

Comparing women

I hope that it is now clear why I place gender and sexuality at the heart of descriptions of 'oriental' societies; why it is that the way in which Mediterranean Muslim women are discussed in both the scholarly and popular literature is embedded within political and economic forces and the structuring of orientalising narratives; and why, as I began my work in Turkey, I placed comparison at the base of those narratives. Orientalist knowledge of women created by women may contain a critique of popular male-derived views of women, but that critique is usually readily assimilated or marginalised. More importantly, western women's writings operate most effectively within the moral domain. They provide the data assimilated into a moral critique of the basic structures of the Islamic community and the place of women in it. Comparison between east and west and between Muslim and Christian women seemed to lie at the heart of both this discourse and of anthropological endeavour. As I analysed my field notes before preparing my dissertation, it was the parameters of similarity and difference between Islam and Christianity that became the central focus.

In the popular literature, the comparison sometimes remains implicit, and the reader may not always be aware of it. When David Hogarth (1925: 45) wrote about village women in Turkey, 'Small blame to them after all if they are ignorant shrews, seeing to what extent they are treated as mere chattels of the men . . .' he was writing as if Christian women in Europe were *not* treated as male chattels and were not regarded as shrews. Certainly we must praise Hogarth for seeing that being treated like a chattel would make a woman shrewish, but the point to note is the way in which the comparison of Turkish Muslim women with their European Christian counterparts is present but unstated. Were Hogarth to have consulted the English women he had in mind while writing so confidently of the Turks, he might have noticed that many European women felt that *they* were treated as little more than chattels, and that they found Christianity a deeply misogynist religion. Were he alive today, he might also learn that many women still feel unhappy with their lot in a masculinist world and that European, American and Australian inheritance, labour and voting practices continue to discriminate against women in important and punitive ways. These implied and unspoken comparisons between Christian and Muslim women are fundamental—the 'Muslim woman' is compared implicitly with an entirely idealised and secularised 'European woman', and set against an idealised modern 'European society' of equals. The Muslim woman always appears disadvantaged and inferior, and women's writings have not yet significantly destabilised these equations. It is also the case that one category is based upon a religious identity (Islam), the other on a geographical one (Europe), which means that the terms of the equation are not equivalent or indeed comparable. Is it the case, then, that because of the relations of power within which both traveller and anthropologist must work, and because of the metonymical collapsing of woman and orient, that an explanation or clear understanding of the situation of Muslim women's lives is impossible?

If one seeks to provided a better and more accurate—a more real—picture of the lives of Turkish women, the problem of comparison appears to require the setting up of more equivalent and less hierarchical terms of comparison. Because of the nature of the structuring of the similarities and differences through which the comparisons are drawn, an anthropologist faces a task as difficult as that of any other traveller in a foreign land. Anthropology is defined as the *comparative* study of social systems and cultures, which makes the task of comparison explicit. But in order to overcome the limitations of orientalist discourse, anthropology (if indeed it stood beyond the realm of orientalist knowledge, as I at first assumed) would need to find criteria for comparison that were other than those embedded within those ways of knowing the truth about women. For this reason, the account of the lives of Turkish women which I worked out within my dissertation was an exploration of the differences and similarities through which comparisons are made. Because of the focus on Islam and the erasure of Christianity from the form of comparison, I began to analyse women's religious practices.

While an accurate knowledge may never be possible, the stripping away of the complacencies and blindnesses by which we know the world is nevertheless valuable in combating the excesses of power. While of its nature such an enterprise is speculative, it need not be ill-founded. The aim of the dissertation growing out of my fieldwork and the field of knowledge within which it was embedded was to speculate upon the grounds on which a more useful comparison might be drawn and differences more safely delineated.

I proposed a model of Turkish society allowing a clearer picture of gender relations as well as a more useful view of social structures. Setting that model in a broader economic and historical context, I used it to throw new light on Ottoman women and to draw out some of those implications for thinking about the Turkish women of today. I outlined a rather different approach to religious beliefs and practices in Turkey, one which, besides illuminating the lives of Turkish women, indicated the direction a comparative analysis of gender in the Mediterranean might take.

The interaction of anthropology and feminism has been problematic, not least because of the difficulties in developing a feminist theory that is cross-culturally valid without being resolutely ethnocentric. It is not clear how a feminist anthropology would look, but I attempted to scrutinise the structures of comparison as a contribution towards a feminism not founded upon western ethnocentrism. Marilyn Strathern suggests that, 'we might hope that feminism and anthropology brought together would look like neither of them considered separately ... feminist scholarship leads to new mixes' (Strathern 1985: 1). But a feminist anthropology would lead, or should lead, I think, to a radicalising of the entire field. To give women their proper place in ethnography is a first step—and in a flourishing literature, the results of that step are now before us. To move on from there requires a working out of the implications, not just for ethnography, but for social theory in general. For surely, if women assume their rightful place, we will have a radicalised total ethnography rather than twin ethnographies carried out according to gender, or accounts of female and male worldviews. It is no longer sufficient to accept male accounts of male worlds which, after all, are usually dominant and expressed in ideologies insensible to gender difference. Male models of those worlds have been challenged: male values, male norms, male notions of politics, and male ideologies need to be reviewed and devalued until women can take their rightful place within ethnography and in a new theory of society. Until this happens, ethnography, like other western knowledges, will remain distorted and oppressive to women. In its analysis of the symbolic construction of gender hierarchy, its links with the distribution and usage of social space, and the way in which I see the possibility of working with different models of gender and sexuality, my own work, carried out in the late seventies was intended as a contribution towards a feminist anthropology. I do not think that gender is, in any sense, 'less than society' (Strathern 1985: 5). Indeed, I have tried to demonstrate in the sections of this chapter on orientalism that sexuality and gender are the key issues and structures of society and ideology in both the eastern and northern Mediterranean because they *are* society.[50] That interpretation provided a model of society and its structures placing ritual symbolism at its centre rather than at its periphery, made explicit its significance for gender in Turkey, and placed gender at the base of social structure. The following chapters set out the elements of that comparison, together with some of the ethnography on which it was based. They also expose the limitations inherent within it and show why it is not sufficient, why another step is necessary.

5 Islam, Gender and Hierarchy

The problems of comparison and difference are nowhere more evident than in the vast literature discussing the doctrines and practices of Islam. The implications of a set of religious doctrines for women are always difficult to unravel and there is no doubt that, like Christian Europeans, many Turkish men say that women are in some respects lesser creatures than men. Some of the preachers at the Friday midday prayer can be heard, for example, expounding upon women's proper (submissive) role. No doubt one could even find a number of women (although I only ever heard one) who would say the same thing. Both women and men would be able to draw on verses from the Kuran to justify their points of view.[51] Both could also cite some of the enormous range of aphorisms attributed to the Prophet which are not included in the Kuran (which is the word of God alone) and which are assembled into the volumes known as the Hadith.[52] But so too would their opponents and these sources are not one dimensional.

As with Christian theological debates, resort to the fundamental texts resolves nothing. While the words of the prophets may be clearly written down for all to see, their meaning is rarely undisputed. Texts, no matter how sacred, have to be interpreted, just as they have to be put into practice selectively. Some theologians, as well as their congregations, recognise that an unequivocal statement like that of the biblical commandment, 'Thou shalt not lie', often requires both interpretation and tact in application, and this is so even though the text itself offers no apparent opportunity for modification, no grounds for distinguishing between white lies and others, nor for distinguishing situations in which truth may do more damage than a lie. Ibsen's play *The Wild Duck* revolves around just this difficulty. Although all texts, sacred or secular, require interpretation, the difficulty is compounded by the way in which they originate. Texts which originate in dreams or prophecy are, by their very nature, often contradictory, ambivalent, unintelligible, erratic or incoherent. Trances, ecstatic states, apocalyptic dreams, visions, and oracular performances do not generally produce coherent doctrines. The success of oracles, for example, often rests upon ambiguity. Those parts of a sacred text which are direct revelations differ in the degree of interpretation necessary from those which claim to be accounts of historical events, chronicles or law. Nor may it be clear whether a mystical text is genuinely spiritual at all; the sensuous imagery of the *Song of Solomon* indicates ecstasy, and is generally read allegorically. Yet it need not be:

> Thy cheeks are comely with rows of jewels, thy neck with chains of gold.
> We will make thee borders of gold with studs of silver.
> While the king sitteth at his table, my spikenard sendeth forth the smell thereof.
> A bundle of myrrh is my well-beloved unto me: he shall lie all night betwixt my breasts
> Behold thou art fair, my love; behold, thou art fair; thou hast dove's eyes.
> Behold thou art fair, my beloved, yea, pleasant: also our bed is green.
> The beams of our house are cedar, and our rafters of fir.
>
> *The Song of Solomon*, 1: 10–17

The complex symbolism of a text like this requires considerable theological commentary and explanation (the changing gender of the beloved and of the narrator is but one aspect of this remarkable text) but this is not the point I want to stress here. Rather, it is simply that the religious text is often literally unintelligible, even though it may well appeal powerfully to other forms of knowledge (to sensual understanding, for example), and that the need for interpretation is characteristic. The New Testament book, *The Revelation of St John the Divine*, is an example of this type of mystical text, while the narrative structure of the Kuran, received by Muhammed directly from God during times of retreat and meditation, is another. As with other sacred texts, because it is a text and because the text originates in prophecy, the Kuran also requires interpretation.

Not only must sacred texts be interpreted, but the relevant or applicable verses must first be selected. Most Jews, for example, reject the biblical doctrine of an eye for an eye (*Exodus* 21: 24; *Leviticus* 24: 20; *Deuteronomy* 19: 21), and Christians hold the New Testament revision of the doctrine to be valid (*Matthew* 5: 38) without it disturbing its application in the case of murder.[53] The fact that it is the word of the Lord does not guarantee it a following. So it is with the Kuran. The verses precluding the collection of interest on loans have always had a variable following, and those forbidding the wearing of silk garments by men, like many other verses, are often ignored. While theological disputes are firmly based upon the Kuran, they nevertheless cannot be solved either by referring to the text alone, or by citing additional texts. The relationship of text and code to daily life is *never* immediately clear.

The verses of the Kuran, the Hadith, or theological arguments about their relevance therefore cannot provide data for sociological explanations of a gender hierarchy in which women are subordinated to men in Islamic societies. Nor is it possible to argue that women in Turkey are subordinated to men *because* of this or that verse of the Kuran. The variety of women's economic, political and social conditions in the Muslim Mediterranean indicates that the Kuran and the body of law said to be based upon it, is not the controlling factor it often seems. Rather than determining attitudes to women, the Kuran can be used to legitimate particular acts or sets of conditions that concern women (and it frequently is) but this use of the Kuran is part of the politics of the operation of gender hierarchy in daily life, a part of the way in which gender hierarchy and sexuality are negotiated and enforced; it cannot provide an explanation of it.

While sacred texts are not to be considered as a source for the subordination of women to men, the broader set of religious practices cannot be so readily exonerated. The Kuran, while central to Islam, is neither the only nor the most important part of the beliefs and practices that make up Islam in daily life. Indeed, accounts of Islam found in scholarly publications, whether those created by social scientists, historians or orientalists of one specialism or another, are basically accounts of the male view of what Islam properly is.[54] Western scholars and travellers, whether working with religious texts or gathering information at first hand, generally rely on male informants discussing texts written by men and representing their male views of their religion. In the male view, all believers have the same responsibilities to God, and the same duties to perform. All Muslims are equal before God and religious laws apply to all believers equally, but men are in charge of women. *Sure* 2: 228 is often cited in support of this position:

> Women shall with justice have rights similar to those exercised against them, although men have a status above women.
>
> (Dawood translation, page 356)

> The women ought also to behave towards their husbands in like manner as their husbands should behave towards them, according to what is just: but the men ought to have a superiority over them.
>
> (Sale translation, page 24)

When women's beliefs differ from those of the men, their beliefs are declared to be 'not Islam' and very likely 'superstition'. The ritual symbolism of women's beliefs and practices is set out in the following chapters; here, I explore the implications of the dominant, male-centred view of Islam for Turkish women.

In Izmir there was a reasonably close fit between the range of doctrines preached from the mosque, Islam as learned in religious schools and Kuran classes, and the practices of the men (in so far as they are known to me).[55] There are always differences in personal understandings and practices, of course, and many of the people I knew in Izmir disapproved of some of the teachings of the religious high schools, finding them too strict, too rigid and too intrusive. And as in all societies, there are many nominal believers, agnostics and atheists. Very few men I knew prayed five times a day, but a great many attended the Friday prayer at the mosque, and this is, I shall shortly demonstrate, very important for the production of a hierarchy of genders. It is Hanefi Islam, in an urban, middle-class form that I present a brief account of here, and one which will be familiar in outline if not in detail to many Turks.[56]

Most who write on Islam, whether Muslims or foreign scholars, put the five obligations of each believer at the heart of the matter and this emphasis is, I think, correct.[57] The obligations are first, the belief in one God and in the validity of Muhammed's mission, and then the obligations to pay alms, to pray regularly, to fast and to make the pilgrimage to Mecca. There is very little dissent about the validity of these obligations, whether or not one manages to meet them. They are also prominent in the teachings of missionary Islam, for they include the most visible acts of a Muslim. A person who carries out these obligations is both a declared member of a community of believers and a financial supporter of it, a full community member in every way. These obligations rest equally upon all adults.

In this sense then, the community of Muslims is made up of equals, and this is supported by the belief that all are equal before God, a doctrine which can be supported by reference to the Kuran. This is the basis for the assertion that Islam is egalitarian. Yet it is also widely held that while all are equal before God, men are in charge of women, and this too, as noted earlier, can be supported by references from the Kuran. Mernissi (1975: 81) considers the Islamic community, the *umma*, to be the male world, a sub-universe of which the women's world is the other portion. But this is only partly so. The *umma*, or community of equal believers, is not so much a male sub-universe as a universe gendered male in which the female has no place at all. The distinction between the concept of the *umma* as the imagined moral community to which all individuals naturally belong, and the society of believers on earth, is an important one if an understanding of the relation of religious beliefs to daily life is to be achieved. It permits the clarification of the ways in which power is deployed through gender and sexuality. Doctrines of equality expressed through the notion of the moral community of all Muslims, the *umma*, help to produce the basic hierarchy of genders which is so important in daily life. The two domains (the moral community and the world of daily life) are connected but in ways which are not immediately apparent. The five obligations of a practising Muslim occupy a critical position in the relations between the two.

The first two obligations of a Muslim are private and not readily witnessed by others. First and most important, is the formal declaration, known as the *Shehada*, that there is only one God and that Muhammed is his prophet. This God, gendered male, is also the god of Jews and Christians but lacks both the patriarchal characteristics of the Christian Father or the feminine aspects of the Jewish Lord. Turkish Muslims recognise most of the Old and New Testament prophets, and some saints, as Muhammed's predecessors. In contrast to Christianity, while holding Muhammed to be the last of the true prophets, Muslims make no claims for his divinity. The authentic voice of God is revealed through Muhammed, but while insisting on the divinity of the message, they grant the essential humanity of its vehicle. Within the Kuran and in the theological and popular texts, Muhammed is presented as a much more robust figure than Jesus. Born into an established family and network of kin, he is orphaned, marries, trades and politics in a refreshingly human way, and a great deal is known about his life, his loves and his offspring. His kin and wives were important in shaping the early practice of the faith and in factional approaches to questions of succession.

Despite great variation in iconography, the Christian Jesus is a much more ethereal figure, sexless, almost genderless; the historical details are few, often contradictory, and stereotyped. The two are very different types of prophet. The difference in iconology is related to the important fundamental differences in attitudes to sexuality between Islam and Christianity which will be dealt with later. The point to note here, though, is that while these differences are important to a comparison of the two religions and thus of their differences, they are not so critical to understanding the gendered nature of an Islamic world. While Muhammed and Jesus differ in the ways in which they embody gender and sexuality, the statement of belief contained within the *Shehada* is formulaic, frequently repeated by all believers (before prayer, for example) but has no specific implications for gender, gender hierarchy or sexuality within the daily lives of Turkish women.

The second obligation, the payment of alms, is also generally a private matter. Alms can be paid either by a woman herself or through her husband. They are often treated as voluntary and the amount paid varies greatly. Alms-giving is, like the affirmation of belief, of little importance for gender relations as both are practised in such a way that they affect women and men identically. The remaining three obligations differ, however. They are much more public and while they bind all believers equally they have important effects on the way a gender hierarchy is produced.

The first of these is the annual Fast of Ramazan (Arabic: Ramadan), which falls within the ninth month of the lunar ritual calendar. Although it can be a tiring and difficult experience, Turks look forward to the fast and enjoy the opportunity for discipline and purification that it offers. While children, the sick, and travellers are exempt from the obligation to fast, people do not seek to avoid it. Some, of course, give up after the first week, but it is the regularity and prevalence of fasting which impresses, not the lapses, and almost every adult I knew tried to fast for the entire month. The conditions of the fast demand that during the hours of daylight, nothing is to enter the body, neither liquid, food nor smoke. It is also a time of daytime celibacy (*Sure* 2: 186–7). In the evening, the fast is broken with a simple meal and prayer, and a fuller meal then follows, often with visitors. Guests are very welcome at this time and in the past the wealthy often distributed food to the poor. The gaiety and light of the nights contrasts with the austerity of the days. For the evening prayers, the mosques are brightly lit with lamps within and on the minarets outside. During this month, night and day are reversed.

The obligation to fast affects women and men differently because fasting requires ritual purity. A woman who is menstruating or who has recently given birth cannot achieve ritual purity. Clearly, no pre-menopausal woman will be able to complete a fast that lasts for thirty days. The days lost in this way, like those lost through illness, are made up later. They are often attached to a particularly sacred day later in the year or to the week preceding the Ramazan of the year following. The obligation to fast, which applies equally to *all* believers, in fact distinguishes women from men, and it does so on the basis of women's bodies and on universally applicable concepts of purity which affect women and men differently. The distinction made is such that the requirements for the legal and successful completion of the fast cannot be met by women. The equal application of this aspect of religious law, then, leads to a firm distinction between women and men, one in which women are characterised by their inability to control the flow of body fluids. The annual Fast of Ramazan, the only major religious feast of the ritual year that is one of the fundamental obligations of the believer, is therefore significant for gender relations and shows how it is that all believers can be equal before God, but simultaneously differentiated by gender in daily life.[58]

Women who fulfil the fourth obligation, the pilgrimage to Mecca (Turkish: *hac*; Arabic: *hajj*) have precisely the same problem. The ritual purity required for the *hac* rites cannot be maintained by women unless they are past the age of menopause. In fact, most women delay going until menstruation is no longer a problem. The Meccan pilgrimage is extremely important to Turkish Muslims and the formal departure of individual pilgrims from their homes and the departure of the annual pilgrimage 'caravans' from the major cities are prominent public events, even though the journey is now by air rather than by camel. The returned pilgrim uses the title of *haci* and is accorded great respect. Although *hac* is an obligation, it is one which not all can meet, and while this fact is recognised it is nevertheless extremely important in the cosmology of Islam. Mecca is at the sacred centre of the Muslim world; the long and arduous rites which are carried out in the universal company of Muslims assembled there are the earthly manifestation of the unified community of believers. There is much more that could be said about pilgrimage and its significance for women but it is important to note that pilgrimage too is important in gender relationships. Because of menstruation, younger women are prevented from participating fully and uninterruptedly in that congregation of believers, in participating in the community at the sacred centre, even when they have the financial means to make the journey.[59]

Like the Ramazan fast and pilgrimage, prayer, the last of the obligations to be discussed, is also of immediate significance for women but, unlike the others, it is both a public gesture *and* a daily one. The call to prayer is heard clearly in every neighbourhood and most of the women I knew liked to try to set apart a little time each day for prayer, even if family responsibilities made the five prayers impossible or even if five prayers were considered unnecessary. Men too liked to pray regularly, but they did so at the mosque. The midday Friday prayer at the mosque was always very well attended, especially at those in the central market. It was on Fridays that the size of the male congregation became evident.

Prayer and gender hierarchy

It is through prayer that concepts of purity assume their central role in the structuring of the Islamic community, the *umma*, and it is through purity law that gender becomes the basis of that structure. Prayer makes a strong statement about the community of believers in three distinct ways. First, while prayer can take place anywhere, the Friday midday prayer, which draws large crowds and is obligatory for men (but not for women), *must* take place in the mosque. Similarly, the dawn prayers in the mosque which precede the great festival days (the Feast of Sacrifice and the Festival of Sweets) are only obligatory for men. In Turkey each of these prayers attracts an enormous crowd of worshippers, even in inclement weather. Women do not attend any of the obligatory mosque prayers. The weekly Friday prayer and the two annual festival prayers are public affirmations of the structural, visible community of Islam and assert that that community is male. Each of these important prayers must be preceded by a total purification, whereas unless major pollution (ritual impurity) has occurred the other, daily, prayers require only a partial one.

The practices of prayer make a second strong statement about the community of believers through regularly excluding women from praying. While menstruating and during the period after childbirth, a woman cannot purify herself. She cannot, therefore, make formal valid prayers, or touch the Kuran, and is thus placed outside the moral

community of believers. A man who is impure is, of course, also pre-
cluded from prayer and from touching the Kuran, but such a state is
voluntary because his pollution could be readily removed. Within the
structures of logic set out in this section of the law, men's bodies
cannot present them with this problem.

The third important point is that communal prayer is valued over
solitary prayer (Kamal 1964: 11; Doganbey 1963: 209). While it is
perfectly legal and acceptable to pray alone, praying in a mosque is
better. Women usually pray at home, often alone, and do not attend
the highly-valued, regular communal prayers in the mosque. In Turkey
there are no mosques specifically for women but there is usually a
place within the mosque which is reserved for women worshippers.
Some women certainly enter the mosque to join the daily congrega-
tional prayers, but there are relatively few of them. Where women are
found in a mosque in large numbers, it is always the case that the
mosque is built on the site of a saint's tomb. Haci Bayram in Ankara,
and Eyup Sultan in Istanbul, are places where women visit in large
numbers and often join in the mosque prayers. In these cases, the
histories of the mosques show that they originated as a service provided
for visitors drawn to the place by the tomb. They come as pilgrims
first, a mosque is then provided by a benefactor, and if the place is
very popular, all the facilities required by pilgrims, religious officials
and teachers grow up. Eyup Sultan grew in that way and still has
extensive pilgrim facilities; another example is to be found at Seyit
Gazi, near Eskisehir, although few pilgrims now make the journey
there. It is as if women enter the mosque under the protection of the
saint; in this, Turkey differs from those countries where women are
never admitted or have their own separate establishments.

The practice of prayer is connected to the gender structures of daily
life in several ways. Most importantly, it is part of the way in which the
community of believers is publicly represented as a community of
males. Because of the requirements of purity law, the public participation of women in the daily practice of their religion is limited.
Furthermore, to achieve the ritual purity required for prayer they must
put into practice those powerful aspects of ritual law which affect
them in such a way that their community is defined as male and they
are regularly excluded from it. The same ritual prescriptions for prayer
and purity are carried out by women and men, but they have very
different gender implications. For the one, prayer is the means of
symbolic and public affirmation of membership within a universal
community; for the other, prayer becomes part of the process of exclusion and subordination on the basis of gender.

In everyday life, then, it is the practice of prayer which makes both
a Muslim and the Islamic community. The concept of the community
of believers, the *umma*, reflects the importance accorded these ideas.
Prayer is the way in which the individual is drawn into the community

of believers, all of whom are equal before God; but prayer is also the means by which women are given secondary status in the world of men, and are regularly excluded from the male community through pollution. In this way, prayer, politics and gender are bound together in the daily practice of Islam to produce important results for women. Through the concepts of pollution established in the processes of purification and prayer, processes which are the same for all believers but which affect women and men differently, a universally valid male model of society is established for *all* believers. Through the law governing the regular practice of prayer, women and men learn pollution categories which define women as secondary and, it will be shown, as in need of control. The degree of 'outsideness' caused by the important, specifically female, pollutions is indicated by the law which forbids divorce during both the period of menstruation and the forty days which follow childbirth.

For many women, the texts of purity law which set out the categories of their pollution become integrated into life through daily practice. To see the significance of this aspect of the way women and men participate in the daily processes of constructing their places in the community of believers, we need to understand a little more about it. Prayer and pollution concepts go together in a particular way, and because of this, purity law is, for many pious Turks, a matter not only of legal texts but of daily practice. It is often asserted that women are more religious than men. It is impossible to verify such a proposition but I am aware from my field experience in Izmir that many urban women try to take ten or twenty minutes from a busy day to devote themselves to prayer. The point is not whether women are more pious than men, but that Turkish women of all classes, regions and situations are often very interested in their religion and pray regularly.

Purity, pollution and gender

Perhaps the pioneer of anthropological studies of pollution was Franz Steiner (1956) but it was Mary Douglas (1966) who explored the ramifications of pollution beliefs in a more systematic manner. Douglas cast her initial work within a fairly tight systems and functionalist framework. This consisted of a grid in which societies could be placed according to the openness of their pollution beliefs. Social reality is probably more complex and more fluid than her formal framework allows and I think that Turkish concepts of purity and pollution are a case in point. They show how fundamental and pervasive pollution concepts are, and how flexibly they can be utilised under varying economic and political conditions. But her concern with specifying and documenting what she called the openness of pollution beliefs points to a very important characteristic of these beliefs—the responsiveness and flexibility which is combined with their persistence.

A medieval view of Izmir. Wall painting in a manor house, Birgi.
(Photo: Ian R. Smith)

Merchant's house, Izmir, c. 1684. From de Bruyn's *A Voyage to the Levant*

Izmir, c. 1830. Lithograph by L. Sabatier

Izmir's harbour, 1979. (Photo: J. Marcus)

Above: The 'Rock of Niobe',
Manisa, 1979. (Photo:
J. Marcus)

Isobel Burton. Frontispiece
from *The Inner Life of Syria.*

Lady Hester Stanhope at Jouni. Not drawn from life. Frontispiece of Dr Meryon's *Memoir of Lady Hester Stanhope*.

Gertrude Bell and Lionel Smith at Eridu, 1926. (Photo: Collection of the University of Newcastle-upon-Tyne)

Violet Dickson in Arab dress. (Photo: H. Dickson)

Thomas Rowlandson, 'Harem', c. 1812

Above: Young woman waiting for the bus. Black Sea district, 1982. Classical orientalising positioning. (Photo: Ian R. Smith)

Visitors to the shrine of Susuz Dede, Izmir, 1979. (Photo: J. Marcus)

Left: Preparing lunch from a newly sacrificed sheep, Birgi, 1982. (Photo: J. Marcus)

Right: Tying clothing to the window bars of the mausoleum of Ishak Celebi, Manisa, 1979. (Photo: J. Marcus)

Below: The shrine on the beach near Antakya, 1979. (Photo: Ian R. Smith)

Above: Pilgrims at Seyit Gazi, (near Eskisehir), 1982. (Photo: J. Marcus)

The House of the Virgin Mary, Ephesus, 1982. Young girl reading testimonials near the discarded crutches of the healed. (Photo: J. Marcus)

Douglas discusses pollution concepts as symbolic systems which work at two levels, the instrumental and the expressive, and she suggests that 'some pollutions are used as analogues for expressing a general view of the social order'. In order to see how pollution concepts relate to 'the social order' (Douglas 1966: 14), that is to say, how what I have called symbolic models of the moral community relate to social structures, it is crucial to analyse that section of Islamic law which is often ignored by foreigners, purity law. When the Turkish material is scrutinised from Douglas' point of view, two questions emerge. Can Turkish purity beliefs reveal a symbolic view or model of the social order of the kind that she claims, and if they can, what can such symbolic models reveal about gender relationships?

The type of symbolic modelling that I utilised in relation to Turkish concepts of purity differs from the symbolic classifications discussed by Needham (1973, 1979) and other scholars working in his tradition. The models I used are not a form of classification but an organising principle on which such classifications might rest. I was searching for something more akin to Bourdieu's (1977) 'structuring structures' per-haps, a way of inserting a sense of causality into the discussion, but without the teleology that causality so often produces. The difference between a 'symbolic classification' and a 'symbolic model', in the ru-dimentary sense that I am using it in the analysis which follows, is that of the difference between a taxonomy and a theory; the one was, I believed, descriptive, the other analytical. While the distinction between description and analysis ultimately collapses, it reflects two different endeavours, two approaches which have differing political intentions. I found this distinction useful in dealing with the complexities of textual law, concepts of purity and their ramifications in daily life, because it seemed to allow an understanding which helped to establish more valid dimensions of difference between Islam and Christianity and to establish the place of Islam, gender and its relation to social structures in both.

It is important to recognise that concepts of purity and pollution, particularly those directly connected to menstruation and childbirth, are only one element of a constellation of symbolic processes through which the body is culturally constructed, experienced and known. But the principles laid down through those laws ramify throughout Turkish culture and are constantly reinforced. Concepts of pollution, that is to say, concepts concerning ritual purity, relate both to the processes of gender construction and to the ranking of genders into a hierarchy (Douglas 1966: 14). Much recent work on pollution refers to Southeast Asian, Melanesian and Polynesian societies, and while the importance of pollution beliefs for the understanding of sex and gender in Turkish society has been noted (Tapper 1983: 81), the relationship between purity, pollution and concepts of gender relations has not yet been explored in any detail.[60]

The law of purity and pollution

The vast western literature on Islamic law deals mainly with inheritance, family and commercial law and usually omits any detailed discussion of purity law (Coulson 1964; Coulson 1971; Coulson &
Hinchcliffe 1978). But it is just this section of the law which concerns
the five 'pillars' of Islam, the obligations of the believer which provide
the basis for the actual practice of the faith as it is understood by
Turkish Muslims. This section of the law carries into daily life the full
force of what it means to be a Muslim, of what it means to submit to
Allah. Failure to understand the significance of the purity and pollution concepts which are written into both Islamic law and the daily
practice of Islam can lead to difficulties in describing and analysing the
relationship of the law to daily life, and in assessing its significance for
social structure.

Islamic law books provide a rich mine of information on purity and
pollution, but three things must be said about using them as a source.
First, in urban Turkey there is not a large gap between the written
canon law on purity and daily purity practices. Although I draw upon
texts to support the analysis of purity law, I use them as a convenient
reference point for daily practice and to supplement material gathered
through observation and discussion. Second, I draw on two Sunni Hanefi
codifications of the law which are readily available in English translation
(Brandel-Syrier 1960; Isik 1975–81). These translated codifications are
remarkably similar in content to the inexpensive popular texts, freely
and widely available in religious bookshops, which explain in Turkish
how to be a good Muslim and how to be a dutiful, believing woman.[61]
And finally, although the translations I used are from medieval texts,
they remain in current use in both Arabic and vernacular Turkish.

In order to pray, the person must be ritually pure. The legal requirements for valid prayer are therefore spelled out very clearly in the law-
books and in the manuals based upon them. Every action, every
movement, every detail of the process is described and circumscribed
so that the believer can have no possible doubt as to the correctness
of the process and the acceptability of the prayer in the eyes of God.
In addition to bodily purity, valid prayer requires the complete concentration of the body and mind on God. This requirement does not
vary greatly from region to region and is, as will be seen shortly, an
important aspect of pollution.[62]

Pollution and purity are the two sides of the same coin, for pollution
must be removed for an individual to be sufficiently pure for prayer
and for other religious duties. Pollutions fall into two legal classes,
minor and major, each of which can be removed by specific techniques
of purification. As is indicated in Figure 1, major pollution results
from a range of ordinary actions; it would be difficult to maintain the
body in a pure state from one set of prayers to another. Unlike the

situation in many societies (Europe or Melanesia, for example), in Turkey pollution is an everyday state that cannot be avoided. Indeed, Turks say that even if you thought you were pure, you probably would not be, and that therefore a purification must always precede prayer, just in case. Because of this, ritual impurity does not necessarily imply moral failure or sin. How, then, is purity achieved?

Purification

The two types of legal purification, the total and the partial, match the two forms of pollution (major and minor). For the total purification required by major pollution, the entire surface of the body must be touched by the purifying agent, which is usually, but not always, water. The purpose of wetting the head and facial hair is to ensure that water comes into contact with the surface of the head and face; teeth and finger and toe nails must be cleaned prior to purification to permit water to flow around and under them; for the same reason, toes and fingers must be spread apart during the process. No nook or cranny may be forgotten or ignored, and the legal instructions are detailed and complex, both on the various parts of the body, and in the discussion of what to do if water is not available.

The order in which the actions of purification must proceed is also clearly specified. Purification of the hands precedes that of the head, the head that of the feet, and in each case, the purification of the right side of the body precedes that of the left. The partial purification which can be seen taking place outside the mosques just before prayer is sufficient to remove minor pollutions. It follows the same principles as the total purification, but is applied to the head, forearms and feet only. In both, however, the water must *flow* over the entire surface of the part of the body to be purified

Whether it is total or partial, however, the essence of purification is that the *entire surface* of the specified parts of the body should be touched by the purifying agent; that the purifier should *flow*; and that on no account should the purifying agent enter inside the body. The importance of this last point is illustrated by the careful instructions concerning organs like the ears, the nose, the mouth and anus; they must be rinsed thoroughly but without any water being allowed to pass from them into the body cavity. The result of treating the body in this way is that the inside and outside of the body are established as two entirely separate domains, domains which must be kept entirely separate and distinct if purity is to be maintained.

Islamic purification rites are often referred to in English as ablutions, a ritual washing. Mary Douglas (1966) has clearly shown the difficulties caused by failing to disentangle ritual from hygiene and pointed to the ways in which ritual prohibitions are constantly justified

Figure 1   Causes of pollution

major impurities	sexual intercourse post-partum discharge menstrual blood touching a cold corpse
minor impurities	excretion urination bowel gas vomiting tears fainting madness and intoxication deep sleep, strong emotions, laughter, grief
forbidden foods	pork blood alcohol animals sacrificed to other gods
unclean places	abbatoirs
the body	nudity discouraged 'private parts' must never be exposed hair requires special control male circumcision
inoperative prohibitions	silk clothing gold jewellery for men gambling and prophesying blowing on knots usury

through recourse to theories of hygiene. In this case their confusion can also be misleading as the phrase 'ritual washing' combines two distinct ideas. The first is the idea of washing in order to be clean through the removal of physical dirt from the physical body, of which the current western obsession with hygiene is an example. The second is the idea of ritual, which in the Islamic rite implies a sacred cleansing quite different from the washings of daily hygiene, one which aims to remove invisible dirt from the symbolically constructed or imagined body. The commonsense distinction between the two types of dirt and bodies, while not sustainable analytically, can be seen in the case of rape, an act which is totally defiling to a woman but one which no amount of hygienic washing can ever remove.

In Turkey the body is cleansed in the steam-bath or its equivalent; while cleanliness is next to godliness it is quite separate from it. Purification in Islamic law and practice is in no sense a washing, and washing to remove dirt is a totally different procedure. All substances, including dirty ones, must be removed from the body surface *before* purification can take place, so that water can flow unhindered across the body's surface (Isik 1981: [4] 22–3). Purification only incidentally removes substances considered physically dirty, its purpose being not to clean but to reassert the integrity of the body surface, to make what has been breached by daily life whole again, and to make sure that the boundary between the inner and outer domains of the body is once again intact. For legally valid prayer, the body must be both clean *and* purified.

Pollution and women

I have pointed to the crucial relationship of the body surface to the symbolic body categories of *inner* and *outer* as they are developed through the processes of purification and prayer. That relationship can be seen more clearly in the situations which are considered to be polluting. Analysis of the categories set out in Figure 1 shows that the major and minor pollutions seem to fall into two groups. There are those caused by a substance crossing the *margins* of the body and those caused by a *loss of control* of either body or mind. Polluting substances are semen, menstrual blood, urine, tears and faeces. In other words, all substances which cross the surface of the body, except for breast milk (which is not mentioned at all and which is a topic I shall return to later) and sweat. This categorisation of the principles underlying pollution differs from that put forward by legal scholars. Isik (1981: [4] 14–16), for example, holds that there are seven conditions which lead to loss of purity. These are:

Figure 2   Legal categories of analysis

1 things issuing from one's front or back
2 dirty things issuing from the mouth
3 blood, pus or yellow liquid which issues from the skin
4 sleeping lying down or falling down suddenly
5 fainting, craziness or an epileptic fit
6 laughter during prayer
7 marital congress

His discussion of examples and exceptions indicates that exudations of the ears and nose are included within the mouth category of polluting conditions. But it is also apparent that only the red or yellow substances which issue from the skin are polluting. Clear liquids are specifically excluded, and although Isik (1981) does not consider sweat within his discussion of clear liquids from the skin, it certainly qualifies under this category and is elsewhere specifically mentioned as non-polluting. While tears, a clear liquid, are held to be polluting, it is their connection with control, their inherent controllability that appears to refocus them into a context from which they might otherwise have been excluded. Similarly, breast milk appears to be excluded on the basis of colour alone, as viscosity does not appear to be used as a classifying characteristic. What is less clear is whether breast milk is considered to be white or colourless, or whether it partakes of both. In women's rites, milk plays an important part and whiteness is, as is usually the case, consistently associated with purity. However, while purifying substances like water are recognised as colourless, it is not colour which is critical to its purifying quality, but movement. I would argue that rather than colour, it is movement which is absolutely critical to understanding the structure of pollution concepts and in the relationship between pollution concepts and gender hierarchy. The importance of the movement of fluids can be seen in the way in which menstrual blood is treated.

While menstruating, a woman is unable to achieve the state of purity necessary for valid prayer, fasting, pilgrimage to Mecca or for reading the Kuran; that is, a woman is unable to participate in the acts of symbolic construction and expression of the universal Islamic community during these processes. Menstruation is in itself polluting because the movement of the fluid across the body boundary cannot be controlled. Ritual purity cannot therefore be restored until the flow of blood stops. The categories set out in purificatory ritual suggest that menstruation is polluting because the boundary of the body is transgressed—an inner substance flows to the outside. Sexual intercourse is forbidden during menstruation (Brandel-Syrier 1960: 32) but no danger to men results from it, nor is any special purification necessary to remove menstrual blood from men; in contrast to some Melanesian societies, menstrual blood itself is not dangerous. Menstrual blood is just as polluting as semen but only because it flows across the body boundary; but unlike semen, its flow cannot be controlled.

The essence of such a formulation of pollution is that of movement or *flow*. For example, 'Ablutions [must be free] from all flowing blood' (Brandel-Syrier 1960: 9). Flow also explains the nature of pollution caused by sexual intercourse, a form of pollution which is equally polluting to women and men. For both, fluids flow and body boundaries are crossed. The pollution which results from sexual intercourse can be removed only by the total purification which reasserts the wholeness of the body, its integrity and control and its separation into two distinct and separate spheres.

The importance of the movement of fluids across the body boundary is shown by the detailed legal discussions of what does and does not constitute intercourse, and what does or does not constitute a loss of purity during prayer. By analysing the detail of the legal arguments and the possibilities being discussed by the legal scholars, it is possible to see that it is ejaculation which is polluting. It is neither intercourse with women nor women themselves which pollute, but any act which results in ejaculation, including anal, animal or homosexual acts (Isik 1981: [4] 32). Masturbation and nocturnal emissions (male or female) are legally just as polluting as sexual intercourse (Brandel–Syrier 1960: 13; Isik 1981: [4] 31).[63] There is a special technique, described in the law books, for discharging any semen that might remain inside the penis and which might otherwise trickle out inadvertently during prayer, an event which would render the prayer invalid before God. Although intercourse is considered to be polluting, my analysis indicates that it is the flow of sexual fluids across the boundary of the body which is crucial.

The fit between the range of observable body fluids and the world of the body constituted through pollution practices is imperfect. A word should therefore be said about the relations between the logics of structuring concepts to the reality they claim to describe and encompass into their totality. Because pollution practices constitute a 'world' through the practices of prayer, that world must be a closed system or structure and it must be encompassing and universal. But because the body is itself unruly, there will always be a disjunction between it and the worlds built upon it. The disjunctions, where they become visible in logic or law, can often be incorporated into the system. In other cases, they can be ignored without the system collapsing or without its truth claims being affected. With menstruation, for example, no woman below the age of ten is legally able to menstruate and any blood loss is therefore *not* menstruation for purity/pollution purposes. Similarly, a woman over the age of sixty-five cannot menstruate and is therefore not subject to menstrual pollution, whether there is blood loss or not. Movement of vaginal fluids occurring between menstrual periods can be comprehended as 'nocturnal emissions' or sexual fluids and as such are polluting; or they can be ignored and defined as not existing and therefore not relevant to purity practices.

In all cases, however, individuals can (and do) work within the frameworks of the structures of purity and pollution, and make individual choices about when and how strictly to apply them. Some will therefore take special care not to break a fast by allowing saliva as a substitute for water to slide down the throat; others will not feel this to be of importance. People argue around the margins of practices but to say that these concepts are therefore not as central and powerful as might at first seem would, it seems to me, be a mistake. It is precisely their invisibility and flexibility which guarantee their centrality; precisely the arguments and variation at the margins that guarantee the consensus at the centre and their significance in the practices of daily life.

The concern with the movement of substances across the body surface is also found in the legal discussions concerning the conditions of fasting. If the fast is to be valid in the eyes of God, it is absolutely imperative that no substance cross the body boundary in either direction. The people who discussed fasting with me never spoke of the possible difficulties caused by weeping boils, enemas or injections, although they were perfectly clear that one must not swallow food, liquid or smoke, and that one must abstain from sexual acts of any kind. Furthermore, they were very clear that one must not seek to circumvent these requirements. But the legal discussions, in seeking to arrive at a position in which the believer could be absolutely certain that the legal requirements are met, must deal with extreme cases and possibilities. And it is in the limiting cases that the underlying pattern of logic comes more clearly into view. 'If the medicine put on the boil on one's skin penetrates in', the fast is broken; 'all the three imams said that the fast breaks when it is known for certain that the medicine has penetrated in, whether it is liquid or solid' (Isik 1979: [5] 40 & 41). If the medicine stays on the outside of the hypothetical boil, then the fast is not broken. The legal concern with the nature of substances and with the structure of the body indicates very clearly that, not only is movement a critical feature of polluting substances, but also the body and its management is of great importance. The reason for this concern, I have already suggested, is the relationship of purity, pollution and the body to the construction of gender hierarchy. If this is the case, the legal concern with the detail of such matters would not be surprising.

The basis of pollution therefore appears as the separation of *inner* and *outer* into discrete, mutually exclusive categories, and the need to keep them apart. The symbolic separation is achieved during the purification which precedes prayer and other major rites. While the process of purification also utilises distinctions between left and right and between upper and lower, these are not the bases of pollution. Once the body is established as separated into *inner* and *outer* domains, it is then correctly oriented towards God (facing Mecca within the mosque), so that the right:left categories become more significant. However, as will be shown shortly, bodily control and concentration of the mind are much more important than left and right, for loss of bodily control during prayer leads to pollution. The concern with control carries through from the structuring of the body (inner/outer) of the symbolic moral community to the processes and organisation of action and daily life.

Women and the left

In the law books and in Turkish practice there is no consistent link between women and the left hand. This is an important difference between Islam and Christianity (where the left hand plays a significant structuring role). In the mosque, for example, women pray in separate space, either behind the men or in a separate gallery; the women's gallery can be on either side of the mosque, or upstairs. Jewish women in the synagogue also pray separately and also frequently above the male congregation. The critical factor is not the spatial orientation to a fixed point that is found in Christian churches, but gender separation. This relationship between the structuring of ground-space and gender contrasts with the practice of the Greek community in Izmir (and in many Orthodox Mediterranean Christian communities) of placing women in church to the left.

It is possible, therefore, that formally gender-segregated societies like Turkey do not use a distinction between left and right to order gender and spatial relations even though in other contexts, the distinction between left and right may well become significant. There is plenty of evidence from Turkey showing the way in which a distinction between left and right marks the crossing of spatial or conceptual thresholds. One moves into a household right foot forward, into a mosque right foot forward, and out of the mosque with the left foot first. One begins an action with the right and ends with the left. One may even go into an unclean place with the left foot first.

In the literature dealing with the Turkishness of Turkish Islam, the veneration of thresholds by the pre-Islamic Turks is often mentioned. In Turkish epics, the expression 'of the left and of the right' is used as a term of inclusion rather than as one of separation or polarisation (Sümer et al. 1972: xiv, 63, 192 n. 40). While it is possible that the symbolic use of a left/right dichotomy in Turkey is a specifically Turkish or Altaic contribution to Islam, it is a usage which is also Semitic (Chelhod 1973). What really needs to be accounted for is not the origin of the use of left and right as a principle of symbolic or spatial organisation, but the Christian association between women, the left hand and impurity, which is, I suspect, implicated in the production of a specific gender hierarchy.

The difference in approach to women and the left in Christianity and Islam can be seen in the different versions of the story of Adam and Eve that are found in the biblical and Kuranic texts. In the biblical version, woman is created from the left side of man and her actions cause the expulsion of all humans from Paradise. The connection between woman and 'man's fall' is usually made explicit. In Spain the serpent is given a female face (Brandes 1981) while the relationship between Eve, weakness and sin is said to be 'deeply rooted ... at the popular level' in contempary Greece (Hirschon 1978: 68). But in the Kuran (*Sure* 2) it is not Eve but Satan who causes the expulsion of man from Paradise.

The Christian story of Eve being formed from the left side of Adam is recorded in some extra-Kuranic Islamic traditions, but in others Eve's leftness is not mentioned. The Kuranic origin myth lacks the strong association between leftness, woman and sinful sexuality that characterises orthodox Christian belief (Reuther 1979: 42). Gnostic texts preserve extra-biblical versions of the Christian origin myth and its meanings while in some of this literature the serpent is held to represent neither evil nor sexuality but divine wisdom (Pagels 1979: xvii). In some of these texts Eve is closely associated with the serpent's wisdom (Pagels 1979: 29) while in others it is Eve who gives life to Adam (Pagels 1979: 30). Indeed the Gnostic literature contains many references to the femaleness of deities and the wisdom of women, as well as to formulations which present female deities as having three aspects. These are woman as wife, virgin and whore (Pagels 1979: 55 ff.), the motif which appears briefly in some accounts of the three Marys at the foot of the cross after Christ's crucifixion. All such doctrines and interpretations were eventually condemned as heretical by the more established churches and, it appears, successfully so until recent feminist discourse sought their revival and revitalisation. The existing evidence suggests that Islam and Christianity drew upon the same range of eastern Mediterranean religious traditions; traditions which circulated extensively in popular forms for millennia, and which were eventually selected from and declared orthodox, institutionalised and enforced. In this case, the difference between the two versions of the origin myth is of great importance to the construction and enforcement of gender hierarchies and for their significance to the women who live within them. In the variation between the two sets of beliefs, one of the critical dimensions of religious difference emerges.

The evidence suggests that the polarisation of left and right which is made in Turkish Islamic ritual and in symbolic space is secondary and, while relatively widespread, weak. The Islamic practice of orienting prayer toward Mecca rather than toward the east weakens the connection between east and the right hand which is found throughout Christianity, and further distances the ritual links between Islam and the solar cults which preceded it at Mecca. The primacy of the inner/outer distinction and the emphasis on bodily control that is written into Islamic law in such detail also tends to undermine the impact of left/right dichotomy. Rather than being associated with other categories in a classification, in Turkey leftness and rightness are associated with margins and boundaries, with changes of state. Most importantly though, unlike the distinction between inner and outer, a left/right dichotomy is not the basis of purity, and does not appear to be integrated into the construction of a gender hierarchy.

In other words, a distinction between left and right is certainly important—it is important in organising action and in acknowledging symbolic boundaries, and left is, as is so often the case (Hertz 1960) associated with impurity. But this dichotomy is not directly related either to the construction of gender or spatial categories or to the relationship between them. In contrast to the categories of purity law, the spatial and symbolic boundaries that are recognised through the deployment of a distinction between left and right are acknowledged by both women and men and affect them identically. They are therefore not important in the *production* of a hierarchical order of genders within the purity/pollution framework analysed here, although they remain of significance in the production of other sets of differences.

Pollution and 'flow'

The polluting nature of the movement or flow of substances across body boundaries is clarified in the legal discussions concerning illnesses which prevent the achievement of ritual purity. These are illnesses like bleeding from the nose or from a wound, incontinence, constant vomiting, and so on. The approach to these illnesses varies in detail and legal scholars seem generally unwilling to exclude from prayer someone who is stricken in these ways. There is much discussion and definition as scholars try to escape the decision which the logic of the legal argument imposes. But a man who suffers from a dripping penis which cannot be staunched is legally polluted. Such a logical outcome of the law is recognised (Isik 1981: [vol. 4] 49), even if evaded. Hence the lengthy discussions concerning when a nose can be declared to be not bleeding, how much vomiting constitutes vomiting, and whether it matters whether you swallow it or spit it out. Although at first sight many of these legal discussions appear trivial or irrelevant, they are crucial to an understanding of the basis of the concepts of purity and pollution; they reveal a deep concern with the body, its structuring and the logical implications of that structuring, a concern which can only be explained by the relationship of the entire series of concepts concerning the body and its purity to the structure and purity of the moral community.

The process of purification and the concepts of pollution to which they refer together constitute a logical system, the most significant components of which are the body, its integrity, its surface and its control. Once pollution is understood in these terms, a further observation can be made. This is that 'flow' is important in constituting water as a purifying substance. Earlier in this chapter, the importance of the flow of water over the body surface was mentioned. During the partial purification (*abdest*) the hands are held up and water is allowed to trickle down the forearms. This gesture is characteristic and necessary, and all mosques make provision for flowing water for these purposes. Similarly, concepts of hygiene also require flowing water. Turks do not regard sitting in a tub of hot soapy water as cleansing, and handbasins rarely have plugs. Wherever water is used, it must flow (Isik 1981: [4] 53). Standing water is unclean and thus cannot render other things either legally or hygienically pure. Water from fast-flowing streams and springs is greatly valued and sought after. Against this background it may seem more comprehensible to non-Muslims that sand, dry soil or even pebbles (Isik 1981: [4] 14) can be used as a purifying agent if flowing water is unavailable. The property these substances share with water is their ability to flow over the body surface in the manner necessary for purification.

To summarise the argument so far: I have suggested that through purification rites, Muslim Turks participate in the construction of their symbolic bodies in regular and powerful ways. In these rites, the first and most important distinction is that between the inside of the body and the outside world. This is the base upon which concepts of pollution rest and, as we shall see, the definition of the moral community which is built upon it. Then comes the spatial organisation of the body into left/right and upper/lower distinctions. Spatial organisation of this kind is not important in defining pollution or in structuring the moral community built upon it. The requirement for *control* however, is constant and crucial. Pollution law rests on three concepts: on the primary distinction between the inner and outer domains of the body, on the need for self-control in order to maintain that distinction, and on the threat posed to that order by flowing substances. The result is a systematic logic of purity/pollution, a logic which is in no sense a grammar but which, like the grammar of a language, can be used without being consciously formulated.

Women, sexuality and control

Understood in this way, purity law must have important implications for Turkish women. Ritual pollution, for example, keeps a pre-menopausal woman from daily prayer and from reading and touching the Kuran; it prevents her from completing the annual fast of Ramazan or any other long fast which she may wish to undertake; and it prevents her from carrying out the complete cycle of pilgrimage rites in Mecca. For this reason alone many women prefer to postpone their Meccan pilgrimage until menopause. Pollution does not absolve a woman of her religious duties, it merely defers them. Although women do not need to make up prayers missed through pollution, fast-days lost must be observed later. The restrictions concerning purification apply equally to polluted male pilgrims, but while male pollution is controllable, female pollution is not. No man is prevented from fasting by unavoidable pollution; all that he requires is a total purification. No man risks the invalidation of his pilgrimage, except through his own controllable failure to observe the restrictions of the pilgrim state. Pollution does not alter a woman's religious obligations, which are exactly the same as those of men, but it alters the ways in which those obligations are carried out.

Pollution concepts also ensure that the relationship of women to the universal Islamic community differs from that of men. They have the effect of preventing women from continuous contact with God and of regularly pushing women outside the community of believers. Most importantly, pollution categories not only establish the structure of the moral community of Islam but also define women as uncontrolled. They do this by insisting on a distinction between mind and body. As women are unable totally to control their bodies through the exercise of the power of the mind, and as lack of control leads to loss of separation, men must therefore control women if the community is to retain the moral order based upon the clear separation of two genders. Community order therefore rests upon male control of women. This point is crucial in understanding gender relationships in Turkey, and it helps explain the way in which theological discussions of gender relationships constantly utilise the imagery of chaos to illustrate or threaten what will happen if women get 'out of place'. The chaos is, I think, a world from which gender separation and its masculinist hierarchy have been lost.

Pollution practices also have implications for women's sexuality. In contrast to Greek Christianity (Hirschon 1978), Islamic pollution law does not define sex as evil or sinful. Although Muslim Turks have clear notions of sin, Turkish pollution concepts are not necessarily related to them. Actions which result in pollution may or may not be sinful—for example, heterosexual intercourse is not a sin but homosexual intercourse is—and many sinful acts are not at all polluting. It is sometimes said that in cases of bestiality (which is also a sin), the victim should be slaughtered; this may be related to the impossibility of removing pollution from the animal.

In most Islamic countries celibacy is not highly valued and the Kuran provides no support for it. Muhammed was himself much married and the legal scholars, saints and mystics who came after him have rarely been celibate. The fast of Ramazan does not entail total celibacy, but a period of celibacy within the day, a realisable goal that seems to stress the value of sexuality rather than otherwise. Neither is there the split between sexuality and fertility that is found in Christianity. In some of the more recent discussions of Islam and women, scholars like Mernissi (1975) have pointed to the very positive value given by Muslim women to their sexuality. In this valuation they have seen both an important contrast with the situation of Christian and western women and a significant western misreading of the situation of Muslim women.

A reading of purity law suggests that Mernissi is right, for the laws do not deny but acknowledge female sexuality. The law books accord female and male sexuality and bodily secretions absolute equivalence, so that, like men, women are also constructed as sexual. However, unlike male sexuality, women's sexuality is located within a body beyond the control of the mind. The need to control that body in order to achieve purity operates in a way that it does not for its male counterpart. The conjunction of a highly-valued sexuality of the individual with the uncontrollable female body has important repercussions for women, for together they become a continuous potential threat both to the symbolic separation on which the moral community is held to rest and a threat to the male control which maintains that separation.

Attitudes to hair—the need to control it, and the way in which hair is a concern of fundamentalist preachers—suggest that hair, particularly women's hair, may be a dangerous substance in the sense identified in Mary Douglas' work. Body hair is strictly controlled by both women and men in Turkey. Women who uncover the face (and very few Turkish women are veiled) often find it much more difficult to uncover the hair; women working within the household generally wear a head-scarf no matter what they do with the hair on leaving the house.[64] But women wear the head hair long, while men wear theirs short. Against the background of pollution law, women's hair can be seen as a rather difficult substance, perhaps ambiguous in its nature. Although it flows across the body boundary and it is uncontrolled, it is not of itself polluting, for it is constantly present and in movement; presumably such a process would be difficult to eliminate. Cutting the hair (or the nails) does not result in a loss of purity (Isik 1981: [4] 16), even if the cut portions fall upon the skin. While hair and nails are singled out for comment, and while it is clear that they are important, they do not seemed to be linked. Indeed, legal scholars do not consider them to be linked to the acts and events of daily life which routinely lead to loss of purity. They may have magical power, but not in the context of purity law. Hair is, however, quite clearly defined as a substance in need of control and it is closely linked to the order of the moral community. Women also defined as uncontrolled, are further identified as such through wearing the head hair long. Hence the fundamentalist concern with women's hair, the concern that it should be tightly tied and concealed from view, particularly during prayer. However, head hair seems to be used to state a lack of control which has already been established elsewhere; like so much of cultural practice, it reinforces pollution categories but does not appear to determine them.

Other body hair is tightly controlled by both women and men. Pubic hair is frequently removed, a process which formerly took place during the steam bath. Underarm hair is also removed and the removal of all body hair is frequently part of the pre-nuptial rites for both bride and groom. Many women also remove any other facial or body hair, a procedure frequently observed in hairdressing shops. Men do not necessarily remove all facial hair although in nineteenth century Istanbul it was Christians who wore head hair long and shaved the face, while Muslims wore the head shaven beneath turban or fez, and the beard long.[65] Indeed, the hair of the male beard has an important role in Muslim texts, in Turkish folklore and in daily life in many Middle Eastern Muslim cultures. Many pilgrims to Mecca grow a beard and retain it upon their return. This is usually a clipped and trimmed beard, as are the beards worn by Turks of varying religious and political commitments. Style of beard has nearly always been a sign of political stance. Untrimmed beards generally appear only with great age or with the movement out of social structure that accompanies sainthood or madness. Not only did men frequently take an oath on the beard (c.f. Lane 1836: 29 for Egypt in the nineteenth century) but the hairs of the Prophet's beard are an important class of relics which does not appear to have any precise equivalent at Christian shrines (even though some representations of Jesus are lightly bearded).

Many discussions of the apparent significance of hair in the structuring of female subordination take some form of psychoanalytical approach. Another possibility would be to take a Douglasian position and assert that the natural characteristic of hair as a bodily exudation is quite sufficient to qualify it for symbolic attention and for it to be classified either as a marginal substance or as an ambiguous one. Such an approach would account for the fact that hair is the focus of symbolic attention, but not for why women's head hair should be long or for why males should preserve their facial hair either in the form of a moustache or a beard; nor can it account for why the ambiguous state should be rendered as threatening or dangerous rather than, say, sacred.

The importance of hair and the ways in which it is used within an engendered culture and society is perhaps indicated by the way in which Turks distinguish head hair (*saç*) from pubic hair (*kil*). While head hair is treated differently according to gender, pubic hair is removed by both. The understanding of the ways in which women's subordination is produced and then represented is important, for it indicates the ways in which sexuality and gender are deployed within a culture, and thus the direction which political action aiming to intervene within those structures needs to take. One of the critical elements conveyed through this treatment of hair is its need for control. This applies to both categories of hair; the danger of hair suggests its links with moral order and the uncontrolled female sexuality which threatens it. Men can and do control their hair, as they are able to control the movement of their other bodily functions. But women do not. They could, of course, if they were permitted to do so, but they are not. Instead they cover the hair of the head with its danger and seductiveness, releasing it only in connection with their reaffirmed sexuality. Clad in their uncontrol, they represent both their power and their danger and their welcomed and valued sexuality becomes the more firmly woven into their subordination.

Earlier I suggested a link between chaos and the loss of gender separation. That link is also there with hair. Fundamentalist preachers focus upon the need for women to control their hair and keep stray tresses out of sight. Their concern with women's hair, its danger and its sexual associations, becomes more comprehensible if it can be set within this type of framework. It is less a method of oppressing women or of inserting them into a gender hierarchy, but more a way of representing their oppression and subordination.

But what then is the precise relationship of the production of a mind/body split, and its use in the structuring of the body through the laws and practices of purity, to the economic and political institutional structures of the society in which Turkish women pass their lives? If purity law divides the body so firmly into *inner* and *outer* domains, is this dichotomy also at the base of what we usually refer to as social structure, of the institutions of society through which a moral community and its practices are enforced? In approaching this problem it is important to see first that there is no simple translation of this dichotomy from its symbolic and conceptual role in prayer into a means of organising social structures or the topographical space within which people live. The inner/outer dichotomy produced through the body is fundamental to social order, but it organises social structures in an indirect but very effective way, not to organise society into two sections of inner and outer, but into two domains of female and male. The distinction between inner and outer is important in social structure, but is not an organising principle of that structure in quite the way that might be expected.

This is the power of purity law, its concepts and its daily practices. It has the power to engender those categories so that the world is filtered through them and organised to support them. The inner/outer body division translates into a dichotomous female/male society. This is to say that inner/outer is the basis for gender construction and that gender then becomes the basis for social organisation. Such a view of Turkish society has some interesting implications for the seclusion of women, a subject that I will deal with in more detail shortly.

Women and the law

I now want to explore the problem of the relationship between Islamic law and Turkish social structure more directly, and to indicate the value of analysis of purity law for an understanding of it. The relationship of law to what they refer to as custom and social structure is discussed by Keddie and Beck (1978) in their influential book on Muslim women. They approached the status of Muslim women by first suggesting that 'The embedding of the position of women in Islamic texts and law may largely account for the conservatism of Islam regarding women's position as compared with other parts of the Third World, where such religious embedding is less deep'. They went on to ask why it is that '. . . the family and personal status aspects of Islamic law and custom have been held onto most tenaciously. Whereas Islamic civil and commercial codes have often been swept away with a virtual stroke of the pen, the same has been true only of family law in Turkey' (Keddie & Beck 1978: 28). Following from this line of thought, their question then becomes:

> ... not why traditional Islamic culture has been more discriminatory toward women than other major cultures [but] why Islamic society has been more conservative in its maintenance of old laws and traditions in this area [i.e. family and women] than have other societies—although others have not lacked conservatism. (Keddie & Beck 1978: 27)

They suggest that the political subservience of most Islamic males 'may encourage men to keep control of the only area they can—that of women and children' (Keddie and Beck 1978: 28). While this last point is important because it points to links between the realisation of masculinity and the domination of women, it is insufficient in itself to account for the dimensions and nature of the relationship between Islam, the family and women. Similar versions of Islamic family law work very differently in different places. Rural women in Morocco work within a framework of serial monogamy and frequent divorce, while elsewhere, practices range from polygamy and concubinage to nuclear monogamy—each equally legal. Here I consider just one aspect of their argument, that of the connection they posit between legal texts, legal change and the status of women.

The question I would ask is this: is the status of women indeed embedded in legal texts in quite the way that Keddie and Beck propose, and if so, why is it that the texts should be so influential? To the last part of the question the traditional answer is that the sacred texts were written into a sacred law and that Islamic law, being sacred, is peculiarly immutable (and helps to account for the inability of Islamic countries to respond to changing conditions). This is at best a partial answer. There are injunctions in the Kuran which are not re-expressed in law and which have been totally ignored; there are those which, while written into law, require either constant vigilance to enforce or are widely ignored; and there are universally observed 'Islamic' customs like circumcision which are neither mentioned in the Kuran nor written into law. The need for interpretation is often met by resort to the Hadith (the 'traditions' regarding the sayings and actions of the Prophet). The Hadith collections are usually classified into categories of reliable, unreliable and false, but even so, in practice they are a flexible body of aphorisms and statements which could be used just as easily to promote change as to support the *status quo*. Therefore, while a 'sacred' textual law may at first seem to encourage conservatism, this should not be assumed.

Some important concepts regarding women and their place in society are indeed embedded in Islamic law, but not quite in the way that Keddie and Beck were proposing. Instead, gender relations are embedded in the law of purity and pollution, rather than in that of the family. Unlike family law, which is constantly subverted in practice and which has the capacity to improve the economic status of many Muslim women through enforcing inheritance law, purity law has been flexible but relatively unchanging and is incorporated into the daily life of Turkish women and men very much as it is written. Most importantly, its laws are often applied without much thought. Purity law is rarely written into legal codes in the same way that family law is and breaches attract no legal sanctions. It is nevertheless widely accepted and followed and its categories are practised not only in the mosque but also in a range of acts embedded in hygiene and the cleanliness of daily life. Family law is usually written into sacred and secular legal codes in great detail, but this guarantees neither its application, its enforcement, nor its consistency.

I did not see purity law as immutable. Indeed, I was certain that interest in it related directly to politico-economic changes. But until the role of purity and pollution beliefs in producing and structuring what are very deep-seated commonsense understandings about the nature of the world and the nature of human nature could be better understood, its response to economic and political factors could not be properly known. As a corollary to this, it seemed to me that the effects of economic and political factors on Turkish women would not be understood until rigorous theoretical models of purity/pollution could be established.

As Keddie and Beck noted, Islamic family law has been discarded only in Turkey. Atatürk's new republican constitution affected Islamic family law radically. It circumscribed the practice of mosque religion, abolished the mystical orders, and starved religious institutions of funds. But it left Turks reasonably free to practise their religion privately through prayer and purification. The new legislation did not touch purity law. The legislation which so altered Turkish society thus left the gendered and sexualised basis of the moral community of Islam intact, and in doing so, it left women and men in basically the same relationship to each other as before.

The production of a gender hierarchy

That relationship is one of hierarchy, and it is in the production of hierarchy that I see purity law as critical. With the body, the essential productive separation required for purity, I have suggested, could only be maintained by strict control of body and mind, a control that women are unable to achieve not because of their bodies but because of structures of purity law applying to women and men to produce bodily differences. As the ritual symbolism of the practice of purity law leads to the male construction of the category of female as lacking in control, it follows that in the male view, females must be under male control if the moral order of the community, that is, gender separation, is to be maintained. It is for this reason that I suggested that the moral community based on gender separation that *could* be shown like this:

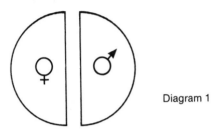

Diagram 1

is actually slipped onto its side to become hierarchical, like this:

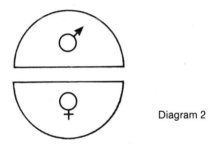

Diagram 2

Hierarchy is achieved at the point at which women are constructed as uncontrolled; their highly valued sexuality renders them vulnerable to the need for external male control. This is the critical structuring intersection of gender with sexuality which creates the potent linkage between body and society through a normative moral community.

A moral community symbolically structured by gender and by separation contains within it the option to structure the actual community structures and space according to the same principles. I think that this is exactly what the Turks do. Women are allocated separate ground-space purely on the basis of gender, and institutional structures are then gender segregated along spatial lines. In this view of Turkish social life and structure, the division of labour (usually referred to as a sexual division in western sociologies), emerges from the division of space according to gender and separation (that is, from purity law), not from economic factors or from specific material relations of production.

The proposition that I make here, then, is that in urban Turkey gender inequality results from the practice of Islamic purity laws and further, that the moral community is based upon gender hierarchy and gender separation. This view of the moral community, which I call a world-view, is a male one, even though it is also held and experienced by women, and it is the realisation of this world-view that is generally studied as Islam or as Turkish society. It is part of what Victor Turner (1969) would call the 'structural' world-view, the structural domain of *the social*. In this male view of the nature of the world, all Muslims are equal before God, but in fact, men are in charge of women—just as is written in the legal texts. Women are definitely not equal to men and they are not equal because they lack control of their bodies and are possessed of a highly valued sexuality.

This is the male view of society preached from the mosque, and it is the Islam that is most easily described by scholars in a variety of disciplines. It is also the dominant model of society, but it is not the only one. In the next chapter, I look at how this hierarchised and en-gendered moral community structures an engendered distribution of space that has both advantages and disadvantages for women.

6 Women's Place, Women's Space

A distribution of space according to gender, restricting women to particular areas, is well documented within both the scholarly and popular descriptions of Turkish life. This sexual division of space, together with the limits placed upon women's mobility, lies at the heart of the moral critique of Islam and occupies a central position in western views of the virtues and vices of Christianity when compared to Islam. The sexual division of space also acts to direct the western mind and imagination inevitably toward the most secret and restricted domain of Muslim life, the harem. The imagination flows into this point of Muslim life—an almost black hole, but one filled with sexualised and perhaps perverse women. This is the point at which religion and women come together in the hierarchy which permits a 'western' moral critique of a universal 'Islam'. And although I do not take it up here, this perverse and sexualised domain of the harem is also highly racialised. This is clearly seen in the use of black slaves in the orientalist paintings I referred to earlier, but it can be seen most clearly in texts on the imperial harem which stress the role of the black (and often very ugly) eunuchs who form the innermost guard of the sultan's women. Those black, deformed and feminised men form a frame or keyhole through which the western imagination approaches the hidden licentiousness and perverse sexualities of the 'orient'. The contrast with the whiteness of the beauties within is usually very marked. Indeed, in all the orientalist paintings I know of, the women within the harem who are 'enslaved' to their lord and master are always white, with black women always being the women's slaves. In these regular juxtapositions of race, gender and sexuality we have very clear expressions of the relations between western visions of its orient, Islam and the vital racism of the nineteenth century.

The lands of the Near East and north Africa are always first defined in terms of the religious beliefs of their inhabitants. Europe and

91

European countries are never defined through religion—it is a geographical west versus a sacralised Islamic domain. No-one writes of the 'Christian city' or 'the sociology of the Christian world', and anyone proposing to discuss urban life in Europe or European culture in these terms would be ridiculed. After all, how could one generalise in such an indiscriminate way? However, it is always held that Muslims are less 'secularised' than Christians and that it is therefore appropriate to describe those cultures and economies through the filter of their strongly held religious beliefs. This is why the western press continues to stress the fanatical religiosity of the Muslim countries, and why they are reluctant to stop doing it. The difference in the construction of the terms of the comparison produces precisely the difference they know and want—the difference that counts, the difference Islam makes. The importance of religion in the relations of power between the various countries allied into a west and those defined as oriental can most easily be appreciated by looking at the ways in which religious fundamentalism in Europe, America, Australia, Israel, Ireland and the eastern European ex-communist states has been presented in the press and among so many experts both inside and outside the universities. The focus and significance accorded to religion as a motivating force of irrationality varies according to whether the people concerned are perceived as friendly or not. Fundamentalist Christian and western sects are discussed as minor aberrations (which they are not), non-defining movements tied to specific social or psychological causes and currents of restricted political significance. The political role of fundamentalist Islam in western definitions of Muslim cultures and societies means that it will occupy an important place in the narrative structuring of orientalised countries and cultures and in the current political climate is represented as universal, irrational, terrifying and mad. And it is Islam which imposes a division of space according to gender, eliminates women from male space in ways which Christianity does not and in the process, creates a site of crucial importance for a westernising imagination.

The harem, the hidden world of Muslim women, has always been the focus of interest and has always tempted the traveller. As I noted earlier, women travellers have been important in bringing this most remote of places into the mapped and known world of western knowledge. The harem has represented the forbidden world of a west and its orient, a realm of sexuality and unbridled licence in which one man rules supreme, the fantasy through which Muslim women become at once sexualised and hopelessly oppressed. Rowlandson's pornographic etching *Harem* (*c.* 1812) illustrates the way in which that inner, secret, oriental domain was used almost as a screen upon which images critical to western notions of sexuality and gender could be sketched. Indeed, Rowlandson's scene is explicitly staged, the suggestion of a tent providing a raised curtain to the serried ranks of naked, provocatively posed, female bodies, with the spectator following the line of sight of the sultan or pasha who is shown seated upon a carpet, smoking, with huge animal-like penis erect. Costumed in an approximation of the garb of the east, this picture shows the ways in which the oriental harem is home not only to the women inside it, but to some very familiar western sexual fantasies. The imprisonment and restriction of sexualised women, a theme currently played out in pornography and rock video clips, is an essential element of the western sexualities, rather than the lives of women who are Mediterranean Muslims. The element of imprisonment and bondage can also be seen in the Algerian postcards analysed by Alloula (1987) and some of the photographs collected by Graham-Brown (1988: 44), and come into play when foreign military invasions are described as liberation rather than as conquest.

Despite its rather simple line and sketching, the Rowlandson scene appears also as a kind of blackness, the blackness I referred to when saying that in the imagination, discussions of engendered space seem to flow toward a kind of black hole. The blackness of race is simultaneously that of voyeurism, the framing of the peepshow or pinhole camera. This blackness focusing on the light within, is also the blackness of barbaric sexualities, those forbidden or rejected in a sanitised west. It is important to understand the ways in which these images of the restricted or imprisoned woman are such an important vehicle for male dominance and enslavement within a western gendered hierarchy in which women are supposedly unrestricted and all are 'free'.

Restrictions upon Muslim women's use of space have served as counter-metaphors for images of imaginary western freedoms, and the metonymical collapsing of dominated cultures into 'woman' has meant that the western gaze has been constantly focused upon the harem in an attempt to locate the reality of the woman at the centre who will prove the empirical truth of the other world of the mythical orient. The closed household, the hidden women within it and the absence of outside scrutiny have meant that to the traveller, the household appears as the most secret of domains and thus a domain of heavily guarded precious and essential truth. The potency of harem imagery results largely from the place that women hold in western knowledge, and the forces of difference seem particularly important in shaping the parameters of this crucial domain. The restriction placed upon women's use of space has provided a convenient site for the working out of western notions of female sexuality, gender relations and Christian doctrines of equality. Feminist questions concerning the status of Muslim women often revolve around the use of space and thus the ways in which spatial restrictions constitute or reproduce systems of domination. Because of the work of women scholars, we now have a great deal more information concerning the ways in which Muslim women of many regions and classes live their lives within a variety of spatial constraints, and the western picture of women's lives is much more realistic as well as more varied.

The spatial placing of women at the goal of the journey east and the restrictions of the harem have also had the effect of producing the feminised east as a largely male reality. In the western fantasy, the absence of women from the imagined daily life of the cities, towns and villages has made that world into an almost entirely male space. The fantasy has come to represent not so much a vision of eastern culture and space as an exact replication of the desired sexual division of western space. The local variations in an engendered division of space found in regions like Turkey cannot mask their profound difference from the variations found in the Christian spatial codings of Europe. Rather than the vast male public domains which characterise the Islamic city as observed through the western eye, and the restricted and reduced female private domains of family life to which few men have access and control, a view in which the male reigns supreme over all space, there is quite a different situation. There is female space, separated but secure in its own right. In the Christian west however, there is no female space, only a female *place* allowed within the privatised domestic domain over and in which men exercise dramatically effective control of their women. The highly valued 'openness' of the western household, in its suburban and nuclear imaginary forms, militates against the satisfactory development of a female domain with women in significant political positions in a 'women's world'. The knitting, quilting, tennis and coffee groups which have been described as women's space in America and Europe are stepsisters indeed when compared to a situation in which women's space is encoded as spatially and hierarchically separated and ranked by gender as it is in Islamic purity law.

The allocation of space according to gender, I refer to as *gender segregation*. But when women are defined as uncontrolled and males as responsible for controlling them, men may try to sustain their concept of male control by reinforcing either the symbolic or the material boundary between the two domains. It is a paradox of gender separation, however, that once men are separated from the female domain, male control of that domain weakens, simply because direct male supervision of it is reduced. This can lead to increasing male anxiety, further attempts to reassert the moral order by moving or reinforcing the boundary between gender domains, further loss of male control, until a situation emerges in which the boundary of the female domain is drawn at the threshold of the household or even at some point within it. This latter pattern I refer to as *seclusion*, and while it is not often found in Turkey, the lives of a small community of Muslim women in Delhi described by Jeffery (1979) provide a current example of it.

Where a moral community, society and its culture is structured in this way, other constraints may also be placed on women's lives; clearly, constraints on women's access to economic and political resources may help to sustain male control of the universal world in which they move. The restriction of ground space, however, need not always coincide with restricted access to political and economic resources. The absolute seclusion of imperial Ottoman women in the seventeenth century, for example, coincided with their access to enormous economic resources and their development of extensive, powerful, political patronage networks.

While I am arguing for the primacy of the gender division and its imposition upon a division of ground space, I do not do so at the expense of excluding material conditions from analysis. On the contrary, a specific politics of gender cannot be understood without a detailed account of their interaction with the social, material conditions of the day and place. The boundary between the two domains of the moral community appears to be a very flexible one, one which responds rapidly to political and economic conditions, but does so in ways which relate to male control of women and their sexuality. A variety of patterns of both segregation and seclusion results from the interaction of the symbolic structures of the moral community with the socio-legal structures by which a gender hierarchy is implemented. The data on Ottoman women, while very limited, illustrate the point.

Purity, history and Ottoman women

The popular orientalised view of Ottoman history, which has it as beginning with a period of medieval glory, followed by a steady decline continuing into the present, has been extensively criticised (Said 1978; B. Turner 1978). Until recently, considerably more was known about the extremities of the time-scale, the ages of glory and collapse, than of the stages by which one became the other. The focus on beginning and end contributed to the often-discussed and characteristic feeling of orientalist timelessness. There were very few detailed studies of the seventeenth and eighteenth centuries and a good deal of what was written 'rest[ed] upon the flimsiest basis in fact' (Owen 1977: 133). The lack of information about these centuries made it easier to visualise the impact of European capital as a relatively recent phenomenon and to conclude, as some did, that what is perceived as westernisation began in the nineteenth century. In such a view, the moral decay of a declining empire was unable to survive the economic and moral challenge of a more vigorous west, with the result that western expertise had to be brought in to help the region to 'modernise'. External economic and political factors are seen as peripheral to the processes of internal decline, while the effects of European capitalism and industrialisation in the earlier periods remain obscured. Some of the difficulties that arise from this approach to history-writing are illustrated by the propositions put forward in an interesting discussion of Ottoman women by Dengler (1978).

To make maximum use of the available range of source material, Dengler collapses time-frames in order to arrive at generalisations about Ottoman women in the Imperial Age. But because the time-scale is so long, it immediately becomes unlikely to be valid. Similarly, perceiving change over the length of time being considered becomes very difficult. Applied to the study of women, this method leads to the thesis that by the end of the fifteenth century the organisation of Ottoman women in society 'appears to have been set very much in the pattern it was to keep until the reforms at the end of the nineteenth century' (Dengler 1978: 229)—in other words, four hundred years of stasis. The view that the sixteenth century saw the institutionalisation of the seclusion of women is fairly widespread (Taskiran 1976: 18); however, to assert that it was during the sixteenth century that Ottoman women became secluded differs from suggesting that the 'social organisation' of women remained unchanged thereafter. Gender hierarchies and patterns of segregation are far more flexible than this.

When seen against the effects of an expansionary European politico-economy on the Ottoman Empire, the timing of the seclusion of Turkish women is interesting. There are a number of chronologies attaching to seclusion, but it is most often thought to have occurred against the backdrop provided by the wave of inflation, probably caused by the influx of cheap American bullion into the Ottoman economy, at the end of the sixteenth century. Institutionalised seclusion of women must be considered against a background of economic difficulty caused not simply by internal political decay or moral decline but by the effects of western capital on a mercantile economy. That for four hundred years thereafter the organisation of Ottoman women remained unchanged is a suggestion difficult to sustain, although it is a relatively common view and one which is fully consonant with the orientalist view of an unchanging orient with rigidly traditional social structures. Nevertheless, it cannot be accepted without more detailed justification. The treatment of change and continuity within western histories therefore has implications not only for overall historical narratives of evolutionary progress, but also for the accounts of past women's lives through which we come to know those of the present. The acceptance of this sort of proposal results partly from the separation of orientalist historians from historians of the west, and partly from the development of a specifically orientalist methodology.

One must ask why such a method is used. Part of the answer is that it produces results which conform to existing preconceptions, so that the conclusions have a superficial plausibility which closes off further questioning. Another part is to be found in the failure to develop a more suitable language for the analysis of women and their place in society. The concepts being used are too general to be of value. It is difficult to say anything useful while 'women', 'status' or 'organisation' are used as undifferentiated analytical categories. More importantly, these methods and approaches avoid the need to work with a theory of gender, sexuality and male power and thus continue to erase questions concerning the role of these factors in producing western knowledge.

The two fields of study, that of the Ottoman and the western family, are motivated by different problematics and therefore need to draw on different sets of empirical evidence and different theoretical approaches. Those differences guarantee the differences of their 'subject', of course, for some of the familiar differences between cultures vanish as soon as they are treated through the problematics and analysis reserved for western societies. The differences involved become clearer if the work of historians of the western European family are examined. These scholars (e.g. Anderson 1980; Houlbrouke 1984; Segalen 1983) have been very conscious of the effects of time and place on family and gender and have produced a series of detailed and specific studies. They draw on work of a variety of western social and political theorists, on Foucault perhaps, or Eco, Baudrillard or Bourdieu; alternatively, on Raymond Williams or even Marx. A number of distinguished social historians have incorporated feminist critiques into their work in ways that are very different from the orientalist work. In sociology, Christine Delphy's (1984) work offers a more radical perspective on the relations between family, economy and gender hierarchy. Historians of Ottoman women might draw on such sources for an alternative theoretical framework—on the work of the social historians of the western European family and on feminist analyses of family and gender structures. A third possibility lies in the anthropological literature on family life and domestic organisation that is found in recent Anatolian ethnographies, together with the extensive anthropological work on gender and sexuality. While this literature also poses problems and suffers from many of the difficulties of orientalisation which occur elsewhere, it offers certain possibilities.

Where sufficiently detailed studies of Turkish family structures exist, for example, they show that precise patterns of residence, household composition, age of marriage, frequency of divorce, number of children, sibling relationships, preferred marriage partners, significance of patrilineages and clans, degree of protection afforded married daughters by the natal family, control of bride-price and so on, are all remarkably localised and probably time-specific (Benedict 1974; Starr 1978; Kiray 1976; Meeker 1971 & 1976; Stirling 1965). While it is true that the anthropological data are often sketchy, dispersed, and sometimes theoretically uninformed, a close reading of the available ethnographies indicates that far from being a fixed entity cast in the patrilineal, virilocal, extended, polygynous, ideological mode, family structure is exceptionally flexible. As a result, the organisation of Turkish women within the family varies dramatically from place to place and time to time. Because of the recorded variability and flexibility, there is now little ethnographic support for the notion of a traditional family, so that attempts to relate changes in family structures to modernisation or urbanisation are not very convincing (Kongar 1976). It may be suggested, of course, that contemporary variability in family structures and domestic organisation in Turkey results from the destruction of traditional structures by the processes of modernisation, and that it was precisely the absence of such factors in the past which led to the general stagnation and decline that allowed traditional family structures to persist. But such approaches assume either that social structure is simply replicated by each successive generation, rather than being actively negotiated, or that social change is produced by external factors and that in the Ottoman case, significant external economic factors were absent until the nineteenth century. Both assumptions must be rejected.

The notion of the late impact of capitalism on the eastern Mediterranean was challenged by Braudel (1972), while other studies (Naff & Owen 1977) also suggest that the processes by which the Ottoman Empire was fragmented and incorporated into the periphery of a capitalist world-economy began at least as early as the sixteenth century. I have linked the growth of interest in Europe's ancient Greek origins to just these economic movements. Rather than painting a picture of economic stagnation and moral decline, there appears to be the possibility of considering the Ottoman Empire to have been subject to the same sorts of economic processes that were found elsewhere in the expanding world-economy, and that the Ottoman 'economic mind' (Inalcik 1970) is not a haven of traditionalism but a dynamic response to a changing world order. Once one has admitted external economic and political forces to a history of Turkey and can work within dynamic time, one can also argue that family structures, the place of women in them and within other social structures, may also have varied in the past. No society has ever been isolated from the impact of its neighbours, the Ottoman Empire less so than most. It is interesting to note how thoroughly the empire has been bounded off from Christian Europe, perhaps the better to stagnate internally.

The task of bounding, defining and differentiating has been efficiently carried out through history-writing; for western observers of the Middle East, the problem has always been one of change and continuity within that history. Whereas 'the west' is perceived as being committed to change through the generation of scientific knowledge and thus to 'progress' (see Jarvie, 1984, for a recent affirmation of this position), 'the orient' was perceived as steadfastly resisting change and, I have noted already, as lacking in the sort of rational thought that permits scientific discoveries and technological advances that lead to 'progress'.

While no anthropologist would now propose such naive unilinear evolutionary schema, the assumptions underlying social evolution remain embedded in much of the literature and are difficult to escape. Polygyny, for example, is usually considered to give way to monogamy as a society modernises, and Turkey has legislated against polygynous unions for precisely this reason. It is also the case that western feminists, Christian missionaries and many social scientists hold the view that polygyny is associated with low status for women (Davis 1968: 133). It follows from such a view that monogamy is the better type of marriage arrangement for women and that in this respect, Christianity is superior to Islam. Again, the matter of difference arises. Questions of social change are set against this unstated comparison between 'orient' and 'west' and 'Muslim' and 'Christian' that is so much apart of the western moral critique of the 'Other' that it precludes finding a useful answer.

A more differentiated language and analysis not only permits a more precise understanding of gender relations, but it also produces a more useful picture of social change. The analysis of the symbolic structuring of gender and space that I presented earlier indicates areas of change that may have been important for women. It allows a distinction between the ways in which changing material conditions react with the structures of gender hierarchy, and the impact of economic change upon the social structures by which a gender hierarchy is realised through practice. The models of the moral community that are generated through the practices of purity law are partly unavailable to ideological critique and partly immune to changes in economic and political structures. In this sense, Dengler's (1978) notion of an unchanging organisation of women is closer to being true; but what is *relatively* unchanging is not the social organisation of a gender hierarchy, but that gender hierarchy itself. It is precisely the social structures and ideologies by which hierarchy is realised that respond to changing material conditions and which cannot be considered as either permanent or traditional.

In addition to the problem of time and change and the difficulties which result from it, historians of Ottoman Turkey also face the problem of interpreting their data. This problem can be illustrated by referring to patterns of women's property holding in Anatolia during the sixteenth and seventeenth centuries. Utilising very interesting material extracted from wills in sixteenth century Bursa, Dengler (1978: 235) notes:

> a marked preference by women to divest themselves of property not related to the household.[66] This last point is even more succinctly put in the seventeenth century Kayseri, where women divest themselves of extrahousehold property three times more frequently [than men].

There is no problem here with the facts of the matter; not only are they attested by figures from Bursa and Kayseri (Jennings 1975), but a much larger set of documents from the courts of eighteenth century Aleppo (A. Marcus 1985) shows a similar pattern. Women tend to sell off land and buildings. But what do the data mean, and how are they to be interpreted?

No amount of empirical data can provide an interpretation of this evidence for women as property owners and property sellers, and it is at this point that the assumptions about the nature of the Ottoman empire, its gender relations and the processes of social change within it, become crucial. If one accepts the set of assumptions usually characterised as orientalist, one would have to infer that the high percentage of sales of property by women means that women are exchanging real property for cash, buying luxury goods and consuming their (or their husbands') capital.

Support for such an interpretation comes from an examination of the items left by women in their wills. From this and from other data, Dengler (1978: 236) considers that 'Their [women's] reading habits suggest a similar predilection for amusement and diversion ... their free time was spent in idle consumption, on promenades, excursions, picnics in the countryside, and at women's baths'. The picture that emerges is pleasant, but it is one in which the women of the urban bourgeoisie of a prosperous trading city were, because of their wealth, largely idle consumers. What the women bought and sold is important because certain versions of decline theory assert that the considerable assets of the Ottoman empire were consumed in luxury goods rather than invested, and that therefore the capital accumulation, which is incorrectly held to characterise European economies at the beginning of the capitalist era, failed to occur in Turkey. The picture of Ottoman women that emerges from this interpretation therefore conforms to decline theory and either allocates women a role in the decline, or makes them an example of it.

But is this interpretation correct? Is it indeed the case that the transfers of land and buildings into consumer goods, into jewellery, mirrors and so forth are really to be considered as a movement of capital from investment to consumption?

In reaching an alternative interpretation, the first point to be taken into account is the nature and practice of Ottoman law. Ottoman inheritance law (as codified in the *Hedaya*) ensured that women in-herited a fixed share of the estates of a deceased parent, spouse or child, and smaller portions from more distant relatives. A daughter received only half the son's share, and wives received only a small share of a deceased husband's estate (Coulson & Hinchcliffe 1978: 46), but if the law was enforced, a woman of the urban mercantile classes would tend to inherit little but often. As there is no primogen-iture in Ottoman law, if there were no countervailing forces estates tended to become extremely fragmented and common ownership of very small shares often occurred. While there may be other factors involved, the law itself will produce this effect. One can observe the same pressures at work in Turkey today. Residence after marriage is often (though not always) virilocal, and it is possible for married women to be pressured by male heirs into exchanging their share of inherited real property for cash or valuables.

As noted above, a widow is not a major beneficiary of her deceased spouse. The bulk of a married man's estate goes to the offspring, which may well mean that the marital dwelling devolves not upon the widow, but in small shares upon her children. Such an estate is then subject to reconsolidation through some of the owners selling to the others. If there is a tendency toward fragmentation and then toward the sale of small portions of estates by women to men, women would tend to accumulate cash or other valuable items in much the same way that men would tend to accumulate buildings and land. If, as seems likely, women in the seventeenth and eighteenth centuries had only limited access to the market place, and if women found it difficult or unsafe to travel long distances to inconveniently located orchards or fields in which they had a small share, there would be an additional incentive for them to divest themselves of certain kinds of property. It is therefore possible to account for the facts, in so far as they are known, without defining women as consumers of assets.[67] Indeed, when the nature of the investment by women in jewellery is considered more carefully, the pattern of transactions seems perfectly rational.

Part of the reason for characterising Ottoman women as consumers is to be found in the nature of the items listed in the Bursa wills, items like jewellery, mirrors and elaborate clothing. In Turkey today, jewellery is largely gold; in the past, clothing and linen was often heavily embroidered with gold and silver thread. Many families still own the older style of wedding dress of red or purple velvet that is encrusted with gold thread and most women own gold jewellery in one form or another. Women acquire gold throughout the life-cycle: they receive gifts of gold at birth, at marriage, at some annual festivals, and on the birth of their children. Women also inherit jewellery from female kin, or receive it by direct gift. The small gold coins which are sometimes given to a young boy at circumcision are often put aside to be included in the wedding gifts that will be made to his bride. Wealthy women acquire more than the poor of course, and are probably better able to retain it, but even quite poor women accumulate considerable amounts of gold jewellery and coin. This gold is not consumed except in emergencies; instead, it is a durable asset in a fluctuating economic world, an asset which is both portable and convertible on demand.

The importance of gold in the economy can be seen in the markets. The bazaars of even small Turkish towns contain large numbers of gold merchants. Gold coins and jewellery are bought and sold at a daily fluctuating rate which relates to the international gold market. Certain objects are of standard quality and weight—bracelets, for example, are manufactured and sold in this way so that they carry regular and known values within marriage exchanges. The customers in the gold markets are almost exclusively women, all of whom have some knowledge of the qualities, weights and age of gold. The goldsmith's guild is a large and powerful commercial organisation, as it was in the seventeenth century (Evliya Effendi Çelebi, 1834, volume 1 (2): 86).

It is at least equally plausible to suggest that urban women in Bursa and Kayseri in the sixteenth and seventeenth centuries also received and purchased gold in the form of jewellery, clothing, mirrors and other valuable items, and that it is this form of wealth which we see being distributed by women to their heirs in the Bursa wills. Clothing was included in registered male estates (Faroqhi 1984: 90) as well as in women's. It should be recalled that Ottoman law granted women ownership and control of all their assets within the marriage, and that the law protected the ability of women to accumulate and control their assets (an advantage not lost on Lady Mary Wortley Montagu). The illegal sale of a woman's gold by her husband was harshly treated by the Ottoman courts (Jennings 1975). Women could also make direct gifts of their jewellery to their daughters, thus passing on wealth through the female line. We do not know whether sixteenth century women did this, but as it is done today, it is clearly a possibility. It is therefore possible to suggest that in purchasing jewellery and clothing, the urban women who appear in the Bursa wills were not consuming their assets but converting a male form of asset into a female form, a form over which they had unequivocal personal control.

Perhaps the most interesting fact to emerge from the study of Ottoman women in Bursa and Kayseri is that some women actually increased their holdings in real property, a fact which theories of idleness or consumption cannot account for. Unfortunately the nature of these holdings is not clear, but the court records of Kayseri show women buying property, women lending money to other women and to men, women trading in cotton and opium, women successfully claiming their inheritances and marriage payments in court (Turkish: *mehr*) and women setting up perpetual trusts (*vakf*) for their heirs.

While there is no doubt that women of the urban elite and of the bourgeoisie enjoyed passing their leisure hours in visits, picnics, at the baths and on walks, and although they may well have enjoyed reading frivolous books, this does not seem to me to be overwhelming evidence for idleness in general. Nor is the case for women as consumers very convincing. What seems to emerge from these fragmentary data is a much more interesting picture, one in which urban women appear as remarkably autonomous within the hypothetical limits of the patterns of gender segregation of the time. Propertied women appear as controllers of their property and as willing and able to go to court to enforce the contractual rights granted through Islamic law. In seventeenth century Kayseri at least, the courts were open to rich and poor, villager and urbanite, Muslim and Christian. Rather than consuming material assets, there is evidence that in some cases women transferred their assets from a male form to a female form, a form which was partible and readily convertible, a form which circulated by gift, loan and inheritance within the female domain, much as land circulated within the male domain.

Had the exchanges been only between men, that is, if men had been exchanging property for cash or valuables, this would not so readily have been interpreted as consumption. The connection between sales of property and the consolidation of fragmented estates would have been more obvious. Indeed, just this point has been made in a large study of the court records of eighteenth century Aleppo (A. Marcus 1985).

Even though the available data are fragmentary, it is nevertheless possible to wrest differing images and understandings of the lives of Ottoman women from it. If the theoretical framework remains constrained by orientalist discourse, if the theory is functionalist and gender-blind, then the image of women consuming their assets will emerge and be considered plausible. If the assumptions of orientalist discourse are abandoned and if theory is taken from a feminist perspective, then an alternative image and understanding emerges. The Ottoman women who appear in the latter perspective are much more active, rational and autonomous individuals than those who appear in the former. They also appear as significantly involved in the market economy. I want to explore women's relation to the market place in Ottoman Turkey in more detail, but in order to do that, it is necessary to take into account the impact of European capitalism on the Ottoman economy.

The Ottoman economy and women's rights

In order to explore this relationship more carefully, I return to my earlier observation that Ottoman history has been better researched at its beginnings and end, than it is in between. I have already noted the effect of this hiatus on concepts of social change, its contribution to both the ideology of the orient as a timeless essence and the conceptualisation of the Ottoman empire as being in the grip of slow economic and moral decline. Considered from the perspective provided by Wallerstein (1974), the causes and processes of economic and social change during these two centuries become more comprehensible.

Put most simply, Wallerstein suggests that as capitalism developed within the 'core' economies of Europe from the sixteenth century onwards, capitalists sought export markets for their manufactured goods from a constantly shifting 'peripheral' zone. I suspect that the notion of the value of economic growth began to gain currency from about this time also, although it only became fundamental with the development of economics as a science. From the peripheral zone, however, the core European economies extracted raw materials, labour and unprocessed foodstuffs. The relations between core and periphery are such that incorporation of a region into the periphery of the capitalist world economy creates the need for new markets, new and cheaper labour supplies, and new sources of raw materials. Such a system, in Wallerstein's view, constantly creates the conditions for the necessity of its own expansion and it is in that context that a culture develops in which economic growth is perceived as vital rather than cancerous.

Zones which become peripheral to the core economies of Europe share certain characteristics and the actual processes of incorporation are remarkably similar over time and region. The internal economies of regions in the process of peripheralisation will exhibit, Wallerstein suggests, political, economic and social characteristics that reflect the response of pre-existing social structures to the economic and political demands of the core zone. Wallerstein's theory therefore can account both for the similarities of the broad processes of expansion and incorporation, and for the specific differences of the eventual accommodation between the core and a particular periphery. Problematic for feminist and non-marxist scholars, his theory nevertheless offers a more dynamic view of historical processes, one in which there is no possibility of an unchanging, resistant, traditional, society.

The ways in which the processes of peripheralisation worked out in Sicily, where the medieval mixed subsistence agriculture was transformed into a mono-culture of wheat (Schneider & Schneider 1976) are interesting. The move there, as elsewhere, was from production of food for home consumption to food production for export to Europe.[68] Changes to the nature and role of agricultural production then led to a need to import food and manufactured goods. In Sicily, the conversion of agricultural land to grain production resulted in both poverty and what the Schneiders describe as 'rural brokerage'. Brokerage describes a set of economic and political relations in which the combination of political instability, rural brigandage and the agricultural export market creates the social space for an economic intermediary between rural producer and exporting urban merchant. In Sicily, armed pastoralists acted as brokers; later, in coping with the demands of nineteenth century industrial capital, their brokerage role was transformed into the institutional structures of the Mafia.

There are many parallels between the Sicilian experience and that of the Ottoman empire, despite the differences of scale and complexity. At the time for which the court records of Kayseri provide glimpses of the lives of Ottoman women, the Ottoman economy had ceased exporting luxury cloth and was deeply involved in the supply of raw materials to the growing textile manufacturing centres of Europe. Although Ottoman governments made every effort to prevent the export of food crops like the olive oil and grain which were needed to provision the Anatolian cities, the demand from Europe and the possibility of high profits from illicit exports (Mantran 1977) ensured that large areas of land in western Anatolia, the Aegean islands and the Balkans went over to large-scale grain production.

As a result of transformations of the rural and urban economies and of the consequent impoverishment which led to the weakening of the bureaucracy, Anatolia, like Sicily, also suffered from serious political instability and brigandage. By the early eighteenth century, the government in Istanbul had lost effective control of most of Anatolia to local lords and banditry was endemic, but this situation was the culmination of processes which began much earlier. Most of the lordly bandit lineages trace themselves back at least to the seventeenth century and it seems that those in Cilicia (Gould 1976) and those in western Anatolia (Veinstein 1976) were involved in the export, legal and illegal, of grain and cotton to Europe.

Rural-mercantile brokerage also became a necessary part of the established pattern of organising Ottoman trade, but, as I noted in discussing Izmir's history, rather than armed pastoralists, it was the Jewish and Christian communities which were able to utilise their language skills, administrative experience, educational advantages and religious compatibilities to move into brokerage. In the sixteenth and seventeenth centuries, both Christians and Jews who appeared in the courts of Kayseri and Bursa were able to enforce their contracts under Islamic law. We know that this was also the case in Aleppo somewhat later (A. Marcus 1985). In these centuries the law was applied universally so that non-Muslims were not necessarily disadvantaged. The merchant guilds of Bursa, for example, were not usually based on religious affiliation and in this bustling manufacturing town, only three specifically Jewish guilds are recorded (Gerber 1976: 84). The 'minority' communities whom the European governments were so anxious to 'protect' stood poised to benefit further from the brokerage role during the period of the penetration of nineteenth century industrial capital.

To assess the full impact of such changes upon women, a very clear picture of the pre-penetration phase of the imperial economy would be necessary, together with detailed information on many aspects of women's material, social and cultural lives. Unfortunately, only the outlines can be determined, and even then, none too clearly, particularly as it is difficult to locate an originary phase precisely. However, it has been noted already that in seventeenth century Anatolia and eighteenth century Aleppo, women had personal access to the *kadi* courts. Earlier, I noted that the institutionalisation of the seclusion of women (Taskiran 1976: 18) took place in the sixteenth century, but it seems reasonably clear that in those years, whatever form institutionalisation or seclusion took, it did not include exclusion from access to legal protection.

The sixteenth century wave of inflation that I earlier referred to (Braudel 1972) was also the economic backdrop for the codifying of Ottoman commercial, land and family law by Ebu-es-Süüd, the Sehy-ul-Islam (*Encyclopedia of Islam*: Abu'l Süüd; Shaw & Shaw 1976: 22). Both the formalisation of the legal structures of the Ottoman state, and the institutionalisation of the seclusion of women, took place against the initial destabilising effects of the penetration of European capital. Although the Empire was prosperous, this was also the era of the Celali revolts and the flight of the peasantry from the land. Despite these events, Ottoman law, based on principles of gender segregation, granted women significant legal rights and protections. The law was formulated and enforced, in the more important towns at least, so that it acted to counter the alternative models of gender hierarchy and control circulating beyond the reach of law encoded in the patrilineal ideologies of tribal, clan and lineage practices.

Sixteenth century Ottoman society appears as relatively open, formally structured by gender and religious affiliation, a relatively prosperous, urban, mercantile economy supported by a food-producing peasantry and an effective legal and bureaucratic structure. Sometime toward the middle of the seventeenth century (Mantran 1970) prosperity decreased overall and the polity weakened. This was when the English first began to sell their manufactured woollen cloth in Anatolia so that by about 1620 all English purchases from the Ottomans were paid for by it. The British largely purchased the raw silk (R. Davis 1970: 195–6) brought overland from Persia to Bursa, whose silk spinning and weaving industry was by this time no longer export-oriented. These years also saw a growing trade in raw cotton grown to feed the European mills (R. Davis 1970: 200 & 204).

Despite the importance of exports of raw materials to the Ottomans, their significance as a trading partner to the core states of the capitalist world-economy decreased dramatically. Anatolia was gradually impoverished. Villages lost their schools (Dengler 1978: 230 & 240 n. 9), and education declined; the quality of the legal scholars, the *ulema*, could not be maintained. Entry to the theological colleges (the *medresse*) was difficult, with the result that government judges and officials were often ignorant of the law (Repp 1977) and had little interest in applying it. By the eighteenth century, appointment to legal and bureaucratic office had become hereditary rather than competitive, so that the *ulema* of this century 'differed substantially from that of the sixteenth' (Zilfi 1985: 320). The widespread corruption caused by administrative collapse fuelled European notions of oriental decline and despotism. In the nineteenth century the economic activities of the European powers produced the final destruction of local economic control, while their political ambitions caused the breakdown of the Ottoman provinces into a reordered series of nation-states, no matter how weak the basis of such political forms might have been. Byron's romance with Greece, Lawrence's adventures in Arab-land and Gertrude Bell's travels in Iraq were part of these dismantling processes.

The penetration of the Ottoman economy by European capital in both its mercantile and industrial phases has implications for the rise of the concept of the nation-state in the eastern Mediterranean, for the rise of a market-oriented dependency elite, a feeble urban bourgeoisie, and an impoverished peasantry, just as it did in Sicily (Schneider & Schneider 1976: 7). The incorporation of the empire into the periphery of the world-economy also had implications for the increasing social visibility and status of religiously defined groups which came to be perceived as foreign minorities with physical and cultural characteristics alien and antithetical to the Ottomans, a structural and representational visibility that was to result in massacres, war and the expulsion of survivors. Is it feasible that the structures of gender hierarchy, gender segregation, seclusion and the social organisation of women's lives could have remained largely unchanged in such dramatically changing times?

Women of the imperial Ottoman family were often granted large and valuable estates which they managed through agents. They established extensive networks of patronage and brokerage and exercised considerable political power (F. Davis 1968). The seventeenth century is referred to as the 'Sultanate of the Women', but in fact the influence of the women seems to have begun rather earlier, about 1565 with the daughter of Suleyman, a widow of the Grand Vezir (Dengler 1978: 237). The mother of Murad III sat on the Council of State and while Mehmet III was on campaign, his mother ran the empire for him. The wives of both these men wielded considerable political power, but in the next century, Kösem Sultan, the most formidable and long-reigning of all, was defeated not by the state authorities who were men, but by another woman, Turhan Sultan (Shaw & Shaw 1976: 204; Dengler 1978: 237). The success of these totally secluded women has caused one scholar to suggest that the men of the imperial lineage at this time were little more than pawns in women's political games (F. Davis 1968: ch. 10). This they were not, but they certainly gained access to powers which in Europe were not available to women. Women of the elite (but not of the imperial lineage) regularly presided over large households of slaves and family, managed their own political and economic affairs through agents, and used some of their wealth to provide public services and endowments for the cities (Bates 1978).

While women may have been discouraged from, and disadvantaged within, the market place, Ottoman/Hanefi law upheld the rights of women to act as autonomous individuals within commercial transactions and marriage in a way that was unknown in England for many centuries. Ottoman women had the right to enter into contracts without constraint and to pursue their claims against defaulters, fraud or illegality, in court. Women, like men, were able to appoint an agent to act and trade on their behalf, and the Ottoman law of agency is particularly well developed. In the Kayseri courts of the seventeenth century women were able to testify on their own behalf, and the courts were open to women on any day (Jennings 1975). Where information exists, it seems to show the courts of this period enforcing the laws that protected women and their commercial enterprises. There are conditions under which neither gender segregation nor seclusion exclude women from political power or economic activity, and the information on Ottoman women illuminates the range of possibilities available within a gendered division of space. The division itself *may* offer advantages to the women working within its structures by providing a spatial dimension to a gendered world.

Gender and separation

I have argued that distinct gender domains are the basis for the social organisation of ground space, that women are allocated ground space that is separate from that of men. If this were the case, then each gender domain could have its separate social and symbolic centre, rather as Victor Turner's theory of the nature of sociality suggests (Turner 1969; Turner & Turner 1978). The mosque is the spatial location of the symbolic 'centre' of the male domain, and we have seen that women are largely excluded from it (J. Marcus 1983). The household is the spatial location of the symbolic 'centre' of the female domain, and there we also find that men are largely excluded. Just as women have no 'place' in the mosque, so men have little 'place' within the household. Just as the mosque is the focus of male rites and just as it is symbolically protected from impurity, the household becomes the focus of women's rites and so the boundaries of the household are ritually protected from impurity.

From the engendering of spatial domains, it follows that the female domain cannot be equated either with a domestic or private world, and the male domain cannot be identified as public. There are public and private spheres within each gender domain. A circumcision rite, for example, is a public event for which women and men may assemble in gendered groups within the household. Under these circumstances the household is not private, as it is open to all other women and hospitality demands that all guests be admitted. It is simply closed to men and they must gather in separate space. The local streets within the domestic quarters and other women's houses are likewise public female space, even though the household forms a very private, symbolic centre on other occasions. The mosque becomes men's private space on occasions, with the market the public male space.

The situation in Turkey differs from that found in many other Muslim countries, partly because of the quantity of ground space available to women and partly because of the means by which gender separation is achieved. Gender separation can be achieved socially as well as spatially. Women learn not to interact socially with extra-household men, or they may use modes of dress to establish a personal female domain within which they are enclosed while moving through male ground space. The degree of harassment experienced by women as they enter male ground space will have a determining effect on their mobility, but in Turkey the streets are not strongly identified as male ground space and women move freely through them. In countries where veiled women are harassed while in the streets, and where the streets are clearly conceptualised as male ground space, separation can be said to have moved toward segregation; where women are forbidden all male ground space, and the boundary of the female domain is drawn at the household door, seclusion becomes complete.[69] Yet even when the boundary is drawn right at the doorstep, women may still be able to move freely through the male ground space in which they have no place. Veiled and secluded women in Turkey and many other places may well visit extensively. Veiling does not necessarily limit mobility.

The question here, though, is not women's mobility or degree of constraint, but the implications of a gendered division of ground space for women's relations to the economy. Delphy's (1984) distinction between 'market' and 'domestic' modes of production is useful because it allows women's labour within the household to be given a proper status. A domestic mode of production will include all those aspects of women's labour that are appropriated by the male household head, but it will exclude women's independent transactions within the market mode which in itself, need not be gendered. Transactions may be between women within the women's domain or between women and men in either the male or female domain. The strongly gendered division of ground space that one finds in Turkey and many Muslim societies can be seen to be neither a necessary impediment nor an overall disadvantage to women's economic activities. Indeed, Delphy's domestic mode allows a much clearer picture of women, labour and the market to emerge.

In a formally gender-separated society with a particular legal system, while women's unpaid labour may be appropriated by the household head, this is not necessarily the case. The situation differs according to class and region, but even among the peasantry, it is sometimes possible for women to maintain control of some of their labour and property and to transact it within the market mode. Among urban women, this is even more likely as aspects of Ottoman law concerning the autonomy of the economic individual, inheritance law and property ownership within marriage have been incorporated into the Republican legal code. The Ottoman legal system differed from those of contemporary Europe, and it is this code that western capital encountered as it penetrated the Ottoman economy. Ottoman law guaranteed women access to an ungendered market mode of production, even though it did not necessarily allow women either access to male ground space or a place within the social structures of the male, mosque–market complex.

Because the male household head is able to appropriate the value of the product of family labour, the location of the productive processes of the market mode of production within the household unit does not and cannot lead to any alteration of gender hierarchy itself. Nor can the participation of women in the market mode of production alter the terms of the gender hierarchy. However, where institutional structures exist which guarantee women's access to and control of such resources as come their way, they are able to appropriate and maintain their limited share of resources and may share in both modes of production, in both the domestic and market modes of the economy. Even if women were able to gain equal or superior control of labour and resources within both the market and domestic modes, there is nothing to suggest that the gender hierarchy would be affected. It is more likely that economic activity would be devalued as 'women's work', or that men would revalue and monopolise the non-material sphere, as Hamilton (1975) suggests is the case among Aboriginal Australian societies. This is why it is so important to distinguish clearly between the hierarchising of genders and the particular set of engendered material relations through which that hierarchy is sustained and enforced.

Without legal protection, however, Ottoman women were forced to surrender precisely that access to property and the legal autonomy as a separate person which to some extent counterbalanced male rights in female labour and services. Without an effective legal and administrative system, women must surrender their legal inheritance rights in return for fraternal protection or ultimate rights of asylum (Aswad 1971; Stirling 1965). Without Ottoman law, *mehr* (paid to the bride by the groom's family), becomes *başlik* (paid to the bride's father); restrictions on movement increase; without effective courts, the ability to employ agents and enforce the contracts made with them decreases; and so on. In such processes (and the precise patterns will vary) women lose their access to the market mode and become part of the domestic mode of production, and the means of male exploitation are increased. This happens quite independently of any removal of production processes from the family or household unit, and does not represent a movement of a 'household economy' from production to consumption.

However, besides Ottoman law, European capitalist economic relations also encountered a strongly gendered, separated, division of space. I have argued that the boundary between the domains of 'inner' and 'outer' and 'female' and 'male' is of great concern within such a symbolic model of the moral community. If this is the case, then any threat to the boundary between the two domains would cause moral anxiety and a move to restore any breaches. It is at this point that the moral critique of Islam accompanying European economic activities within the empire, the critique focused on the status of women, becomes important. For while the economic penetration of the male domain by European capital caused great economic stress and disarray, the European moral critique aimed at the female domain. On the one hand, it called for the liberation of women from the household, from enveloping clothing, and from restrictive marriages; on the other, it demanded the admission of women to the male spatial domain. The moral critique challenging the basis of the Ottoman moral community was eventually accepted by the modernising elites who sought change, development and renewal after the European fashion. Such a critique, when accompanied by the strength of capitalist trade and politics, could only lead to the 'reactionary' reassertion of the value of gender hierarchy and separation and to attempts to develop an Islamic form of modernisation.

The welfare of Ottoman women then, was very directly related to the economic situation which underpinned the legal and political institutions of the empire. When the towns were prosperous and the bureaucracy well trained and paid; when the educational system was working; when women could maintain control of their material wealth and could deploy it within the market mode of production and within both female and male domains, then women prospered within the overall constraints of a gender hierarchy and male control. This argument does not hinge upon the notion of the household as a productive economic unit (although the household may have had this function), for the evidence from court records of Kayseri (seventeenth century) suggests that women's trade and its associated activities were only partly household-based. But women clearly had some access to the economy outside the household, despite limitations placed on their mobility, education and choice of occupation. Indeed, it may be the case that the economic changes resulting from the effects of European capitalism led not to the loss of an important role in the household economy for women, but to their restriction to it. What seems to have been lost is the limited access to the extra-household economy, the market mode of production, together with the loss of personal autonomy conferred on women by the Ottoman legal system. This in turn may have led to the creation of a household more resembling the private, domestic, female domain with which capitalism and industrialisation in Europe is so strongly associated.

Reinterpreting a past

I return now to the initial proposition that, in order to understand Ottoman women, it is not sufficient to use conceptions derived from western discourse and that different questions altogether need to be formulated. We cannot ask simply 'what were Ottoman women's lives like?' and expect to get a useful answer. This is because the answer relies not upon the data but on their interpretation. In posing the question in this way, the data will inevitably be interpreted within the terms of western, Christian thought and the framework of a broad discourse usually termed 'orientalist' which has not yet been transcended, even in the scholarly literature. Dengler's essay on Ottoman women is a case in point—it is rich in data but weak in method and thus in the inevitable interpretation. I began by asking what effect the processes of the incorporation of the Ottoman economy into the periphery of the developing world economy had on gender hierarchy, and on the access of women to the market mode of production. Despite the relative poverty of the source materials, these are questions which can now be addressed on a theoretical level.

What is striking about the data from Ottoman Bursa and Kayseri is that women appear as such active agents in pursuit of their interests. Existing data cannot tell anything of the degree of seclusion of Ottoman women, and indeed it is difficult to know what is meant by statements about the institutionalisation of the seclusion of women (Taskiran 1976: 18). To discuss a particular form of gender separation in such terms, besides being too general and undifferentiated, is to leave questions concerning women's lives entangled in an unspoken comparison between the status of women in Islamic countries relative to that of women in 'the west'. The origin of the custom of veiling the face, a custom often confused with the practice of seclusion, is one example of such concern, and there is an extensive popular and anthropological commentary on its functions. The Turks maintain that seclusion and veiling were learned from the Persians and/or from Byzantine Greeks (Ekrem 1947: 73), while the Egyptians maintain they learned it from their Turkish overlords (El Saadawi 1980: iii), but no-one is very clear about how or why veiling or the seclusion of the previously unveiled and independent Turkish women came to be accepted.[70] The possibility of the veil as a symbol of gender separation is clear, but the causes of the seclusion of women remain more mysterious. The Ottoman data however, suggest a society in which women and men operated in separate symbolic and spatial domains, one in which a symbol of separation that did not interfere with mobility would have had its uses. As I noted earlier, it is inherent in the notion of gender separation that male attempts to increase separation may result in increased male anxiety about control and dominance rather than less. This, I suggest, is what happened.

As mercantile and then industrial capital penetrated the Ottoman economy, the economy was reorganised from manufacturing towards exporting raw (rather than processed) materials for the core markets, the peasantry was impoverished, until in the nineteenth century a 'super-westernised' (Mardin 1974) dependency elite formed, and Anatolian women lost the protection of the discredited religious law that had guaranteed their access to the market economy and control of their estates and persons. In the process, the boundary between the female and male spatial domain was drawn ever closer to the household doorstep. The economic and political shocks felt by what I have called the market mode of production were translated into the ideological realm, into a discourse on purity, morality, gender and modernity. This was even more the case than the theoretical propositions allow, for the penetration of capital was accompanied by a western critique of the foundations of the Islamic, Ottoman moral community—the critique of the status of women in Islam which presented all Muslim women as oppressed chattels and which even today remains central to the discourse of domination that characterises not only orientalism but the press (Said 1981) and popular western misunderstandings of Islam.

But is there any evidence that economic and political disruption and unrest had these particular repercussions for Ottoman women? The reason for thinking that the increasing incorporation of the Ottoman economy into the capitalist world economy had direct repercussions on the ground space available to women is that the political disturbances which were related to the internal stresses caused by this process seem to have been followed by new regulations aimed at restricting women. One example of such a conjunction of events is the Patrona Halil revolt of 1730. Artisans rebelled against westernisation and against economic policies detrimental to the bazaar (Olson 1974; Mardin 1973). Following this incident (in which artisans eventually aligned themselves with the Sultan), new sumptuary regulations for women were introduced and enforced, and a number of women accused of corrupting public morality were drowned (F. Davis 1968: 304 n. 1).[71] A passage written to describe the moral decay of society by a contemporary of these events illustrates two themes. First, it shows the penetration of western culture into the Ottoman elite; and secondly, it illustrates the way in which some men reacted to women's behaviour.

> And ladies of upper standing and girls would let themselves be lifted into the swings by mightily built youths ... and would show their garments while on the swings and sing merry songs. The bird brained women would be inclined to such pleasures and some would obtain permission from their husbands and some would not. And they would claim that these were human rights and would leave for the amusement parks and would force their husbands to give them money and if not, would ask for divorce and would take this matter into their own hands and thus there were no more than five honest women left in any one quarter ... Thus were the ways of the people with regard to women, eating and dress subverted. (Mardin 1974: 433, citing Aktepe, 1958)

Later moves towards westernisation, usually referred to as 'reforms', provoked similar responses. In the nineteenth and twentieth centuries, the Tanzimat and Young Turk periods both saw legal action aimed at restricting female ground space and dress (F. Davis 1968; Ekrem 1947: 74; Berkes 1964: 380 & 386; Emin 1930: 233). There is an example from World War I in which 'Enver Pasa sacked a commander at the Dardanelles because he had seen his daughters sunbathing on the Bosphorus' and in 1917 a committee began to discuss, as a measure of public policy, the correct length of women's skirts (Mardin 1974: 434). These are rearguard actions to be sure (and were paralleled by discussions of the same topics in Europe), but they point to the link, not between reform and reaction, but between real economic and ideological attacks from European capital, and Ottoman attempts to maintain the basic structure of a moral community by controlling the place and ground space of women.

Women and their space

Studies of space and time are currently receiving considerable attention from geographers, philosophers and anthropologists. Feminists too, have been concerned with space, partly in the battle to demolish the distinction between an inferior inner female domain, and partly from the concern to interpret ancient symbolism and ancient female deities. Many of these latter interpretations need to draw on psychoanalytic theory, simply because no other grounds for interpretation exist; the social context upon which meaning relies is largely absent from the ancient archaeological record, even where texts can be located. In her attempt to reinterpret some of the ancient female deities, Rich (1977: 97–8) tries to wrench the psychoanalytic concept of inner space out of those patriarchal meanings which rely precisely on the series of dichotomies elsewhere identified as part of women's oppression, to understand what woman's inner space might once have been and what it might therefore become again, when ours once more. And she notes the way that women's bodies can be conceptualised as space, 'a space invested with power, and an acute vulnerability . . .' (Rich 1977: 102).

Part of the anthropological interest in space stems from the concern with meaning that characterises many recent ethnographies—from the notion that cultures are best understood as systems of meaning which are produced by material and historical conditions, the structures of which are negotiated by individuals with intentions and varying degrees of freedom and success. Although it is tempting to think of such systems as closed and discrete entities, this is never the case; the word 'system' is an analogy and, like all analogies, breaks down when pushed to the boundaries, for otherwise it would be not an analogy but the thing itself. This conceptual problem becomes important when thinking about space, because space is not experienced as concrete, either in its physical or social forms, and because it can only be thought about through its structures and by analogy. The notion of 'the universe' is a case in point. For everyday purposes, the universe is thought of as a system of stars and planets governed by physical laws of matter, gravity and so forth; that is, space and the universe are thought of as a bounded entity and must be represented in this way. But by thinking of the universe as analogous to a bounded system, it tends to become a thing, like an apple, a hoop, an ellipse, or whatever analogy is experienced as most accurate and most comfortable to think; and if the universe is bounded, then the logical possibility of the existence of other universes exists. But the universe is not a bounded system and the physics of astronomical systems, when pushed to extremes, leads to great difficulty; the possibility of another universe is rejected by astronomical physics. It is very hard to think of unbounded spaces or unbounded systems, yet the universe is one and so is a society or culture.

Geographers approach the problem from a slightly different point of view, but generally seem to opt for a notion that space is not concrete, but consists instead of relationships. Is space to be viewed as an entity, is it causally productive, can it be distinguished from matter if it has structure or is it merely relative (Urry 1985: 21)? Some opt for a view of space that is four dimensional, that is, that space has three dimensions plus that of time, and go on to argue that 'time–space entities' actually produce 'empirical distributions of social activities within time and space' (Urry 1985: 22). Such notions of time and space, intended to be non-anthropocentric, try to focus on both space and time as entities independent of persons. This is to say, they try to get away from focusing time on the individual, away from the tenses that are found within language, and also away from the focus on the person in space and society. People do not make systems, systems make the people. This, then, is what geographers like Urry want to do to time–space: to find some way of thinking about it which is not trapped in the present, but which takes space to be a set of relations between entities (Urry 1985: 25) and which sees spatio-temporal location as one of two 'crucial interpellations' in the processes by which systems of meaning constitute individuals. The effects of the spatio-temporal interpellation he explores in some detail, but the effects of the second interpellation are never mentioned again. The second crucial interpellation is gender.

Urry's neglect of gender and of its intimate relationship to the structuring of space is far from unusual, but the more interesting thing is that he mentions it at all. Why does he think that only these two factors are important in the processes of constructing the social individual, in constituting the subject? Is class location less fundamental to the constitution of the subject because it is in some way less real, less firmly based in biology or physics, and if so, how do space–time and gender differ in nature and role from class position as constituting factors? How, indeed, do socially experienced space–time and gender acquire their interpellative abilities and how do they differ from those of class?

The significance of space for gender relations or a relationship between space and gender emerges in many discussions which begin with space itself rather than with gender. Gender comes into focus more by chance than intention: Bourdieu, for example, did not set out to study gender in Kabyle society but to study power, space and time in the processes of daily life (Bourdieu 1977). Yet much of what he says about space is intimately connected with gender and neither space nor time could be understood without their relationships to gender (in his discussion of union and separation [1977: 124–30], for example). The two are clearly very closely related; the analysis of an Islamic society in which there is an explicit ideology of gender separation and an explicit allocation of space by gender highlights the importance of an analysis of space for an understanding of the ways in which women move within their society. It is also important to be able to assess the significance of the allocation of space by gender for the actual mobility of women and its implications for their access to political and economic resources. What is less clear is how space is to be dealt with in an analysis, how and when social and physical space are to be distinguished from each other, and how space is going to be held to relate to the models of culture, society, ideology and symbolism that anthropologists usually work with. These issues are canvassed in considerable detail in a recent discussion of the semiotics of space and gender in a Kenyan village society (Moore 1988), but a number of difficulties remain.

There is no particular symbolic or social division of space inherent within the male model of society with which I am working, no principle or concept of separation by which space could be divided, and thus no challenge to the division of space by gender. The clear and definite categories of Turkish purity law assist in the development of a clear, bounded model of the community and in the logical development of its potentialities. Any attempt to translate the notion of gender separation into social organisation entails a social division of space. Gender segregation is the social pattern that results once the formal option offered by a symbolic model of the community based on gender separation is put into practice.[72] The division of space according to gender is therefore implicit in, but not entailed by, the male model of society. I have noted already that Turkish women are rarely secluded, but that topographical and social space is clearly gender segregated and women and men do not mingle socially. Women are able to move freely on the streets without fear of male harassment, and they are also able to travel long distances by bus safely, even when unescorted. They are able to leave the house to visit friends, relatives and neighbours or to attend shrines and they are able to shop within the central markets. Women in small towns, however, are sometimes excluded from the market place, and in these cases men do much of the daily shopping.

The absence of women from the markets is found not only in small-town Turkey but in many other parts of the Muslim Mediterranean. In Cairo, Wikan (1980) describes the ways in which men buy clothing and women themselves only shop locally for essential food. In Turkey, and in many other places, women are to be seen in the markets, shopping for themselves. But while women may sometimes enter the market space, they are almost totally excluded from its social and occupational structure. There are very few women shopkeepers in Izmir's central market, and no small manufacturers, merchants or wholesale traders who are women. There are barbers, but no hairdressers.

Women have much greater access to trades and commerce outside the central market area. The contrast can be seen in the shoe trade. The busy shoe industry of the central markets is organised largely upon apprenticeship lines and the various phases of shoe manufacturing are broken down into specialities. Workshops are small and often run by a single proprietor with some family labour. The new shoe factories located on industrial estates on the outskirts of town however, often utilise female labour. As relatively 'unskilled' labour, there is no apprenticeship system and wages and conditions are controlled in part through national labour and trade union legislation. Similarly, women are more readily found as shopkeepers in the suburban shopping centres of large cities.

In the central markets, men can sit quietly in tea houses, playing backgammon or cards, and use the tea-houses as either clubs or offices. There are no such recreational facilities for women within the markets, and women rarely enter coffee shops or tea houses. In the cities, some restaurants and cafés provide a 'family room' in which women may eat without sitting among the largely male clientele, but these are not places in which to linger, so that there are few opportunities for women to sit quietly or rest and relax in the central markets. In Izmir, the new buildings on the edge of the central markets provide tea and cake shops which cater for more prosperous women, and these stand in marked contrast to the general structure of the central market in which there is no real place for women. Women may enter the central market space, but they have no place there; the central market is a male structure, a male recreational centre tied tightly to the mosque from which emanates the male model of society. Indeed, mosque and market form one space, which is essentially male.

The economic and ritual importance of mosque and market for each other derives from the earliest days of Islam.[73] Mecca was an important town on the trade route leading from the southern shores of Arabia to the commercial centres of the Roman empire and Muhammed was himself a successful trader within this network. The

caravans of the ancient spice trade passed across the Arabian peninsula from shrine to shrine, each shrine having a particular time of year
in which animosities were forbidden and at which the peace of the
market-place was ensured by the gods. It was at this time that the
merchant–pilgrims arrived for the great fairs, some of which were held
within the towns, others outside.

The location of the market is important for there are differences in
the nature and significance of the cults attached to shrines which depend
on their location, but regardless of whether important markets and
their shrines lie inside or outside the town, the link between commerce and religion, and between merchant-traders and pilgrimage, is
intimate. Pilgrims frequently trade their way to and from pilgrim shrines;
merchants accept pilgrims as fellow-travellers and require the protection
of the gods if a peaceable market and the facilities for animals, goods
and travellers are to be established and maintained. Fees and taxes
paid by merchants for their facilities support both the material and
spiritual infrastructures. The mosque–market complex that characterises the towns of the eastern Mediterranean region illustrates this connection. Women are absent, then, not just from the mosque but also
from the market which grows symbiotically within its shadow. What I
propose here is that the mosque and its markets form a spatial centre
to male ground space, one which expresses the link between ground
space and the moral community it structurally represents. Women have
no place there at all, and as a result of gender separation are allocated
their own space.

The women whom I met and mingled with in Izmir lived very
separate lives and rarely sought the company of men. Women socialised with other women; they did many things together and developed
friendships within their own domain. Because of the particular form of
patronage politics which constituted the government of the day, male
access to resources depended upon extensive social networks and even
extended kin relationships were generally insufficient. In Izmir,
friendship as well as kinship was needed to form the networks that
were critical to obtaining access to economic and political resources.
Consequently, school and university friendships became critical, as did
neighbours and unrelated people from one's home town. The formal
visiting patterns of urban women (Dobkin 1967; Good 1978; Aswad
1971; Benedict 1974b; Tapper 1983) need to be seen against this background, as they permit male access to female networks. They also
place women at important nodes of male power; a male has access to
women only through his wife, mother or sister and an understanding
of the particular intimacy of mother–son and sister–brother relationships would need to take this aspect of the structural position of women
into account.

The domain of women in Izmir contains a wide number of relationships, among which kin are important but not exclusively so, and it is

a domain which is by no means isolated from the male one. Indeed, there are broad areas which are shared. Just as Izmirli women may enter the male mosque–market space and yet have no place there, men, whether employed or not, have no place in the household. They must leave the household and meet their friends in the tea house, card-shop or mosque, if not in the office or workshop. Should a man be at home when women visitors arrive, he will leave. During the day there is no place for him there. This is the absence which presents the possibility of the structuring of a female domain and space in which women have responsibilities and some autonomy. Unrelated women and men do not mingle socially, polite speech forms are neutral and distancing, and most public rituals (marriages, circumcisions, prayer, visiting, and so forth), are gender segregated. It is quite possible for women to visit and to receive visitors without the senior male of the household being aware of it. Women visit neighbours casually, they visit kin in other towns and villages, they visit for life-cycle events, for a variety of religious rituals, they visit shrines for solace or for help, and they also participate in a round of formal, structured visits, usually on fixed days of the week (the *kabul günü*). Whether in the workforce or not, urban middle-class women lead extremely busy lives.

The female domain, then, centres on the household, but the household is not 'private' and cannot be described that way—it is the spatial centre of women's public, sociable and religious lives. In small Turkish towns female ground space can include all the residential quarters. Women move freely within their domain; men are restricted to the mosque–market place. In cities, women may enter the mosque–market area, but they have no place there. In cities, men too, move freely in the residential quarters, but they may not enter the centre of the female domain, the household. The female domain, like its male counterpart, has its internal, partly autonomous, social structures—its power structures which give senior women control of juniors, mothers power over sons, and mothers-in-law power over new brides. There is a structure and a set of norms which values age and experience over youth and nubile sexuality, a structure in which age can bring women certain compensations and which provides a secure and valued position for the elderly.

The analysis of Turkish purity law and practice offers a new approach to the empirical data of gender separation, segregation and seclusion. Indeed, the common representation of eastern Mediterranean family life as a private or inner domain of women set in opposition to a public or outer male world, reflects European cultural classifications. This is also the case with those discussions of the seclusion of women which point to the ways in which the female body is held to be impure and purity held to be associated with men. Turkish women cannot be construed as either pure (and thus in need of male protection) or 'impure' (due to the specifics of their biology). They are both, and so are men. Pollution is not necessarily sinful and can be dealt with quite readily in daily life. However, it would be quite possible to use ideologies of female purity or weakness to bolster the social division of space or the gender division of society; it would, I think, be more difficult to add notions of female impurity, although it is not impossible.

Just as the male world-view can be located at the centre of the male domain, the mosque–market complex, so a female world-view can be located at the centre of the female domain. And just as one set of ritual symbolism from among many can be shown to be of critical importance for the construction and reproduction of the male world-view, so one set of household rites from among many can be shown to be of critical significance in constructing and reproducing a female world-view.

7   Women's Rites

The literature on Turkish woman, like the feminist literature on western women, is quite unequivocal about gender inequalities. Turkish women have less education, make fewer and less important decisions, have more constraints placed upon their behaviour and movements, and they are socialised into submission to men (Cosar 1978; Kandiyoti 1977). Men are better educated at every level, better dressed, make most of the important decisions, occupy most of the better jobs, move freely and travel more widely than women.[74] Men have sexual freedom and know that they are superior to, and in control of, women. In addition, the punishment for adultery falls more heavily on women; brothers occasionally kill their sisters for real or imagined crimes of honour; and kidnapped women may be obliged to marry their abductors once virginity can no longer be assured (Starr & Pool 1974).[75] In other words, women are embedded in a gender hierarchy.

There have been, however, a few bright spots in the generally gloomy picture. There are, for example, suggestions that despite the structural inequalities suffered by Turkish and other Muslim women, they are nevertheless psychologically independent and assertive in a way that their American sisters are not; that Turkish women are not emotionally dependent on men (Fallers & Fallers 1976); that seclusion might offer some benefits to women as well as disadvantages. These observations should not be dismissed as apologies for an otherwise unsavoury system of exploitation; they reflect a real uneasiness with existing ways of looking at Muslim women and a realisation that the comparisons being made might be far from appropriate.

It is clear that Turkish women are by no means confined to the house and in fact they travel widely and safely when means permit and, most importantly, move through the streets unharassed. Indeed, the combination of gender segregation and the allocation of ground-space to women which I discussed in the last chapter is sometimes

121

thought to lead to the development of a separate 'women's world', a world sometimes referred to as a 'sub-society' (Tapper 1978) with its own 'subculture' (Sutton, Makiesky, Dwyer & Klein 1975: 598).[76] It has been the perception of a women's world and its structures that has led to the reassessments of the situation of Muslim women referred to above.

Yet the sense of shock which the encounter with the 'oppressed' Muslim women of Turkey and other places produced in women observers from Europe and America provides the basis for one of the major structuring tropes of western women's texts on the orient. The shock of discovery relates to the discovery of the 'truth', in both the popular and scholarly literature, and is thus a technique which legitimates the text. The discovery that the formerly unknown person, group or culture has strengths not explicitly recognised within dominant narrative schema is part of the process by which anthropology claims to arrive at an understanding of people or cultures that stands outside the existing parameters of knowledge and grows specifically out of relations of power. Yet this structuring of the other as unknown and different is in itself an expression of the power of knowledges which produce both the unknown and its difference. For if they were like 'us', they would be, like the map so detailed that it covered the whole world, 'us'—not different but the same. Yet they are not us, so they must be different. There could be no surprise at, for example, women's strength, if the observer came in order to study a group of women perceived as powerful. The location of strength among the dispossessed or deprived therefore grows out of that dispossession and powerlessness and the specific, western knowledges through which those peoples are represented. The perception of a women's world or sub-society flows directly from structuralist theories which ignore both the ways in which relations of power are deployed within gendered space, and the effects of adding context to analyses which are inherently directed away from the broader narrative structures of race, gender and history that are at work.

Women observers cannot be immune to these powers or their positions of privilege within them. Indeed, their crucial position as observers of the world hidden from foreign men makes their role in the production of knowledge a particularly important one. The sense of shock at the autonomy and independence of Muslim women recorded by women observers as being part of their initiation into the world of women must therefore be recognised as a legitimating trope which in itself demands investigation. To recognise the experience as a trope is not to deny the experience. In my own research, this feeling was very strong and it posed many problems for me, particularly those of how to determine the extent, nature and deployment of gendered relations of power without converting the difference into a homogenising similarity that blocked explanation. Pervasive, crucial but indeterminate, neither the empirical nor the interpretive literature seemed to provide a useful understanding of either the subordination or power of women. Indeed, removed from their identifying and locating details, many of the descriptions of women's lives that I read could have applied equally well to women in many parts of the world, particularly to those of Australia, Europe and America. It seemed as if it were the location of Turkish women within a world of Islam or in a Middle East that in itself provided the parameters of difference which I was seeking to explain. Once those geographical markers were removed from the text, little remained to identify women's oppression as differing distinctively from that which I experienced myself within the Australian family, workforce and educational systems.

This sense of the familiarity of subordination in turn raised the question of the universalising tendencies of some areas of American feminist politics of the late 1970s, a question made particularly potent by the mobilisation of Iranian women in support of the Ayatollah Khomeini. Claims of universal sisterhood made at this time sometimes obliterated the important political and economic differences between women, ignored the role of western women in the economies and politics of domination and again imposed western knowledges of gender, sexuality and political priorities upon women who were embedded in very different cultural economies.

But there was another point growing out of this, one not concerning the well-documented power relations which lay behind the feminising of the orient, but one involved in creating the object of scrutiny and constructing the problem which it comes to represent. This is the notion that a particular behaviour is a cultural characteristic rather than a personal one, particularly those activities which Europeans might wish to define as criminal or unnatural. The killing of sisters by brothers, for example, is widely regarded within the ethnographic literature as a geographically and religiously specified cultural response to social structures within the family which focus on the brother–sister relationship in a way that is not found outside that culture area. The definition of these murders as cultural rather than personal would insist, if applied more widely, that the regular bashings and killings of wives by husbands must be treated as an analogous cultural event, and one which is similarly approved and understood within, say, Australian culture. The processes of creating the distinction between culture and person and then of defining particular events or behaviour as cultural practices rather than as personal aberrations, is one of the ways in which difference is constructed and manipulated to produce comparisons which state not simply difference but inferiority. The concept of culture is itself embedded in the hierarchical structuring of difference and the politics of knowledge and because of it, the search for what is sometimes called a more 'scientific' analysis of the differences between women is the more difficult, and the 'truth' of difference ever more elusive.

Partly in response to the perception that Muslim Middle Eastern and Mediterranean women were far from the abject slaves of their men (Ardener 1972), and partly in response to western feminist criticism of anthropological methodology (Rogers 1978; Tiffany 1978; Tilly & Scott 1978; Quinn 1977), students of Middle Eastern societies began to point to the possibility that separate women's worlds might generate separate models of the world. The determination of previously neglected women's world-views of the nature of the moral community might help to overcome the male bias in the literature, provide alternative ways of interpreting existing data, and also explain how women perceive their subordinated position in society as a whole. If Turkish women, for example, could be shown to hold models of either their world or of the universal Muslim world that differed substantially from those of Turkish men, then a more complete ethnography would come into being. In addition, with the discovery of competing world-views of the moral community, it would be possible to see whether the implications of male ideologies of female inferiority might to some extent be ameliorated through the allocation of separate space. My initial encounters with Turkish women were of a kind which immediately raised the questions concerning women's power that were engaging other scholars, and for precisely the same reasons. As well as growing out of a common literary background, my own work in Turkey was therefore set against this common intellectual background and experience. I, too, set out on the search for a female model of society in the hope that such a project would provide the necessary explanations of the unexpected forcefulness of Turkish women noted by scholars like the Fallers (1976) and Nancy Tapper (1978).

If it could be shown to exist, a female world-view, however, could never be the precise equivalent of the male world-view, simply because the male world-view is dominant, supported and legitimated in myriad structural ways, and because women practise the purity law from which it is derived throughout their daily lives. I believed that a female world-view could be derived from an analysis of Turkish women's rites, but that it was a subordinated one, held in addition to the male one. The women's model of the moral community for which I provide evidence presents an alternative construction precisely at those points at which the hierarchy of the engendered male model is established. The female world-view puts birth at a central position, but the symbolism associated with it is not that of uncleanliness or pollution, but of purity; it places motherhood at the centre of being female and of femaleness.

In addition to presenting a view of birth that is nonpolluting, the female world-view also challenges the canonical laws of the mosque regarding death. In canonical law, the corpse is regarded as extremely polluting. Turkish funeral practice is very much in accordance with canon law. The corpse is excluded from the sacred space of the mosque itself and lies instead in the courtyard. Prayers for the dead are held beside the coffin and are brief; the body is then carried to the grave-yard at the brisk pace required by the law for a rapid burial without further lamentation. While women generally lay out the polluting corpse and shroud it, they are excluded from the funeral prayers at the mosque and all displays of emotion are discouraged.[77] Islamic doctrine in Turkey is very firm on death, and the funeral rites become a very controlled and male-dominated event. Bloch and Parry (1982) con-sider a female association with death rites to be nigh on universal, but Ottoman canon law as practised in Turkey seeks to break that nexus. The law is only partly successful on this point, for although the funeral rites are effectively allocated to the male domain, the very important major commemoration of each death takes place within the house-hold, at the centre of what I have called the female domain. At the point of death, as with birth, there is a confrontation between the female and male domains and between the world-views associated with them. During this confrontation, the connection between birth and death and birth and resurrection is reasserted by women. Given the significance of redemption, of life after death, within both Christian and Islamic doctrines, a female challenge to male control of death is important.

Women and the dead

It was the use of a poem celebrating birth as a death rite that first drew my attention to the *mevlüt*. A *mevlüt* is a formal performance of the medieval Turkish poem, the *Mevlidi Serif*, describing the birth and life of Muhammed.[78] For women, the complex relationship between con-cepts of death, fertility and redemption set out in the poem offer a way of integrating their lives and concerns into both the Islam of the mosque and the series of shrine and household rites which form an important part of daily life.

The series of household visits, prayers, readings and *mevlüts* which commemorate the dead are quite different from the funeral prayers of the mosque.[79] They allow women access to an important rite of pas-sage and are part of the intricate network of visits and reciprocity by which the structures of the female domain are negotiated.[80] In addi-tion, cemeteries in Izmir are often pleasant, shady places where women like to visit, to picnic, to sit and reflect, and to pray for the souls of the dead. In the past this activity may have been more frequent, as a visit to a cemetery was a legitimate reason for leaving the household. Women rarely attend the mosque prayers for the dead and the burial but they are neither excluded from tending the dead nor from the cemetery itself; and they are not prevented from performing household death rites.

A *mevlüt* is generally held at seven and forty (or possibly fifty-two) days after death, and then annually. Wealthy families will often give a *mevlüt* in the mosque, in which case the audience is mainly male, the singers professional, and the performance less participatory. But the majority of *mevlüt* ceremonies are given by women in the household. To give a *mevlüt* is a meritorious act and while the hospitality offered during the performance varies according to means, the performance itself, whether in the mosque or in the household, is explicitly open to all. It is nevertheless a rite which is of particular importance to women, and one that is prominent for them, both in death rites and through the symbolism of the poem and its performance. A *mevlüt* is not a body of ritual symbolism known to and accepted *only* by women, but one shared with men. Rather than two discrete, bounded, sets of gender-segregated rites, the *mevlüt* offers a range of beliefs and practices which receive varying emphases according to gender and location. Just as purity law is shared by women and men, so also is the *mevlüt*. While any exclusively female rite risks being declared superstitious, the *mevlüt* does not, being widely accepted as a legitimate act of worship by both women and men alike. While occasionally men express reservations as to the legality of its performance on particular occasions, it is rarely dismissed as superstitious, even when aspects of its non-Islamic nature are noted.

The *mevlüt*, however, is central to women's household rites. It offers an alternative world-view, one which is distinctively, although not exclusively, female. The ceremony begins with the arrival of women guests. They are welcomed by the hostess but, as is the custom with formal visiting, each guest must then greet all women already present, so that after finding a seat, a guest is greeted in turn by all subsequent new arrivals. In Izmir, *lokma* (small doughnuts in syrup) are often served to the guests, each usually receiving three. Smoking is forbidden, as it is in the mosque and during the Fast of Ramazan. When the singing is about to begin, women put on their special white (occasionally pastel-coloured) *mevlüt* scarves. *Mevlüt* scarves differ from those for prayer in that they are longer than they are wide and are worn loosely thrown over the hair, rather than tightly tied. This means that the hair remains partly exposed rather than fully restrained, as would be the case for formal prayer. This difference nicely illustrates the contrast between the two sets of religious occasions. When all are settled and the children quiet, the performance begins.

The singers are generally women and they alternate, the lead singer taking the more important verses, pausing now and then to ask if extra verses are required. Each singer keeps a collection of her own verses, some printed, some handwritten, and there is considerable variation in each performance. The guests form a chorus to the professional singers and sing the refrains; the chorus also sings the *Merhaba* which welcomes the birth of the baby Muhammed, and it provides the intermittent *amin*s which build up to the final crescendo. In this way, even though the atmosphere of the *mevlüt* is generally rather sedate, the women provide a framework upon which the professional singers hang the narrative. It is the women's role as chorus which helps to give the performance its unity and dramatic quality; everyone present shares not only in the recounting of the events but also in the drama of the miraculous events themselves.

One of the major sections of the poem deals with the Annunciation and Nativity of Muhammed, events in which women have the major roles. Part of this section of the poem is actually spoken by Emine, the mother of Muhammed; her direct speech gives the account of her vision an immediacy that heightens its emotional appeal.[81] In Kuranic accounts of Muhammed's birth there is no claim for a virgin birth; his father is referred to, though briefly, and it is only as the hour of birth approaches that Emine learns of her special blessing. Three women, one of them Mary (the Mother of Jesus), announce that Emine's son is destined to be a prophet. They give her a miraculous cold white drink to ease her birth pains and a white bird flies down and strokes her back. At that point in the narrative, Emine loses consciousness until the birth is over.

This most important section of the poem is broken by several choruses in which everyone joins. As the singers tell of the white bird stroking Emine's back, everyone stands and moves around the room touching the shoulder of everyone present. They are careful not to omit anyone and are particularly concerned to include any strangers. The room is transformed by the turning of the women as they move about, smiling and stroking the shoulders of everyone there, white scarves fluttering gently. The famous *Merhaba* follows, the chorus of welcome and greeting that greets Muhammed's birth, the chorus in which everyone joins. This part of the performance, its central focus, is both enjoyable and moving. I am certain that it has far greater meaning for women than for men. It is not only that in the narrative sequence of the text Muhammed's progenitor is replaced by women, but that the ritual action of the performance of the text brings birth into focus as an entirely female event.

During the final verses of the poem, the participation of the audience increases steadily. Women interpolate *amin* more frequently and emphatically, until at the end of the poem the performance achieves a dramatic and moving intensity. When the lead singer calls the final *Fatiha*, the prayer for the dead, the sudden peace as each woman prays silently is all the more striking.[82] Women pass their hands over their faces, then sit back and pause for a moment before beginning to speak to their friends. The hostess offers her guests rosewater for their hands and hair, then serves rosewater s[h]erbet (cordial) topped with slivers of roasted almonds, and offers cigarettes.

As with all texts, there are a number of possible readings. The one I present is a women's reading, one in which the action highlights those events of greatest concern to women, the events they say they like and enjoy, and which are linked into the themes found in women's other household rites.

The possibility of varying readings of the poem can be illustrated briefly by considering its opening moments. It begins with the statement that Adam was the first person granted the Light of God; it passed from him to his wife Eve, then on to their son Seth and from there on to Abraham, Ishmael and Muhammed. Each of the prophets listed is of fundamental importance to Muslims (except perhaps for Seth), particularly in the Meccan pilgrimage rites. It is possible to emphasise the role of Adam in Muhammed's spiritual lineage and thus his role in establishing and legitimating Islam. Or it is possible to emphasise the role of Eve as Adam's wife and as mother of the prophets. Eve is a popular and revered figure, often referred to as the Mother of Humanity; until the 1920s her grave near Jeddah was visited by pilgrims on their way to Mecca.[83] The Christian connection between women, sexuality, sin and the Fall of Mankind is absent from the Islamic Eve, for in the Kuran it is Satan, not Eve, who causes the expulsion of Adam and Eve from Paradise (*Sure* 2). In both the Kuran and in the extra-Kuranic traditions which amplify this story, Eve is a very positive mother-figure.

In fact, her place in the prophetic succession is significant to women; it is her role of mother which fits in with other aspects of women's ritual symbolism. The narrative places woman clearly and unambiguously at the beginning of the world; it emphasises Eve's role as mother rather than her role as wife (although she is often seen as very helpful to Adam); and it does not connect her with sin. This is, I think, how many Turkish women perceive Eve. Men would certainly not deny Eve's role; it is a matter of emphasis rather than of absolute contrast and it seems quite clear from observation and conversation that women respond to the female imagery and symbolism of the Eve narrative in a way that men do not.

A number of points emerging from an analysis of the household *mevlüt* suggest it presents a reasonably clear female world-view, one that contrasts with the male world-view at its most critical point, that at which a gender hierarchy is established. The first point is that these events are essentially egalitarian and open to all, and that the openness is also, as will shortly become apparent, characteristic of women's symbolism. The second point is that the turning and touching of the women at the moment of Muhammed's birth seems to replicate the circling movement found at tombs and shrines, and is perhaps related to the circling of the Mevlevi *dervis*-es, although this has yet to be established.[84] More importantly, it is an inclusive rite, an act of mingling; there is no separation of social or cultural categories here—quite the reverse.

And thirdly, there is the use of the colour white, a colour which in other contexts is widely associated with purity, in the white of the Meccan pilgrim's robe, for example. The bird which eases Emine's birth pains is white, and although the white bird carries no explicit gender loading, the reenactment of the bird's arrival indicates its close connection with women. The miraculous drink given to ease the birth pains is also white; in other contexts this white, life-giving drink is located in one of the fountains of Paradise. The close association of women, birth and whiteness in this context stands in direct opposition to the association of birth with the polluting blackness and loss of control which results from the categories of purity law. The *mevlüt* therefore falls into a class of well known rites which combine fertility symbolism with death and which, like them, have implications for gender relations (Bloch & Parry 1982; Bloch 1982).

Women and the flow of life

In the central life-giving episodes of the *mevlüt* and their reenactment is to be found the ritual symbolism of a distinct world-view, a univer-salistic one that is woman-centred, in which women are construed as mothers rather than as wives, and one which specifically marks death by referring to its transcendence by birth, a transcendence which is, in this context, purely and exclusively female. The term I use to describe the transcendent life process is *flow*. Flow highlights the distinction between the male and female world-views that I am proposing. In the male world-view, the flow of substances across conceptual or physical boundaries results in impurity; the flow of semen, menstrual blood or tears leads inevitably to pollution. This type of flow can only be prevented through control of body and mind, a control only partially accessible to women. But transcendent flow, the flow of life that comes into view in the *mevlüt* rites, is also important in defining water and blood, substances critical to notions of purity, sacrifice and hygiene. For flowing water is pure and purifying, but standing water is impure and unable to purify. This is set out in purity law as well as being carried out in daily practices of hygiene. And flowing blood is pure, while stagnant blood is impure and renders a carcass unfit for human consumption.[85] Naturally, animal blood is forbidden as food and in practice is never eaten. These are life-flow concepts, concepts concerned with a set of symbolic structures and beliefs about purity that do not focus on boundaries and control, and are diametrically opposed to those expressed through the purifying ritual practices of the mosque.

In the female world-view that I am proposing, one that is found at the centre of the female domain and which stands in direct contrast to that of the mosque, the flow of life, expressed in a massive body of folk ritual and symbolism, is both life giving and pure and, for women, female. This is the opposite of the hierarchical world-view of purity law. Whereas in the male world-view the mingling of categories leads to pollution, in the female view of the world it does not. Rather than hierarchical, the female world-view, like so many of those formed in opposition and within dominating relations of power, is egalitarian.

Emine's loss of consciousness and reawakening after birth is also very significant. Within this imagery of death and resurrection through birth lies the notion of the continuing flow of life despite death itself. It seems plausible to interpret this dramatic and dramatised moment of the text as offering the opportunity for both a transcendent and compassionate reading of childbirth. Within local narratives, the same event and imagery also surrounds the birth of Isa (Jesus) to Mary the Virgin.

There is also the absence from the poem of Hatice, Muhammed's first wife and first convert, a woman greatly esteemed and revered in other contexts. She bore him no children, as she was 'old' when she took him as a young husband. But also, I think her absence strengthens the presentation of women as mothers, for it is Muhammed's mother, Emine, who has the central role. At the same time, the focus on women as mothers leaves aside the politics of sexuality which conceives of young women as wives, as bearers of a dangerous sexuality, and as subordinate to males and to mothers-in-law as mothers of sons. It is along the lines of sexuality that conflicts between women for the favours of men flow, and this divisive aspect of masculinist power relations on subordinated women's worlds and lives is left submerged and deflected. As a result, the *mevlüt*'s world-view is egalitarian and unified; it focuses on women as mothers and the opportunity motherhood provides for both power and respect; and it expresses an important series of concepts concerning the flow of life through women's redemptive procreative powers.

Within engendered cosmologies which focus on women's procreative role and powers, there is often a significant iconology representing the appropriation of those female powers by men. In the *Mevlidi Serif*, for example, during the Annunciation scene, Muhammed himself is described as God's Mercy, a term which is closely connected to the symbolism of rain. Muhammed is often said to have one hundred names. Of the many names available, it is interesting that it should be this one which is used just at the moment of birth, for analysis of women's shrine rites and of folklore suggests that rain, transcendental flow and fertility are very closely connected. Rain, defined as flowing water, is considered to be particularly pure, purifying and fertile.

Women and pilgrimage

Perhaps it was no accident that early on my own journey out to the orient I should gravitate to Izmir's most important shrine, and that from within my own journey to the margin of my culture, I should seek to know the Turkish women who regularly journeyed out of their own mundane constraints.

The most conspicuous of their journeys was the regular Friday climb up the small hill surrounded by high-rise buildings to visit the tomb of Susuz Dede.[86] If the weather was fine, each Friday two or three hundred women made the journey out from their homes, climbing past the foodstalls and the line of gypsy fortune-tellers to reach the tomb on top of the hill. At the top, the hill was covered by groups of women praying, carrying out the ritual of the shrine and eating the midday meal. Women talked freely among themselves and listened to each other's problems. The sacredness and power of the place was acknowledged not with awe or quiet respect, but by active participation in ritual: the noise of prayers being recited, the bustle of the crowd at the tomb, the slaughter of cocks, children playing, the shouting of drink-sellers and the constant reading, singing and conversation produced a noisy, friendly, pious and supportive atmosphere that was both relaxing and enjoyable.

Since my first visit to Susuz Dede in 1978, the crowd of women at the tomb has grown steadily larger and continues to do so. It is now much better organised: there are more food vendors, more watersellers, more gypsies and more beggars. The slopes of the hill have been terraced and planted with trees and shrubs and the municipality has taken on the responsibility for watering them. This important aspect of the religious lives of Turkish women has sometimes been ignored while the women who go to shrines like Susuz Dede are regarded as ignorant, superstitious and probably heretical. Yet every small town has a shrine like Susuz Dede and the larger shrines have national reputations. Men are often very disparaging of women's religious practices and clerics particularly so, for they are often regarded as un-Islamic. Yet there are clear and obvious continuities between shrine rites and those of the mosque that indicate the need to consider the shrines more carefully. They are clearly important to many women, and if these women consider themselves Muslims, it is difficult to declare that their ritual life lies outside the bounds of Islam.

I visited a great number of women's shrines in Turkey. They ranged from very small local shrines known and used by the women of one neighbourhood only, to well-established city shrines like Susuz Dede and the shrines of the great Turkish saints, Mevlana Celal ad-Din Rumi (Konya), Haci Bayram (Ankara) and Eyup Sultan (Istanbul), which women and men all over Turkey knew of and visited. Even when these shrines are attached to a mosque, women remain an overwhelming presence at them, and their rites overwhelmingly women's rites, aimed at women's concerns even though men may participate in them. At Susuz Dede three or four men sell their services as *hoca* (religious teacher)—they sell religious tracts, sacrifice the cocks brought to the shrine by women, and for a fee recite sections from the Kuran. But men rarely visit this shrine as pilgrims as Susuz Dede is not one of the recognised 'saints' of Islam.[87] So the space at the top of the hill becomes a women's space within which men have only a very limited place. Within that space, women act independently of their men; through the ritual of the site, they act to take control of important aspects of their lives. They are concerned with difficult health and financial problems, with housing, fertility and education. At the tomb of Susuz Dede they seek contact with the power of God and through ritual, to bring that power directly to bear on their lives. There are several women *hoca*s there, too, who advise newcomers of the procedures, act as consultants to those in distress and pray with those who need it. They also sell the candles and reels of cotton that are used in the rites there.[88]

Women visiting the shrine in search of help usually make a conditional vow—in return for divine intervention they will make a sacrifice of some kind. It may be the sacrifice of a cock or a sheep, with the meat going either to the poor or to one of the *hoca*s; it may be the donation of some other gift to the poor, but frequently it takes the form of a distribution of sweets, sugar cubes, rosewater or bread among the women pilgrims present at the shrine. The poor among the crowd may be able to accumulate significant quantities of sugar and bread from these distributions, but for the majority of the women the sugar collected in this way has a purely sacred value which can be carried from the shrine and utilised in other environments.

The distributions weld the crowd together into a community of women. It is essential that a distribution be made to as many of the women present as possible, and every effort is made to include everyone. Like the touching of women during the singing of the *Mevlidi Serif*, it is a rite of inclusion which generates contacts between women who are otherwise strangers. It establishes unity on the basis of a shared gender and common gender politics, and it helps to create the open, friendly, welcoming atmosphere that characterises these occasions, despite the incredible bustle. The distributions among women also make manifest the effectiveness of prayer and ritual at Susuz Dede, for they are made only when a request has been granted. To a newcomer to the shrine it is therefore immediately clear that this is a powerful, as well as a congenial, place.

At first sight, the rites carried out at Susuz Dede are very simple, a first impression which is quite misleading. It is important to recognise that the classifying of women's rites as 'simple', 'crude' or 'primitive' is essential to being able to define them as superstitious and un-Islamic. The easy dismissal of women's rites as superstition is crucial to maintaining a set of gender relations in which women are subordinate, and denies that women's rites are, in reality, deeply integrated within Turkish culture and Islam.

On arrival at the tomb, most women consult and pray with a female *hoca*, buying the necessary cotton from her. The cotton is unwound from the wooden spool as women walk clockwise around the tomb, praying as they go. The prayers are often intensely personal. As the unwinding is completed, the empty spool is thrown down the side of the hill.[89] It is then usual to sprinkle a bottle of water onto the top of the tomb, together with the reiteration of the appropriate prayers. Some women light a candle or two at the fire which burns at the head of the grave, and those seeking fertility for themselves or another may make and hang a small cradle of rag and string on the branches of a small tree. At the end of these rites, a personal prayer (*dua*) is spoken aloud and the vow made.[90] The first pilgrimage is usually followed by two more. While some women are making their supplications at the tomb in this way, the others are carrying out their vows. In addition to the distributions being made, there are cocks being sacrificed, recitals from the Kuran and singings of the *Mevlidi Serif.*

Many aspects of the ritual and supplications at Susuz Dede are regarded by Turkish men as superstitious and non-Islamic. The making of cloth cradles, the building of stone houses, the use of stones and trees in divination and the use of reels of cotton, for example, are held to be totally pagan and well outside the realm of acceptable Islam. They are nevertheless remarkably widespread among the range of pilgrims (both women and men) at Turkish shrines. Furthermore, the sacrificing of cocks at graves is forbidden in the Kuran, even though it is lawful on other occasions. The making of vows at graves is condoned in the Kuran but the use of candles and the other aspects of women's rites found at tombs is condemned. Candles nevertheless have an established ritual usage in Turkish mosques; Ramazan and the five annual (lunar) Festivals of Light, the Kandils, utilising precisely this imagery. Even at shrines at which men are present, and even when a variety of practices defined as superstition are very much in evidence, men will still sacrifice sheep on sites associated with particularly important holy men. This is the case at the graveside of the Imam Mehmed Birgevi (in Birgi), for instance, where the shrine is much better organised and large parties of women and men regularly sacrifice sheep as the result of a vow, and where women carry out a variety of other rites.[91] In this case, men pray formally in the small mosque in the graveyard, and women sing the *Mevlidi Serif* in a separate cottage built especially for the purpose. At Birgi, the sacrifices are often those of men giving thanks for divine intervention. It is important to note the ways in which, despite their disapproval of women's rites, men are familiar with and active participants in a set of ritual performances that they might want, on some occasions, to classify as pagan or sinful. The break between mosque law and pilgrim practice is far less abrupt than might at first be apparent.

The presence of men at pilgrimage shrines ranges along a continuum which in Turkey is aligned to the degree of acceptance of the shrine within the ambit of mosque Islam. At Eyup Sultan in Istanbul, where men visit the saint's tomb, the mausoleum stands adjacent to the mosque and is surrounded by a suburb of linked religious buildings. Large numbers of women regularly attend the formal mosque prayers, particularly on Fridays. At Birgi, a much less developed site, but one which nevertheless boasts established terraced picnic facilities, a tea-house, a small mosque, the women's room and a slaughter house, the family groups break up into women and men and ritual is carried out accordingly. Yet whether men are a noticeable presence or not, and whether men approve of women's presence and activities, women maintain their place, their access and their separate rites at all Turkish shrines.

The shrines therefore provide islands of women's space within the landscape. Men are largely absent from them and within them the universalistic doctrines of Islam provide the opportunity for women to construct a women's world. They also allow women the pilgrimage, a journey out from the household centre and its social structures into the liminal world of the shrines in which a set of universal, unifying and transcendental values are reaffirmed as emphatically those of women.

Nostalgia, superstition and women's rites

There is no doubt that the first encounter with women's rites at pilgrimage shrines can create the illusion of the universality of ritual experience, a feeling of the eternal value of women's primal concerns. At these shrines women are praying for help with life, birth and death, with the primordial female functions of the body and culture. The immediacy of their pleas and the direct action taken in connection with them seems primitive and unfamiliar to Muslims and Christians alike who have been reared within a different, more constrained, religious commitment. Women's 'paganism', too, fits into western views of Islam itself as a dangerously 'primitive' (barbaric, bloodthirsty) religion, so that no matter which path you take, you risk slipping away into un-civilisation. The sense of difference and its relations to familiar tropes of a 'primitive' world is, of course, an illusion, as is the sense of continuity and timelessness that underpins it. The different religious register of women's shrine rites, its movements and aims, also runs along a continuum, one which stretches across the variety of women's religious practices and into those of men.

The shrine of Hizr, set sternly on the beach near Antakya, provides a good example of the ways in which women's beliefs can be denigrated as unorthodox while simultaneously being locked into a set of symbolic concerns that, although subterranean, are nevertheless of national significance. Hizr's shrine centres on a massive rock in the centre of a sandy beach. A cupola has been built over the rock and around it there are two circular walls separated by a short passageway of perhaps six metres. Beggars sit along both walls of this corridor, so that all entering have to run the gauntlet of outstretched hands, entreaties and pleas of the dispossessed. Inside, between the rock and its walls, is about six metres or so. It is a small shrine which on the days I was there was relatively congested. Into the side of the rock were cut some small niches while others occurred quite naturally. In the niches were sometimes candles, sometimes trays of burning aromatic gums and seeds. Close to the wall of the shrine stood the remains of an old tree. Bark and most branches had long since gone and the remaining wood had the patina and polish of what must surely have been millions of hands. The remaining twigs or stumps of branches were used as hooks, so that bags containing Kurans or other books could be hung there. One of the bags contained dozens of matted balls of human hair. Outside the shrine were feathers and feet, showing that sacrifices had been made there.

When I first visited the shrine of Hizr, which I shall discuss in more detail shortly, the sense of straying into another world was very strong; and in one sense I had. Like all pilgrimage shrines, this was a place apart, set outside of social space, somewhere beyond social structure. But what it was not, was a monument to the past. The noisy presence of the margins of society, the beggars, the focus of the shrine on a rock, the burnished tree trunk, the burning aromatics and lumps of hair hung carefully on the tree—each of these elements conjured up memories from two important narrative worlds. The first was of the ancient rites of primordial tribal Greeks, their tree worship, sacred groves, sacrifices and libations, nymphs and naiads. The other image was of the unplaced and unspecified *primitif*, the feeling that in the bodily exuviae, muttered prayers and circumambulations of the rock, one was looking at what must have been the earliest of human behaviour, an element which had survived here, down on the beach at Antakya, far from the control of the state or the clergy.

It is easy to assimilate the women at the shrine to these past worlds, to see them as exemplars of the lost *primitif*, as outside of culture perhaps, and as tied into their eternal bodily concerns. In a sense, these women become exemplars of the ruins of the past that western travellers put so much time into locating and mapping, in proving that the ruins of the past were indeed superimposed upon a much less friendly present. They also become part of the present wave of nostalgia for those pasts and their ruins. The line between past and present can then become continuous, eternal, and it is not far from this point to the eternal maternal of the would-be matriarchs. It is important to specify the western narrative discourses into which the women and the shrine of Hizr can so readily fit, for only then can first impressions of a journey into those pasts be scrutinised and clarified. In this sense, nostalgia, the desire for depoliticised pasts, is a male discourse on the ruins of the eternal feminine.

Yet it would be wrong to consider these women and their ritual symbolism as being exemplary in this way. Like everyone else, they live in a present that is part and parcel of today's world, and their lives and beliefs are embedded in relations of power with the state, a global economy and men, just as are those of all other women. Their precise relationship to these powers and discourse is, of course, specific and personal as well as structured and general. But it is nevertheless there and because of that fact, their actions and beliefs must be set in the present world, not in that of a past.

8   Women, Islam and Superstition

I have repeatedly pointed to the way in which women are located at the centre of Euro-American narratives of oriental life, and to the crucial role of questions concerning the nature of Islam in those narratives in creating the grounds for a moral critique of Islamic nations. I have also shown the ways in which Islamic purity law is implicated in the construction of a fundamentally engendered moral community in which much of women's religious practice moves beyond the mosque. The result of the conjunction of these two sets of genderised views of the nature of the world is that women, as in European societies, will be regarded as 'naturally' more religious than men. Given the peripheralisation of women in each of the institutionalised state-supported eastern Mediterranean monotheisms, the form often taken by women's religion, among Muslims and Christians alike, will be defined as superstition. This definition of women's religiosity has the effect of again classifying Muslim women, already feminised through orientalist narratives, as irrational and emotional. It is a point on which Muslim men and western scholarship can readily agree.

Most Turkish women who visit shrines in search of companionship or help are well aware of the distinction between acceptable Islam and practices which men define as superstition. Some women try to make their pilgrimage in such a way that it conforms to the official view, one which is expressed on official signs at the more popular sites. But to visit a tomb and pray for the soul of the dead is regarded by all as a meritorious act, complete in itself. The women at Susuz Dede and the other shrines will certainly offer prayers for the soul of the occupant of the tomb, but they also seek direct access to the power of God that is evident at that place. This too is legal. Most women do not discuss the legality of the rites they are performing—they are taken for granted and legitimated through their continuation. When the matter is raised, as it was at the mausoleum of Ishak Çelebi in Manisa, one of the women there pointed out that none of the rites was really Islamic. The heated discussion she provoked was eventually resolved by an authoritative statement from one of the older women. She was, she said, *hoca* and *haci*, both a religious teacher and a Meccan pilgrim—clearly a sensible, educated and pious person. It was her view that God was everywhere (and here I paraphrase her words)—that could not be denied. And just as that was true, so it was also true that there were many ways to God and that God alone knew what was in the heart. God was here, at this place too, and he would understand the actions of those who believed in him.

This formulation was accepted by all but the woman who had provoked the discussion. She remained unwilling to be convinced of the Islamic legitimacy of the rites, yet she continued to participate. In this discussion, a fair representation of commonly held views and positions on this subject could be seen. Such discussion is uncommon at the shrines and in this case was provoked by my interest in activities which some women knew I would regard as superstitious. At Susuz Dede, my presence sometimes provoked similar discussions, although more frequently people simply tried to explain why it was that they came and how it helped. On one occasion, the young students from the nearby *Imam-Hatip* (religious) college came on a zealous journey to inform the women of the errors of their ways. The boys asserted that there was no-one in the grave and that the rites were pagan. When the boys tore the cotton from the tomb and kicked the candles into the fire, they were ignored. Despite their brashness, the women dealt patiently with them, and to support their own views produced arguments similar to those of the Manisa women. At about this time the tomb was broken up and substantially destroyed, probably by a missionary gang from the school, but within three weeks it had been rebuilt, bigger, better and stronger than ever.

There is also the matter of their 'simplicity' or 'primitiveness'. Women's rites are often described as crudely instrumental or as utilising 'primitive' notions of transference. The implication is that in more developed sets of beliefs concerning the sacred, the direct action of the primitive world is replaced with more refined, intellectual and sophisticated sets of ideas in which the gods become ineffable rather than representable. The way in which Christianity replaces the original blood sacrifice with its symbol or metaphor, the communion rite, exemplifies these arguments. The Catholic dogma on transubstantiation *insists* on the reality of the transformation of wine into blood and bread into flesh during the rite of communion. Nothing could be more simple or direct than the transformation required. But it is the context which is important. Where particular simple and direct relations between symbol and substance, action and result, are acceptable to a large institution of considerable power, they become complex mysteries unknowable to *man*. Where analogous simple and direct rites or beliefs take place beyond the reach of the institutional structures of religions, they are declared superstitious, primitive and non-Christian or non-Islamic, as the case may be. When women seek to participate actively in their religion, and to do so without the mediating controls of a clergy in order to stress matters of concern to *them*, their behaviour will be decried and denigrated.

The principal rite at Susuz Dede is the sprinkling of water onto the grave and it is this activity which is most immediately dismissed as superstitious. Yet if the sprinkling of water is set within its broader symbolic context and the structures of transcendence, it loses its difference and becomes part of the broader context from which it has been artificially separated. A detailed analysis of that context and the series of metaphors and metonymies through which it works, suppresses any sense of difference in its narratives, and thus of its quality as superstition. Indeed, the rites at Susuz Dede lose their sense of isolation and become part of a narrative shared by women and men, mosque-Islam and shrine-Islam, so that difference dissolves.

As Turkey moves ever closer to Europe, and as gender relations become ever more enmeshed in an economy and knowledges which disadvantage women, women's shrines continue to grow. The ritual and beliefs expressed and represented there differ enormously from the fundamentalist mosque-Islam so feared by 'the west', with which it is sometimes confused. It is, perhaps, reassuring to find women so committed to the universalising and transcendent values of life, particularly when these values are so frequently ignored. These are the values dismissed as superstition.

The field of symbolism and the narrative structures in which Susuz Dede's rites operate is, in fact, a very large one. Analysis of that field shows that the beliefs surrounding Susuz Dede are neither more nor less primitive or superstitious than any other beliefs, that Susuz Dede is neither isolated nor different from important elements of Islam. The extent of that field and the unity of its narrative structures is nicely illustrated in women's rites at a shrine in southern Turkey, a shrine of Hizr—the Green Saint.

Women enter the shrine through a corridor along which beggars sit imploring alms. They light small fires in niches cut into the rock of Hizr which forms the focus of the rites, and on them they burn aromatic resins and seeds or light small candles. As they do so, they pray or read from the Kuran, and then circumambulate the rock. Locks of hair are sometimes placed in the bag hanging from the tree, while cocks are sacrificed outside the shrine walls. The shrine is often crowded, with the young men idling outside on motorcycles or bicycles boldly eyeing the girls. From the restaurants nearby, loud music reverberates along the beach.

Hizr and the narrative structures at shrines

Hizr, the saint of the shrine at Sammandag whom I mentioned in the previous chapter, has a long oral and documentary history. Hizr's shrines are found throughout Turkey and the Middle Eastern Muslim world, much as shrines to Mary are found throughout the Christian world.[92] Legitimated by a Kuranic account (*Sure* 18: 59–81), Hizr narratives are elaborated in the Hadith, popular tales and stories, and in the oral literature. Hizr frequently appears in dreams and visions (I met several women who had seen him in this way), and he is particularly known for his sudden appearances with assistance for those in distress.[93] The cycle of Hizr legends also interacts with western millennial narratives and British orientalist fictions.[94] Most recently it has been reworked into archaeology through the search for the location of 'the two seas' of Hizr's narrative (Bibby 1970).

In the Kuranic version of the Hizr narrative, Moses begins a journey in search of the land where the two seas meet, a space of eternal life.[95] The place will be marked by a spring and a rock. Arriving, he fails to realise that he has reached his goal and so continues onwards. A miraculous sign sends him back, and this time he meets an unnamed man, popularly identified as Hizr. Moses asks Hizr to teach him everything he knows but a condition of this knowledge is that Moses shall ask no questions. During their travels, Hizr's three strange deeds lead Moses to break his promise three times. Hizr finally explains the meaning of his actions and vanishes.

The Hizr narrative is structured as a journey out to a sacred centre, a pilgrimage.[96] The narrative structure of pilgrimage can be mapped onto a location and in visits to shrines it is expressed spatially. The Kuranic text defines pilgrimage as difficult, makes clear the need for a spiritual guide and shows that the disciple owes absolute obedience to the guide (in this case Moses to Hizr). The responsibility for failure to recognise or reach the goal of the journey lies in the lack of self-control of the disciple/pilgrim, a privileging of bodily control found also within purity law. This model of the pilgrim's search for truth is found within all other forms of mystical practice, particularly in the *dervis* (dervish) and guild rites and initiations.

Most importantly, the Kuranic narrative also links the goal of pilgrimage to the grave. But the two seas of Moses' journey (supposed to be the material and spiritual worlds) are joined together by the Spring of Life, by everlasting life rather than death. For those not able to drink of the waters of eternal life, immortality arrives only with death. Rather than denying life, the grave reaffirms it. Ya Sin, the most frequently read *sure* of the Kuran at Susuz Dede and other shrines, also promises eternal life. The Hizr cycle of legends is very strongly connected to pilgrimage, embodying the redemptive focus of the tomb that characterises many, but not all, shrines.

Like Susuz Dede and the majority of saints, Hizr is gendered male. Usually represented as a virgin, whether he is married or not, his potency and power cannot therefore rest upon his sexuality. The characteristic of celibacy within marriage reflects a context in which sexuality is highly valued and saints frequently married. Having drunk of the waters of eternal life, Hizr appears as a very old man or as a beardless young man.[97] Both forms deny his sexuality through his virginity and mute his gender. In both, eternal youth and eternal life, Hizr denies the finality of death and provides an image of the continuity of life's flow and the life-giving promise of redemption. The contrast with Christianity, where celibacy marks total self-control and sexuality is sinful and demeaned, is very great. In Christian hagiographies, the combination of celibacy with marriage is associated not with men but with women, and is generally part of a resistance to marriage and its inevitable sexuality. This difference is important as it reflects the range of contrasts revolving around the body, its control and gender hierarchies in two very similar sets of religious beliefs.

Hizr falls into that class of 'saints' discussed by Mernissi (1975: 109) for Morocco who do not meet patriarchal stereotypes of masculinity, who are celibate, unmarried, outside family and social networks, eat raw food, either discard or reduce their clothing, and leave the body intact but uncontrolled. Mernissi interprets these characteristics as a male protest against the exploitation of women; however, around the eastern Mediterranean at least, other readings of these structural transformations appear possible. Within the iconography of these saints there are grounds for suggesting that, for example, the emphasis on celibacy, structurelessness, the natural world and the natural body is part of a process of establishing a female aspect of the dominating male, rather than an emphasis on the value of the female element itself. The characteristics of these saints could be seen as a re-appropriation of the female, together with all those values and qualities allocated to the subordinated female by men, into a recognisably male world. Despite their feminised gentleness, these idealised and completed males are nevertheless cannibalising saints who have ingested the feminine aspects of a 'new' masculinity. It is precisely this re-appropriation which characterises the sexual and gender rearrangements found within millennial movements, whether those of originary Christianity, Islam or New Age millenarianism.[98]

The recent resurgence of Catholic and Protestant Marian shrines throughout the Christian world needs to be seen in this context, too, for many of the characteristics of Hizr are to be found in Mary—her virginity, her propensity to appear in times of trouble, her geographical spread, her eternal youth and her associations with God's mercy and healing tears. The historical circumstances of Mary's rise and current popularity suggest that a hardening and redefinition of gender categories and their boundaries occurred just at the time that the Catholic church attempted to shed some of its purity law and other remnants of superstition, thus splitting the eternal feminine from the male in what must be seen as a distinctively modern development. Her nineteenth century rise also accompanied the establishment of the distinctively modern sciences of sexuality and the new definitions of heterosexuality which created the lesbian 'deviance' with which science and orientalist discourses on the 'east' were jointly obsessed.

Hizr's contrasting characteristics, his age and youth, his greenness, and his connection with death, have made him something of an enigma to European commentators. The explanations and commentary put forward in the *Encyclopaedia of Islam*, for example, suffer from the limitations of the Frazerian assumptions within which they are set. Rather than see him in his living and historical context, his meaning is determined on the basis of types of characteristics and the internal consistencies between them. This approach classifies Hizr with other 'green men' (with Robin Hood and the Green Knight, for example) and then seeks to determine their common origin as 'vegetation gods' through their actions and internal characteristics. A folk-memory of some kind is essential to this type of theory, resting as it does upon the notion of 'survivals'. It is a form of explanation in which meanings are located at the source and then assumed to be fixed through time. They assume that the characteristics of the saint originated in the original (and thus) natural characteristics, these being the simplest analogies to draw. Thus green, in recognition of a primordial colour code, *must* indicate vegetation, and so forth. These views are linked to the hope that if only history could show what the earliest practitioners of a rite or users of a symbol did with it, then the 'real' meaning would stand revealed for all time. Within such a framework, it then becomes possible to assert that the present bearers of the symbols and rites being discussed actually understand them instinctively but use them incorrectly. In other words, certain people are deprived of the possibility of understanding these aspects of their lives and the truth of their actions is known only to certain western scholars. Such methods have been long discarded, but they seem to reappear whenever the subordination of 'oriental' culture is being reinscribed. In the case of Hizr, the location of meaning at source has led to a search which has pushed back his origin to beyond the Babylonian era and left it lost in the mists of still more ancient time.

Hizr's greenness has particularly intrigued scholars and, as Corbin's (1970: 56) account of the work of Ibn Arabi testifies, has remained puzzling to this day. Some of the contradictory elements (*Shorter Encyclopedia of Islam*: al-Khadr) to be found within Hizr's structuring characteristics suggest that he is concerned with the origins of the encultured world. But if his character is seen as a set of paired characteristics resolved within the single unifying icon of his person, then he appears as a much more generally recognisable universalistic and transcendental figure. The basic Hizr pattern has, however, a regularity not obscured by the wealth and variety of local detail. Some of these paired attributes are written into the Kuranic narrative—land *and* water, for example, as seen in the rock and the spring of life—while others are developed historically and regionally outside the limits of the Kuranic text. Not a collection of contradictions, Hizr is a set of paired characteristics. The most important of these are:

life : death
water : earth
fertility : virginity

These three oppositions are transcended by immortality, rain and androgyny, and their transcendence represented through the potent colour symbolism of greenness that is Hizr's name and thus the totality of his transcendental content. The name 'Hizr' means 'Green Man', 'the Green', or 'Greenness'. His potent greenness is taken up not only by Islam as its sacred colour, but by those charismatic millennial prophets seeking to usher in the new and reconciled engendered world which Hizr promises. Hizr's immortality results from his drinking of the Waters of Life. The contradiction between his fertility and virginity is resolved through his explicit androgyny, while the water/earth opposition of the Kuranic story is transcended through the rain, which is also his life-giving, life-flow fertility.

Hizr's connection with rain occurs within the Kuranic text, and is elaborated in the extra-Kuranic narratives. In the Kuran, Hizr is described as 'One of Our servants to whom we had vouchsafed Our mercy'. Turks often speak of rain as 'God's Mercy'. This identification between rain, mercy and immortality occurs in other verses of the Kuran:[99]

> He sends forth the winds as harbingers of His mercy, and when they have gathered up a heavy cloud, He drives it onto some dead land and lets water fall upon it, bringing forth all manner of fruit. Thus He will raise the dead to life. (*Sure* 2: 57 [Dawood translation])

> And among his signs another is, that thou seest the land waste; but when we send down rain thereon, it is stirred and fermenteth. And he who quickeneth the earth will surely quicken the dead; for he is almighty. (*Sure* 41: page 391 [Sale translation])

The connections between rain, mercy and Hizr can also be seen in the way in which, in pre-Republican Turkey, formal rain prayers were offered up from the Hizr shrines which dotted the countryside at that time (Hasluck 1929: 100).

In the three pairs of oppositions and their third transcendental, unifying characteristic, rain holds a position of central importance. Connected both to fertility and immortality, rain underwrites the colouring of transcendence as green. As I noted earlier, green has many powerful connotations, some calendrical and agricultural, some mystical, and some powerful. Green is widely used to signify spiritual power and authority. It is also frequently the colour of tombs. The tomb of Susuz Dede, like many similar tombs, is painted green, as is that of Rumi in Konya. Kanuni Süleyman (Suleyman the Magnificent) preferred green robes (de Busbecq 1927: 50), a preference drawing on precisely that potent mix of power, fertility and transcendence. Further afield, the threat of rain in nineteenth century Mecca caused the muezzins to chant the call to prayer to the tunes of popular erotic songs (Snouck Hurgronje 1931: 69). The sometimes puzzling transformations enclosed within such acts can be comprehended when rain and the powers of fertility are brought within the field from which meanings are being determined or derived.

The hill on which Susuz Dede stands in Izmir is probably an old Hizr shrine, although this knowledge is certainly not part of the current set of narratives focusing on the tomb. Whether this could be shown to be historically correct or not, the hill, its outsideness, its name and its rites (the sprinkling of water onto a green tomb of a transcendent figure) suggest that Susuz Dede is a localised version of themes, symbols and meanings which are fundamental and widespread in Turkey and which are strongly associated with Hizr. Biographical detail and personality traits are not essential to a transcendent Hizr-like deity representing the universalistic themes characteristic of pilgrimage shrines. In the many narratives within which Hizr appears in Turkey, his personal characteristics remain obscure. However, the development of much better documented biographies at some shrines often means that the detail will conform to the underlying template rather than challenging its basis. In such cases, the extra detail adds to the ambiguity and transcendent characteristics of the biography rather than removing them.

These processes can be seen at work in the narrative cycle concerning Yunus Emre, a popular mystical poet who wrote in the vernacular of his day, and who dates from approximately the thirteenth century.[100] Even a preliminary reading of the literature concerning the life of Yunus Emre indicates his structural similarities to Hizr (Huri 1959; Schimmel 1975: 329; Araz 1978). Like Hizr, his life is cast within the form of a pilgrimage with its tripartite structure, and like Moses in the Hizr narrative, he learns of the need for a guide and for strict obedience to him. Yunus Emre shares also Hizr's muted sexuality and gender and the familiar tropes of rain, its divine mercy and greenness.[101]

In turn, the associations with greenness, rain and pilgrimage link both these characters into a much broader field of iconology, particularly that concerned with Paradise, gardens, flowing water and immortality. In the Kuran (*Sure* 76), God says directly, 'But the just shall drink of a cup of wine, mixed with the water of Cafur, a fountain whereof the servants of God shall drink . . .' (Sale translation). In a note to this verse, Sale states that this water is white, just as is the liquid given to the mother of Muhammed in the Mevlidi Serif. Another of the fountains of heaven is named Selsebil and is associated with youth perpetually in bloom.

The body of water symbolism is vibrant and immense and I do not want to do more than indicate this. It is utilised in sacred texts, throughout a range of mystical poetry, within secularised concepts relating both to fate and to forms of cleanliness expressed as hygiene. As I noted earlier, drinking and washing water should *always* flow, for otherwise it loses both its purity and its purifying power. This is so whether the water is in the mosque, a garden, the household or a spring. The use of water in formal gardens is important in determining sacred space. Similarly, the structures, concepts and form of pilgrimage are fundamental within those texts dealing with the search for knowledge and truth, whether that knowledge is set within a sacred or secular context. The journey out towards the sacred place and its dangers is often interwoven with the symbolism of water that I have already referred to. Rumi makes consistent use of water imagery within his mystical poetry as does Yunus Emre:

> The rivers all in Paradise
> Flow with the word Allah, Allah
>
> (Schimmel 1975: 332)

> The divine sherbet we have drunk, Elhamdulillah;
> The divine ocean we have crossed, Elhamdulillah;
> Collected were we, and became a spring, we spread and became a river;
> We streamed into the ocean, and overflowed, Elhamdulillah.
>
> (Huri 1959)

It is common, too, to see water sprinkled behind those leaving on a long journey, whether on pilgrimage to Mecca, the journey to the barracks for young conscripts, or a holiday. '*Su gibi tez git, tez gel*' is the blessing that accompanies the sprinkling of the water on these occasions, 'May you go and return like flowing water', that is to say, without let or hindrance.

Both Hizr and Yunus Emre are structured within this complex field of associations and evocations. They offer a wide range of associations determined by each individual's knowledge and experience, and knowledge of them cuts right across class, regional and status boundaries. Susuz Dede's character, as yet only vaguely defined in biographical terms, is nevertheless distinctively defined through his structural and symbolic characteristics. He draws on a vast metaphorical and metonymical field of meanings and locks into it at a point of great power—its greeenness. The sprinkling of the water, the rain of God's mercy, the opening of the life-giving flow of fate and the bringing of these forces to bear on aspects of women's daily lives through a local pilgrimage keeps the grass growing on his tomb a lush green, right through the hot summer months.

Pilgrims to his tomb do not remark on the similarities between Susuz Dede and the well-known and loved figures of Hizr or Yunus Emre, but when the parallels were pointed out, they were accepted readily, if with some surprise. Few of the women at the smaller shrines discuss the meaning of their rites, but it is clear that they are deeply involved in them and that far from being the superstitious acts of ignorant women, they are set within a broad but not unlimited narrative, ritual and metaphorical context of considerable complexity and range. This is also true for the other rites practised at the tomb.

Unlocking the flow of life

God's mercy is manifested most directly at Susuz Dede through the sprinkling of water onto the tomb. The most important characteristic of water is that it should flow unimpeded—it is the flow of water which guarantees its purity. Rain, as water flowing from God, is water in a particularly pure and life-giving form. The importance of the flow of water cannot be over-emphasised; the unravelling of spools of cotton thread at Susuz Dede refers also to this concept of unimpeded flow. As the cotton is unwound, it is wrapped around the tomb until, on a busy day, the headstone is all but smothered. As the end of the cotton approaches, the spool is thrown down the hillside. The unwinding of the thread is explicitly stated to refer to the opening of fate, the same fate that in other contexts is conceived of as the rush of flowing water to the sea. At the shrines, flow is often expressed as fate, *kismet*.

Once fate is understood as the process of life to which the concept of flow is essential, it can be seen to have a logical corollary—flow can be blocked. There is therefore an extensive ritual vocabulary concerned with both the loosening and blocking of the flow of fate.[102] Women pilgrims at Susuz Dede say that the unwinding of the cotton is performed to 'open' their fate. Cotton is also unwound at other shrines. At the tomb of Haci Bayram in Ankara, for example, where it is impossible to encircle the mausoleum because of the positioning of a mosque against its wall, at the call to prayer the cotton is unwound from its spool and the loose hanks waved through the air.[103] But the essential loosening of the action is preserved, even though the thread cannot be bound directly onto the saint's tomb. At other shrines, the opening and directing of fate is achieved in other ways. The use of locks (and keys) and knots is very widespread. Like the opening of the cotton, the unlocking and unknotting usually takes place at a moment of power, one that might be identified by the muezzin's call to prayer or simply as the middle of a particular day.

At the mausoleum of Ishak Çelebi, for example, women gather in the courtyard beside the mosque some time before the Friday midday prayer; those seeking help tie garments (men's ties, underclothing and handkerchiefs) onto the bars of the mausoleum's windows.[104] Many of the garments also have a small padlock locked onto them. At the call to prayer, the garments are unknotted from the bars, the padlocks unlocked, and the garments woven back and forwards through the bars as women pray for help and make their vows. In these actions, women seek the release of blockages and impediments to their fate, and to bring God's power to bear on specific aspects of their lives. Locks and garments are also used by women at Haci Bayram's shrine where, as some women unloosen their cotton, others wave garments in the air or open and close padlocks. All are described as ways of opening fate.

The opposite of the loosening or opening of one's fate is expressed most commonly through the knot. Knots can be most frequently observed on trees at small shrines (Christian, Muslim and Judaic) throughout the Mediterranean lands and across Europe and Asia.[105] Scholars of an earlier generation, like Westermack in his classic *Pagan Survivals in Muhammedan Civilizations* (1933) and Hasluck in his *Christianity and Islam under the Sultans* (1929: 262), considered these knotted pieces of cloth to be clear signs of what they saw as a 'popular cult', an aspect of folk belief which predated and fell well outside the realm of legitimate Islam. Their views were supported by Muslim scholars. There is no doubt, of course, that knotting has a long history and that the use of knots at shrines is by no means confined to Muslims. On the other hand, ritual knots are found in a variety of other, more acceptable, circumstances.[106] They are extensively used in guild and dervish rites and are important in the ritual symbolism of healing rituals—in childbirth, for example. In addition, the concepts of flow and fate to which they refer are found throughout the mystical, folk and religious literature. In the case of the Meccan pilgrim robe, the law states that it must *never* be knotted or tied. The power of knotting is recognised in the Kuran where blowing on knots, a recognised sorcery technique, is banned (*Sure* 113 [Daybreak, in the Sale translation]; Donaldson 1973: 12–14; Zwemmer 1939: ix–x). However knotting, closing or binding is rarely (J. Szyliowicz 1966: 105) motivated by evil intent. Its benign use in cases of, say, pregnancy, where taps are carefully closed off in order to prevent untimely abortion, or in the binding of the cotton thread onto the tomb of Susuz Dede in order to bring God's mercy onto the direction in which fate should flow, are an essential aspect of the practices of fate, openness and flow which I have been describing. The knotted shreds of cloth found so frequently on trees and tombs are usually put there after prayer and as a memorial that a conditional vow has been made. The person tying the knot seeks an interruption of fate.

Fate, then, consists not of hopeless resignation to the will of an omnipotent god offering redemption only through suffering (the Christian view frequently employed to denigrate Muslims trapped in the apathy of Islam), but of a view of the nature of the world in which daily life is seen as a continuing process or flow. Interruptions to the flow of fate occur through human folly or intransigence, or through the will of God. Prayers for help at such times are, at shrines, accompanied by rites which express the hope that the blockage to life's natural process will be removed, that fate will be opened so that the flow of life may proceed unimpeded. These concepts underpin the rites not only at Susuz Dede but those at many of the other shrines frequented by women right across Turkey.

Men also refer to fate; it is by no means an exclusively or even overwhelmingly female concept, nor is it one completely excluded from the mosque. However, shrine rites make manifest a vision of a moral community which is unified rather than divided, one of equals, one which focuses on life and death and the transcendent birthing role of women in both. This is a view of life as process which flows along reasonablly predictable structural channels, one which minimises death, emphasises immortality and thus the continuity of life and the world itself. It is as if death is denied and the process of life is seen as leading straight on to Paradise and eternal life, or, as Isik (1975–81) would have it, to 'eternal bliss'.

Promises of paradise

I have already mentioned that the Kuranic text most frequently recited at women's shrines is verse 36, named Ya Sin. While some women read it for themselves, it is more usual to commission a male *hoca* to recite it. These recitations are greatly enjoyed and women gather round to listen and participate. It is rare to hear any other verse of the Kuran used at the shrines; on any one day Ya Sin might be recited dozens of times. Ya Sin, greatly loved as it is, is constantly associated with death, so it is appropriate for it to be recited at tombs and shrines. It promises salvation to believers and is recited at the bedside of the dying and at the graves of the recently dead. Its use at Susuz Dede is therefore not surprising.

A clue to its popularity can be found in one of the cheap editions of Ya Sin that are readily available in religious bookshops throughout Turkey. In mine, bought at Susuz Dede, the introduction quotes two statements attributed to the Prophet. The first is that, 'in My Kuran are my seven names, Muhammed, Ahmed, Ya Sin, Taha, Müdessir, Müzemmil and Abdullah'; while the second is that '*Sure* Ya Sin is the heart of the Kuran'. These beliefs can also be found in Eflaki (1976) and therefore go back to at least the fourteenth century (although not necessarily in an uninterrupted lineage).

As in many cultures, purity in Turkey is frequently located in the heart; good women are described approvingly as 'clean-hearted' or simply 'clean'. In the 'heart of the Kuran' are seven sections, each one ending with the word *mubiyn* which is translated from the Arabic into the Turkish *açik*, open. Ya Sin contains the same themes, metaphors and imagery found in other aspects of the rites at Susuz Dede, most particularly of course, those concerning immortality, transition and openness.

Ya Sin begins with two warnings to unbelievers and a promise of eternal life to those who submit. A vivid picture of the resurrection follows:

> One sign of the resurrection unto them is the dead earth: we quicken the same by the rain, and produce thereout various sorts of grain, of which they eat. And we make therein gardens of palm-trees, and vines; and we cause springs to gush forth in the same: they may eat of the fruits thereof, and of the labour of their hands. Will they not therefore give thanks? Praise be unto him who hath created all the different kinds, both of vegetables, which the earth bringeth forth, and of their own species, by forming the two sexes, and also the various sorts of things which they know not ... It is a sign unto them, that we carry their offspring in the ship filled with merchandise ... (Sale translation)

A promise of resurrection follows, with a picture of paradise which specifically includes men and their wives. The promise of resurrection continues throughout the remaining verses of the *sure*, together with a statement of the validity of Muhammed's mission. The final verse again stresses the resurrection:

> Wherefore praise be unto him in whose hand is the kingdom of all things, and unto whom ye shall return at the last day. (Sale translation)

The conjunction of this vision of immortality with that presented through Hizr, Yunus Emre and Susuz Dede is clear. In dealing with resurrection, Ya Sin utilises the same concepts and symbolic structuring that can be analysed from the ritual focusing on the tomb at Susuz Dede.

The value and power of Ya Sin is explicitly accepted by religious officials. Isik collects a number of traditions which stress its value and gives ten legitimate uses for this *sure*, each concerning the righting of a wrong. He quotes, for example, the following *hadith*:

> If the Yasin-i sharif is said in the presence of a Muslim who is ill, the angel named Ridwan will bring him sherbet from Paradise. He will give away his soul sated with [holy] water. He will go to his grave sated. He will not need water. (Isik 1979: [5] 93)

Within this *hadith* the place and power of the heavenly waters are quite clear. The reverse aspect of the healing and merciful power of heavenly water is its absence in hell where thirst is one of the tortures of the damned. Isik (1979: [5] 93) also cites a *hadith* to support the practice of giving a sip of water to the dying in order to prevent

Satan offering a deceptive drop and thus leading the dying person to perdition.

In those sections of the Kuran dealing with Paradise, life, death and immortality, the references to the power of water and its relations to rain are consistent. The references in Ya Sin to these elements are vivid and compelling: 'One sign of the resurrection unto them is the dead earth: we quicken the same by rain . . .' and these images are consistent with those found elsewhere. In *Sure* 37, for example, it is expressed like this:

> But as for the sincere servants of God, they shall have a certain
> provision in paradise, namely, delicious fruits: and they shall be honoured:
> they shall be placed in gardens of pleasure, leaning on couches, opposite
> to one another: a cup shall be carried round unto them, filled with a
> limpid fountain, for the delight of those who drink . . . (Sale translation).

Ya Sin is read at death, or when a person is near death, for two reasons. First, because of the comfort offered through the promise of resurrection, and second, because of the important connections with water which I have cited. The sprinkling of water upon the tomb of Susuz Dede is one of the most important actions performed there and its direct connections to the continuous recitations of Ya Sin are clear. However, at other shrines the transcendental themes are expressed in other ways.

Ya Sin is not read only by women, nor is it read only at Susuz Dede; its popularity and significance is widespread. But like the *Mevlidi Serif*, it is read often and with pleasure by a great range of women. It is always to be found at shrines, and in that context is part of that broad model of the world which is constructed and presented to women through their shrine rites. In Ya Sin, men, and women as wives, are promised a place in Paradise: 'they and their wives shall rest in shady groves, leaning on magnificent couches'. What Ya Sin does is to condense a set of symbols and ideas into a synthesised promise of eternal life, and offers it specifically to women as well as to men. These themes are also found in the household rites and women's festivals which are located away from the shrines. However, it is at pilgrimage shrines that the transcendental, universal and unifying aspects of the moral community are emphasised. At the same time, the outlines of a female community are forged through the communal participation in rites which are specifically female and through the lowered cultural and structural barriers between them.

Nearly all the time that a pilgrim to Susuz Dede is making her supplicatory rites at the tomb and the distributions are being made, Ya Sin is being read. A pilgrim moving through the throng will hear excerpts and echoes of it as she proceeds. The recitations, which might be simultaneous if the day is a busy one, form a background to her other activities, a background which may be almost unperceived but which states repeatedly: life, fertility, resurrection, immortality, Paradise, women. For women as well as men are at the centre of the world described in Ya Sin, a vision which stands in stark contrast to the Meccan pilgrimage rites in which the vision of the moral community that comes into view is, despite its explicit expressions of equality, resoundingly male.

Women participating in a recitation of Ya Sin are therefore legitimating the flow and openness that are expressed through the sprinkling of water, unwinding, unlocking and opening that are found in actions not necessarily authorised by a sacred text or law. Through Ya Sin, women participate in the heart of their religious beliefs and its most venerated text, and they do so in a way which expresses communality and solidarity. The themes of Ya Sin are those of particular concern to women and form an important part of a female view of the world and a model for it. It is a world in which women act independently and as individuals seeking to take charge of their fate, a world in which men are peripheral, which is woman-centred and open.

Fire, sacrifice and the blood of life

In the rites that I have described and discussed so far, I have set out the ways in which beliefs, actions and concepts which are not unique to women are nevertheless welded into a framework which concerns their specific interests. Both fire and sacrifice, however, are much more clearly associated with the activities of men, and both the slaughtering of cocks on the site and the presence of a fire at the foot of Susuz Dede's tomb are clearly forbidden in Islamic law.

Isik's formulation on shrine rites is one which would be widely supported.[107] He phrases it like this:

> A vow to kill an animal must be for Allah's sake. It is permissible to give the meat to the poor and to present the *sawab* [benefit] for it to a wali or to an exalted religious (dead) person. In other words one must do [make] one's vows as exemplified: 'If I attain this wish of mine, I will kill a sheep for Allah's sake at Eyyub [Eyup Sultan], give the meat to those poor people who are neighbours of hadrat Khalid, and present the *sawab* [benefit] to his soul.' *The animal shouldn't be killed near the grave.*[108] Also, our religion does not lodge [accept] such things as fastening pieces of cloth or string on tombs, or burning candles on tombs ... Dead people do not need candles. A believer's grave is a garden of Paradise. It is in *nurs* (haloes [holy light or the light of God]).[109] And a disbeliever's grave is a ditch of Hell. It is full of torment. Candles will not rescue him from torment. (Isik 1979: [5] 59–60)

In the most male of Turkish pilgrimage shrines, that built around the grave of Eyup Sultan (the visionary founder of Istanbul), the religious law on sacrifice is observed. Sacrifices are carried out away from the grave in the places specifically designated to receive the animals. However, in order to be legal, the distance from grave to butchery does not need to be great, and at small but well-established shrines like that at Birgi, the larger animals at least meet their maker about fifty metres from the grave.

At Susuz Dede the most frequently sacrificed animal is a cock (*horoz*), often a white one. Although a sacrifice may legally be carried out by any believer, woman, man or uncircumcised (Brandel-Syrier 1960: 157) it is widely believed that it is unlawful for a Muslim woman to slaughter. Sacrifices at Susuz Dede are always carried out by a male *hoca*. If a sheep is to be killed, and this is rare, the pilgrim usually brings a more competent male to carry out the task. However, all Turkish men are required to sacrifice once a year, and most are able to carry out the correct procedures for killing a sheep if required.

The sacrifices at the shrine are regarded as good and beautiful and great care is taken that the animal feels no pain. If it gasps as it dies, the sound is interpreted as 'Allah', when this occurs, everyone is pleased. The blood *must* be allowed to pour away and often, as with the *kurban* sacrifices, a spot of the flowing blood is placed upon the forehead of the person dedicating the animal to God.[110] This transfer of the living blood is illegal under Hanefi law (Brandel-Syrier 1960: 150 ff.; Ali 1950: 731–33) but frequently performed.

The essential feature of a sacrifice (and of slaughter for meat) is that the blood should flow. This can be deduced from pollution categories but it is also seen this way by legal scholars and participants. Isik (1979: [5] 59), in discussing substitutes for conditional vows, says that there is no substitute possible in the cases where a sacrifice has been promised, for sacrifice (*kurban*) requires the shedding of blood. The 'shedding' defines the deed. While it is possible to substitute three fat sheep for four thin ones, as the value of the intention is unimpaired, it is not permissible to substitute a non-sacrificial action like the distribution of clothing to the poor. For the vow to be completed, blood must flow and therefore the substitution must be limited to a sacrificial animal.

Like water, blood becomes polluting when it stops flowing and is therefore unlawful food (Ali 1950: 729; *Sure* 2: 173, 5: 3 & 16: 115). Stagnant blood in the veins of an animal renders it unfit for food, and blood kept and made into pudding or sausage is similarly stagnant and impure. Blood flowing from the animal is not impure and can be placed upon the body. Indeed, the characteristics of blood are precisely parallel to those of that other life-giving force found at Susuz Dede, rain. Sacrifice, which is here legally defined as the shedding of blood and which is performed in response to a successful vow, concerns the flow of blood, the flow of life itself. In the complex web of meanings surrounding the tomb, if forms a pair with the water that is also such a prominent part of the ritual there.

Although many men disparage women's shrines, there is little in this part of the ritual that they can object to. As cited a little earlier, Isik states that 'A vow to kill an animal must be for Allah's sake. It is permissible to give the meat to the poor and to present the *sawab* for it to a wali [saint] or to an exalted religious (dead) person'. It is legal to make vows, legal to make distributions in fulfilling them and legal to sacrifice an animal too. Placing blood on the forehead is illegal but widely practised. It is the performance of the sacrifice beside the grave that constitutes the main problem and this locus which canonical Islam seeks unsuccessfully to sever. If the shrine grows, the location of the sacrifice will probably change, simply because of the increasing degree of organisation. However, even at much better established shrines, it is common to see feathers close to the tomb indicating the prevalence of this illegal behaviour. It is clerics who find it unacceptable, rather than the general populace, and it requires a degree of clerical intervention to prevent it. In their sacrifices then, women are very close to the letter of Islamic law but stand just outside it.

This is not the case with fire, however. Neither the *hocas* nor the pilgrims were able to provide any explanation for the presence of fire at Susuz Dede and in fact, although there is a constant stream of women lighting candles from it and standing them around it, very little attention was paid to the flames. Yet it was there every Friday without fail, despite the absence of fuel on the hilltop. So initially the fire posed something of a puzzle.

The clearest source of the ritual use of fire (and here I also embarked upon a search for origins), lies in the pre-Islamic religious beliefs of Iran which focused on a sacred flame. In the Izmir region there are a number of villages of Alevi Turks who trace their origins to Iran, who formerly made provision for the lighting of a sacred fire in the mausoleums for their dead and who use fire to celebrate Nevruz, the Persian New Year.[111] Alevi Turks are widely regarded as heretical Muslims or pagans, largely due to the absence of a mosque in their villages and the relation of their beliefs to the Zoroastrian cult which preceded Islam in Iran. Although a minority group in Turkey, they are nevertheless politically significant and Nevruz is a festival known to all Turks. In more precise terms, the Alevi might be considered heretical Shi'ite Muslims, with a long and interesting history.

Within Alevi rites, fire is intimately associated with the dead. At Nevruz, Alevi Turks put on their best festival clothing, traditional dress if possible, and all go to the cemetery for a festive meal. Family groups sit around the graves of the ancestors, with the younger unmarried men usually forming separate groups a little to one side. Beside each group of graves is a small alcove in which, until 1978, the fire was lit. After 1978 most people started going over to gas, an interesting move open to varying interpretations. This fire is not at the head of the grave, as it is at Susuz Dede, but it is essentially connected to it.

The Alevi say that at Nevruz they like all the family to be together, living and dead.

The sacred fire here refers to the bloodline of the family, the blood-relationships between individuals, a community which is not destroyed through death. The year begins with an assertion of the eternal links between those making up this community. Among the Alevi, as with other Muslim Turks, these blood links are predominantly patrilineal.

In the past, fire has also been important in other ritual contexts, in the place accorded it in Bektashi ritual, for example. The hearth (*ocak*), and the fire upon it, was the focal point of the room in which the main rites were conducted (Birge 1937: 178). The Janissary soldiers, closely connected to the Bektashis until their destruction, were organised in *ocaks* and were required to transfer their total loyalty from family to their new military *ocak*. The Ottoman censuses were also reckoned in hearths rather than individuals, and it is clear that the hearth and its fire were of considerable significance. However, the Bektashi dervishes, one of only two mystical orders originating in Anatolia, although at times powerful and widespread, were themselves of considerable heterodoxy and drew on elements of the beliefs preceding them, whether Byzantine Christian, Iranian or Shi'ite Muslim. They were not so far from the Alevis and the similar groups that flourished on the outskirts of the canonical Islam of the Ottoman state, particularly during the years of conquest.

There are therefore plenty of sources to which one might look for both the origins and meanings of the fire at the head of Susuz Dede's grave but to do so could mislead. While the historical spread of religious practice is interesting, in this case it serves to establish simply that fire, too, is part of a much larger field of shifting and inter-related concepts, and that it is neither isolated nor incomprehensible.

Hidrellez and the milk-line

Despite its pagan and heretical connotations, fire is also a feature of a May festival, widely celebrated in Turkey, called Hidrellez. Again, this is a festival widely celebrated across Turkey which has little to do with the Islam of the mosque. In the context or field of beliefs associated with women's shrines, Hidrellez is particularly relevant. While today Hidrellez celebrations are partly the province of children, it is also, like many European May festivities, a festival of young women. In the past it was very much a women's festival. Hidrellez is understood as marking the beginning of summer (Tugay 1963: 286). It occurs approximately forty days after the vernal equinox at the setting of the Pleiades (Gökalp 1978: 215) and was formerly used to separate the Ottoman calendar into its two halves. It is usually said that on the night of Hidrellez, Hizr and Ilyas (joined in the name Hidr and Ellez) fly through the sky performing miracles (Kalças 1977: 77). In Gökalp's (1978: 211) version, Hizr covers the sea and Ilyas the land. Ilyas is linked to mountain tops and springs but this connection is not always made.

Like Hizr himself, Hidrellez presents something of a puzzle. The conjunction of rites seen as a problem begins on the evening preceding the festival day, with bonfires lit in the streets over which everyone jumps. The jumping of bonfires is found all over Europe but usually at midsummer rather than in May (Garnett & Stuart-Glennie 1891: (1) 121–2; Megas 1963: 133 & 134). Frazer, in the vast amount of information gathered on fires, considered the jumping a rite of purification (Douglas & MacCormack 1978: 225) and, set against this background, Hidrellez becomes a midsummer festival that has lost its way during its incorporation into its Turkish context.

The date is also confusing. In the Christian calendar, May 6 is St George's Day. The cult of St George has been popular among Anatolian Greeks since medieval times and the famous rock churches of Cappadocia are frequently decorated with the figure of George mounted on a white horse, a serpent-like dragon at his feet. This has led some to identify Hizr with St George (Hasluck 1929: (1) 100; F. Davis 1968: 226) even though George's cult tends to be strongly masculinist; in Crete even aggressively so (Machin 1982, unpublished paper).[112] It is difficult to associate his dragon and warrior iconography with either a universalising women's festival or with the sexless and gentle Hizr. Yet others have approached the festival through etymology. In this case, Ilyas is identified as the Biblical Elias (Garnett & Stuart-Glennie 1891) and Elias derived from the ancient sun god Helios (Megas 1963). While the sun connection might reinforce the thesis that the festival was really a midsummer celebration, his marriage to a rain god is less explicable.

In fact, when considered as a whole, Hidrellez rites also have a clear and recognisable structure in which women move out from the women's structural centre of the community (the household) to its outside, in a movement analogous to that of pilgrimage. Unlike the journey out to a pilgrimage shrine, however, there is no specific location on which to focus, just as one gets away from it all by going out to the countryside. Neither is there any concept of the sacred attached to the movement out. When women lived more closely secluded lives, this was nevertheless an occasion on which they left the household legitimately and for their own pleasure. Ottoman women went out, cast off their restrictive clothing, feasted and played games in the warm summer air. One of the most popular pastimes was swinging, an activity which might seem unremarkable today, but which to secluded women (and to men) represented almost total freedom from constraint and which, as noted earlier, was the focus of considerable male disapproval. These are the attributes of play which were formally found at medieval pilgrimage shrines, the characteristics of what the Turners (1978) call liminality. There is 'release from mundane structure, homogenisation of status, simplicity of dress and behaviour . . . and individuality posed against the institutionalised milieu' (Turner & Turner 1978: 34).

If Hidrellez is conceived of as a rite of passage with the festive meal outside the household as the liminal phase, then the evening rites can be seen as a phase of separation for the journey to come. It is at this point that the fires are lit in the darkness and that women and children jump over them, marking the end or death of the old year, the sinking of the Pleiades, and the beginning or birth of the new year to come. The night hours are passed in preparation for the morrow and for the dawn which ushers in the first light of the new year. At this powerful new dawn women attempt to discern their fate for the coming year, using many and varied methods. The next solar interval, midday, is marked by a feast and it is this meal that is located outside the household, in the countryside. Then, at the sinking of the sun, women make their way slowly home.

The focus on the dawn during Hidrellez may at first sight seem non-Islamic, but this is not the case. The most important prayers of the religious calendar, the two major canonical feasts, are preceded by dawn prayers which almost the entire male population attends. The Hidrellez festivities of women, held mainly in the household, therefore need to be contrasted with the male mosque prayers celebrated at other times of the year. These rites use the household as a structural centre for a women's domain which is the equivalent of the mosque at the centre of the male domain.

Most written accounts of Hidrellez claim that the 'traditional' or 'real' Hidrellez lunch consists of a whole roast lamb and many informants say the same. The wholeness of the meal is interesting, as in Turkey meat is rarely eaten whole in this way; it is much more usually cut into small pieces and served as kebab or meatballs. Informants stress this wholeness. The other distinctive feature of the lamb is its roasting, which stands in contrast to the way in which the other distinctively female food is boiled. Aşure pudding, for example, is an unprocessed vegetable and grain dish, boiled to the consistency of porridge, then sweetened and spiced. The other distinctive feature of this meal is that it is always accompanied by the drinking of milk.[113] This is very striking, as in Turkey *ayran* (a mixture of yogurt and water) is generally preferred to milk. However, milk linkages between individuals, based on suckling, are widely acknowledged and are written into Islamic law where those suckling at the same breast are defined as siblings. (This was the basis of Harold Dickson's claim to his Arab identity). The milk-line, running through women, parallels that blood-line running through men. At Hidrellez women assert their claims to wholeness and cooked food, and reaffirm the value of the milk-line which stands opposed to the blood of kinship law and custom.

Table 1   Elements of ritual symbolism: Susuz Dede and Hidrellez

SUSUZ DEDE	HIDRELLEZ
fire	fire
rosewater	rosebushes
fate	fate
outside	outside
Hizr	Hizr
sweets	meal
water	milk

These three features of the Hidrellez meal stand out strongly from the mass of detail recorded for the varying performances of the rite. As a women's secular movement out of the structures of daily life, it is perhaps not surprising to find a number of similarities between the rites at Susuz Dede and Hidrellez. These are set out in Table 1. The similarities make it possible to understand both Hidrellez and Susuz Dede more clearly. They show that women's rites draw on a common set of symbolic structures and that these are not simply the superstitious remnants of a past poorly remembered, but draw on and are integrated into the symbolism of Islam as understood by men. They help to show that while Hidrellez is indeed a solar festival, the derivation from George and Helios is spurious. And it shows that women's rites maintain their focus on the unifying wholeness of the moral community to which they belong and on the importance of the process of life, its uninterrupted flow. Hidrellez allows a mild reversal of the social structures in which secluded women lived and affirmed the value of a world of women. The table also shows that the fire at Susuz Dede is much less an anomaly than it first appears. Not only do women use fire in other ritual circumstances, but it is used in conjunction with Hizr. There is no real need to search for the origins of its use, although if these were traced to aspects of Iranian religion, the connection with death and immortality certainly exists.

In contemporary Izmir, Hidrellez rites have lost much of their relevance for women. The old Ottoman year has been replaced by the reformed Christian calendar. Children now light the fires in the streets at dusk and jump over them; 'maidens' are often too demure, or too sophisticated, to join in. Perhaps as a result of the egalitarian discourse of recent years, the outdoor meal in the countryside which no husband dared forbid his wife attend has become a family picnic in the park; swinging is still popular, but mainly for children. The absence of seclusion and the emphasis on a nuclear family cuts across the bonds between women, reduces the significance and importance of the rites and allows their colonisation by men.

But the fire at Susuz Dede burns on, and while it too, appears to be of limited significance, it is certainly not the anomaly it first appears. It is thoroughly uncanonical and, with the candles that pilgrims light at the fire, would be roundly condemned by many.

The candles that form a large part of Christian worship, both at shrines and inside the church itself, are absolutely forbidden by the stricter interpreters of Islam.

> ... our religion does not lodge [accept] such things as fastening pieces of cloth or string on tombs, or burning candles on tombs ... Dead people do not need candles. A believer's grave is a garden of Paradise. Candles will not rescue him from torment ... (Isik 1975)

Despite such exhortations, candles, too, burn not only at Susuz Dede but at large numbers of graves and mausoleums around the countryside.

The vandalism and the attitudes the boys were learning in their religious schools, illustrate the ways in which the gap between women's rites and men's is often perceived. For many of the women, that gap does not exist, and the horrified responses to suggestions that the shrines are non-Islamic show clearly that the women there consider themselves perfectly orthodox in the practice of their religion and its duties. I have also shown how the rites are part of beliefs and practices which are widely spread throughout the population and that their strength and meaning relies, in fact, on precisely this integration. So my analysis, too, suggests that the gap perceived by religious scholars is manufactured. Many of the rites and beliefs found at the shrines would be perfectly acceptable if carried out elsewhere.

A women's model of the world?

Within the ritual and narrative experience of Turkish women at pilgrimage shrines a symbolic world of women can be seen—an egalitarian world, one in which birth is central and in which birth and the flow of life processes are presented as transcendent at the point of death. It is a circular and seamless world of whiteness, purity and female fertility that is opposed to the blackness of the polluting blood of menstruation; it follows a milk-line linking women to each other through the breast; but it is also a world which cannot close itself off against competing views. Its lack of an outer boundary results from its universalistic nature: a world which admits all has no firm line to delineate itself from the rest of the universe. Purity law, on the other hand, presents a very clearly bounded model; the practice of purity law defines community membership through exclusion. The openness of the female world-view may help to explain why Christian and Muslim women were able to share the same shrines in Izmir right up to the final invasion by the Greeks. It is certainly the case now that foreign women are welcomed at women's shrines when their entry to the mosque can be more problematic—there is no guarantee that foreign women entering a mosque would be ritually pure. Whereas Turkish women generally meet the requirements for ritual purity both at shrines and for *mevlüts*, this is not the focus of the occasion and strangers are welcomed.

However, the openness and universalism of the female world-view poses no challenge to the dominant model and women's rites are regularly classified as superstitious. Women can never discard the categories of purity law, at least not this side of ecstasy or madness, and neither the *mevlüt*, as it is performed in middle class Izmir, nor the shrine rituals are ecstatic. The openness of women's models perhaps makes it easier to hold two conflicting models of the world and it may also make the female world-view less of a threat to the dominant male categories of community and moral order. Such egalitarian universalism may also be a poor base for women's political action, although the mystical orders of dervishes utilised a male version of the same sort of model for intermittently successful political action.

The Christian churches have integrated pilgrimages and saints' shrines into the structures of ecclesiastical control in a way that is not the case in Turkey today, although in the past the shrine rites of the Turks were thoroughly integrated into the mystical religious institutions and practices of the Ottomans. Very important implications for women flow from the differences in Muslim and Christian womens' world-views and the relations between women, pilgrimage and the religious institutions of Islam and Christianity that are inscribed within them. In turn, these differences relate to those of purity and the ways in which they operate to produce gender hierarchies through the alliance of sexuality with masculinist power.

9 Gender and the World of Difference

Perhaps the most striking feature to emerge from the analysis of women's rites in Izmir was the way in which doctrines or ideologies of equality appeared crucial to the construction of hierarchies and their structures of oppression. This was the case no matter where those hierarchies were being produced and reproduced, whether those sites of generation were described as sacred or secular, no matter whether they were those of Islam, Christianity or any other universalising religion, monotheistic or polytheistic. The structures of difference, being also necessarily those of hierarchy, were key areas for the analysis of gender hierarchies in particular.

The overwhelmingly gendered nature of the realities those worlds contain must be taken into account. We live in a world not only engendered but in which there appear to be no alternatives to that engendering. It is the appearance of naturalness that provides the challenge for analysis, and it remains the task of anthropology to try to tear it away. While it remains impossible to step out of culture, to the extent that masculinist social theory ignores the structuring significance of gender it will be entirely unable to offer an approach to culture that does other than maintain culture's own taxonomies and hierarchies. The addition of context, the task of anthropology, will not in itself displace those taxonomies.

The metonymical collapsing of the categories through which the world is known into those of ranked, characterised, heterosexualised and enforced genders indicates the fundamental importance of feminist theorising and perceptions to analyses of societies and cultures. The almost total refusal of the major recognised male cultural theorists of international standing to even begin to engage with feminist theory indicates the privilege that is at stake. We can also begin to see why it is that binary categories, with their polarising and built-in exclusions, are always the language of power.

160

Writing the difference

I have stressed the ways in which my approach to my research in Turkey grew out of an established literary tradition and I have located the intellectual trajectory of anthropology within the broader narrative structures of that literature. I have shown how the verification of those narratives through observation, travel and research is subverted into a process that tends to confirm rather than disturb the overarching theories of race, gender and evolution within which they are set. This is because of the comparisons, usually unspoken, through which other societies and cultures come to be inscribed into western knowledges.

Because the classifications which underpin these comparisons are structured by and through authors in order to produce the differences they claim to describe objectively, and because those classifications are held in place through relations of power, there is no possibility of reaching a 'true' or 'objective' or 'scientific' cultural classification. Many people find this perception of the way in which knowledge is, by its very nature, totally political, profoundly disturbing. However, an awareness of the political nature of all knowledge permits us to deconstruct and re-read the narratives through which we know our world. In other words, once the political nature of all knowledge is accepted, the critique of all knowledge becomes possible—the nature of knowledge is both oppressive and liberating simultaneously, and the possibility of justice rests upon this characteristic. It is important, therefore, not to allow the destabilising vertigo caused by the loss of the notion of timeless and unchanging universal truths to provoke a retreat into a view of knowledge which cannot offer the possibility of critique, but to turn instead to exploring the liberationary possibilities which this approach offers.

My research in Turkey was carried out very much within the theoretical perspectives offered by a variety of writers who are generally referred to as structuralist. My approach to the problems of comparison that emerged from analysing my data on the religious beliefs and practices of Turkish women therefore used structuralist theory as a springboard. While today that work would have been carried out differently, I still find aspects of it useful. It is useful in combating misconceptions about the nature of Islam and its impact upon Turkish women, and remains fruitful in its attempt to focus on the integration of the body into the processes of engendering the worlds in which we live. I have tried to show how others' misconceptions about Islam *and my own research* grow out of the common narrative structures through which knowledge is created and imposed as the truth.

So that I can discuss its implications for our knowledge of women and religion, I now want to make clearer my structuralist approach to the nature of the comparisons at work. I worked largely with a model of society worked out by Victor Turner, particularly those aspects of it which are explored in the book written with Edith Turner, *Image and Pilgrimage in Christian Culture* (1978). Early in his work on African religions, Victor Turner proposed that all societies, no matter what their economic or technological base, had two fundamentally important dimensions. These he referred to as the domains of 'structure' and 'anti-structure'. In his view, the structural domain contained everything that we usually consider as the social structures and institutions of daily life—the families, political parties, kinship relations, economic relations and the religions of the churches, mosques or temples. He saw each domain as having a 'sacred centre', with the institutions of the churches, mosques or temples which lie at the sacred centre of the structural domain, putting out a series of models of the nature of the world which supported the social structures of his structural domain. In addition to the social structures within which we all live a great deal of our lives, he saw all societies as having a domain which lay beyond these structures. This is his anti-structural domain, and at *its* sacred centre he places the pilgrimage shrine. The social world is therefore conceptualised as consisting of two domains, neither of which can or does exist independently. For the student working with women at pilgrimage shrines, in a region in which pilgrimage is a central and compelling rite, this sociological and structural model of the nature of society offers immediate possibilities. It is equally clear, however, that Victor Turner's model makes no mention of women and allows their continued subsumption within the universalised male. For this reason, Turner's sociology remains resolutely male and gender-blind, without being gender-neutral. The effects of its gender-blindness become more apparent when he and Edith Turner attempted to account for the gendered nature of the Catholic pilgrimages devoted to Mary. This is not a matter that needs any elaboration here, and in fact, I shall shortly make use of some of their very interesting insights into the sociological nature of pilgrimage shrines. When I came to use the Turner model of structural and anti-structural domains, I attempted to gender it—to write gender into it, while leaving the model otherwise intact.

For reasons which are clear from the analysis of Islamic pollution law and its use in producing a sexual division of space, I came to consider that the sacred structural centre of Turkish culture, the mosque, and the sacred anti-structural centre, the pilgrimage shrine at Mecca, represented a dominant, but male, model of society. In gendering Turner's sociological model, I sought female structural and anti-structural sacred centres to correspond to the male ones, on the basis of an analysis of women's ritual symbolism locating them in the household and at women's shrines. I also considered that some hierarchy had to be injected into this view of the social world, and that the male and female models differed in their boundedness. The male model was a tightly bounded and closed model of the world, while in its concern with universal values the female model was necessarily open.

It was this distinctive feature that helped the male model to retain its dominance and the female model to continue as subordinate. This set of perceptions allowed the following models to be drawn up.

In this view of the nature of Turkish life in Izmir the women's *mevlüt*, with its focus on death, transcendence and non-polluting flow, is the structural equivalent of the mosque prayers and their focus on control and polluting forms of flow. The important pilgrimage rites at Mecca offer all participants a universal view of the world of Islam that, despite an explicit reference to equality, refers to men. It is the equality of all Muslim men that comes into view in Mecca, not the equality of women and men. The structural equivalent to these rites are, I argue, those that take place much closer to home, the journeys of women out of the household to their local pilgrimage shrines.

While the male model of the moral community of Islam is a closed model, one which claims to be bounded and discrete in that it admits no other possibilities, in the daily practice of Islam, in the mosque as elsewhere, the reality is variable. It is here that we glimpse the value of these models of the world, for they too assist in polarising and differentiating to produce the differences which order the world in which they live. The practice of any set of beliefs is always extremely variable, and in Turkey there is a continuum of both that lies between the male and female sacred centres. I have set out the outline of this continuum in the diagram which follows so that the accepted canonical festivals of Islam (which are also set out in the chart) act as the link between mosque and household rites, while the gap between the Aşure household festival through which household centres are reaffirmed, is bridged by the set of mosque rites called the Kandils which, in Turkey, are accessible to women. It is because of this overlapping continuum of practice and participation, one which is also seen in the range of pilgrimage practices, that I consider Turkish Islam of the late 1970s as both relatively flexible and encompassing. Changing political conditions readily challenge this flexibility, of course, and the models themselves cannot determine their realisation.

The development of structural models, both the analytical model of the sociologist and the indigenous models analysed from the ritual symbolism I observed, was intended as a first step towards finding an approach to understanding Islam and its effects on the lives of Turkish women within the framework of difference in which comparison had emerged as a central problem. These models implied a set of questions that could be used to interrogate Christian society and culture—that is, they try to make explicit the often hidden basis of the unspoken comparison. But just as I had focused my study of Islamic women on a single region, I wanted to make a specific comparison with Christian women and to treat them sociologically in a precisely parallel way. The closest and most obvious Christian women for comparison were the Orthodox Greeks who had lived close to the Turks for nearly five

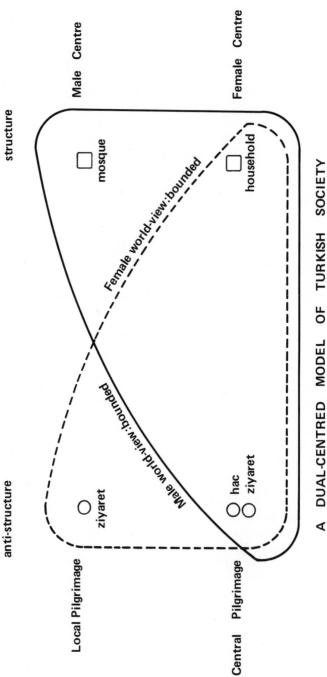

A DUAL-CENTRED MODEL OF TURKISH SOCIETY

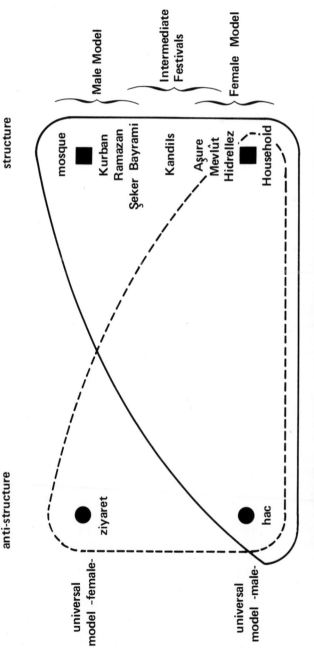

DUAL-CENTRED MODEL OF TURKISH SOCIETY: MAJOR RITES

hundred years, and the Catholic Christians who lived around the shores of the northern and eastern Mediterranean. Naturally, my remarks remain speculative, but as they indicate some interesting possibilities it is important to draw them out into the open. Just as for their Turkish sisters, pilgrimage plays a very important role in Mediterranean Christian women's religiosity.

The discovery of Meryem Ana

The sacred journey to a shrine is an important part of religious life in each of the major world religions. In Islam, the annual pilgrimage to the holy city of Mecca has a singularity in its established institutional role which gives pilgrimage a conspicuous centrality not found among the Christian churches. Yet pilgrimage remains a living and vital aspect of European Christianity in each of the major churches which is particularly associated with women. That the majority of pilgrims to Mecca are men does not mean that pilgrimage is any less important to Muslim women. However, because of the differing institutional locations of pilgrimage within the accepted dogmas of Islam and Christianity, and because of the differing symbolic logics involved in determining gender hierarchies, the significance of pilgrimage shrines for Christian and Muslim women varies.

The practices of women gathering at the shrine of Meryem Ana (Mary the Mother), Our Lady of Ephesus, just thirty miles south of Izmir, brings out some of these points of similarity and difference. The shrine's history also shows the degree to which origin and development are determined by political and economic factors rather than by the dynamics of the pilgrimage process itself.

The search for the House of the Virgin Mary at Ephesus began as the direct result of visions experienced by Anne Catherine Emmerich (1774–1824).[114] Her visions took the form of accounts of the daily life of Christ, his mother and his disciples. She described the clothing they wore, their physical characteristics, what they were eating, whether they looked tired or happy, and what they were doing. They read like a vivid account of a good dramatic film of the life of Jesus. At Easter she saw sorrowful scenes of death, while at the Feast of the Assumption of the Virgin she saw detailed scenes of the life of Mary. It was during one of these visions that she witnessed the death of Mary at Ephesus (Emmerich 1954).

The first interest in locating the Virgin's house at Ephesus came not from Emmerich but from the Daughters of Charity in Izmir in the late 1800s. One night, as they listened to a reading of Emmerich's visions, they begged their Lazarist priest to try to find the site of the house that Emmerich so clearly described (Deutsch 1965).[115]

The House of the Virgin Mary at Ephesus was discovered in 1891.[116]

It is therefore part of that 'dramatic resurgence' (Turner & Turner 1978: 203) enjoyed by Marian shrines during the nineteenth century. The new nineteenth century cult of the Virgin focused entirely on Mary herself, elevating her to new heights. She stood alone, dissociated from her godly son, glorified in her own right but with the emphasis on her virginity. In the nineteenth century the Catholic church accepted the doctrines and festival of the Assumption of the Virgin (into heaven), and a number of new elements entered her cult. I have already mentioned the discursive shifts in sexualities and genders taking place at the time to which this phase of Mary's cult must be related. This pilgrimage shrine therefore originated in response not to local but to European factors. Although on a site noted for its connection with the Ephesian Artemis and her incorporation into a strongly supported Byzantine Mary, the present shrine actually originated in European Catholicism and in the relations of Catholicism to industrialisation and the challenges to the gender and sexual relations of late nineteenth and twentieth century Catholicism.

The growth of pilgrimage shrines

A successful pilgrimage shrine can, and often does, grow in response to factors which have little to do with its origins. This is one of the reasons for considering the origin of a shrine to be relatively unimportant outside its legitimating miracle. Islamic and Catholic shrines, however, grow in ways which have implications for their functions and for women. Islam and Christianity cope with pilgrimage in rather different ways. A spontaneous journey 'out' of the structures in which church and mosque are implicated is a threat to established clerical power networks. Christianity has a doctrine and a system of practices which is able to capture new shrines and rapidly incorporate them into the institutional fabric of the church. Islam has no such doctrine and the relationship of Islam to pilgrimage therefore differs. The dimensions of this difference can be seen by following the growth of Meryem Ana a little further.

The first organised pilgrimage to Meryem Ana took place in 1896, when 1300–1400 pilgrims are said to have travelled from Izmir to the shrine (Thierry 1979: 15). The pilgrim guide-book (*Guide de Pélerin à Panaghia Capouli avec Plan de la Maison*), printed in 1896, assumes that the shrine is fully established and authentic. The authenticity of the site, however, despite the efforts of the Lazarists, was far from accepted and Mary was more usually said to have died in Jerusalem. Many pilgrims visited her grave there.

The claims of Ephesus were put forward on behalf of the Bishop of Izmir (Senior n.d.) and eventually were successful. The details of the struggle which led to the acceptance of Our Lady of Ephesus over those of Jerusalem have been collected by Deutsch (1965). Plenary indulgences cannot be granted to pilgrims unless a site is declared genuine, and plenary indulgences are essential if a shrine is to develop an international reputation. Because of the small size of today's local Christian community in Izmir, Meryem Ana relies almost entirely upon the international tourist/pilgrim trade for financial support. In 1961 the Pope granted plenary indulgences to pilgrims to the House of Mary at Ephesus (Deutsch 1965: 134) and in November 1979, Pope Jean-Paul II, a devotee of the Virgin Mary, visited the shrine himself (*Le Flambeau*, January 1980).

The growth of Susuz Dede

The steady growth of Susuz Dede since the 1960s and its focus on a grave illustrate differences in the developmental processes of two shrines within the same region, both of which, within the Turners' framework, might be seen as responses to industrialisation or secularisation. Susuz Dede remains entirely voluntary and completely outside the ambit of the mosque. Meryem Ana, with plenary indulgences now granted, has moved towards being incorporated into the clerical organisation of the church. The presence of a priest and several nuns at Meryem Ana helps to ensure orthodoxy, while the Catholic doctrine of the intercession of saints assures the pilgrimage shrine and its practices of an integrated place within the legitimate bodies of dogma, doctrine and performance which make up the church.

At Susuz Dede, the men present at the shrine are there to read the Kuran and to perform the act of sacrifice. They are not religious scholars or mosque functionaries, although they sometimes claim to be, and their presence cannot still the irregular practices of the pilgrims. Within Turkish mosque doctrines, no doctrine of intercession has been accepted, and the basis for a cult of saints within the mosque is therefore weaker. Lacking a doctrine of intercession, the concept of sainthood is correspondingly weakly developed. Religious scholars and many pious Turks reject the practices of women pilgrims at Susuz Dede and shrines like it, and consider them unauthorised and pagan. These factors lead to Susuz Dede being outside social and ecclesiastical structures in a way that Meryem Ana is not.[117] Pilgrimage shrines like Susuz Dede therefore offer women a place and a space of their own that Marian shrines do not. The definition of their rites as superstitious reflects their relative independence. The links between the purity categories of the structural centre and those of the shrines also differ between the two religions. While both shrines are fully anti-structural in the Turners' terms and, at both, universalistic and egalitarian models come into view which at first *seem* to offer women greater equality, this is more the case with the Turkish shrines than it is with those devoted to Mary.

Mary is, perhaps, a special case, for she lacks a Muslim counter-part. Throughout Christianity, however, she occupies a critical role, and while that role varies greatly according to time and place, her presence and her flexibility demand attention. In some of the popular literature on the gender of the gods, it is assumed that the presence of a female god indicates the particular prominence of women in the societies which honour her. But the relation of the gender of the gods to the gendered hierarchies of mortals is rarely straightforward and is often bewildering. While Mary has indeed offered comfort and pity to generation after generation of Christian women, she is nevertheless deeply implicated in their subordination. Her occasional appearance as a black Mary should probably be taken as indicating the collapsing of her total subordination to the will of God into submission to the will of men. It needs to be placed within the iconology of blackness and slavery which also racialises her and may hint at the terrifying blackness of the womb so feared by Christian men.

One of the interesting things about Mary is the genesis of her current Catholic cult and its emphasis on virginity. The Orthodox Mary retains much of her earlier identification with motherhood and fertility. The contrast is important because not only did Mary's current Catholic popularity as Virgin emerge from the secularisation often associated with industrial capital, but the move from motherhood to virginity came at the time at which the move to rationalise Christianity saw the expulsion of superstitious practices from the institutional church. In one sense, this pushed the saints and women's beliefs out of the church and towards the anti-structural domain. In another, the increasing rationalisation of knowledge saw the removal of some formal purity constraints from official dogma. The churching of women to remove the impurities of childbirth, for example, was disparaged and ritual pollution became something of the past. Christian (1972) gives a good description of the priests' efforts to stamp out this type of practice in rural Spain. While many of the more obvious markers of purity beliefs are now excluded from Mediterreanean Catholic ritual, because purity beliefs are so complicit in the creation of gender hierarchies, these changes in dogma seem to have created a need to re-focus on purity and women's bodies elsewhere. This is where Mary, always implicated in the visible manifestations of motherhood without sexuality, becomes important. Her reframing as Virgin brings an element of sexuality into the field of symbolism surrounding her.

I have already pointed to the ways in which Islamic pollution law does not, in itself, define sexuality as sinful, and shown how sexual intercourse pollutes women and men equally. This is not the case with Christianity, where the Eve narrative indicates quite clearly that Eve's sexuality is responsible for Adam being thrown out of the Garden of Eden. Had Eve not tempted Adam, all would have been well. In this context, sexuality is represented as sinful, an enduring theme of

Christian hagiography and society. Priests, monks and nuns are celibate, saints are celibate, and the only way of purifying yourself before
God is to reject sexuality altogether. All this tempting sexuality is
located in women. Those tempted to think that such beliefs are of the
past need only look at the rock music videos currently produced to sell
popular music to young people to see the continuing prominence of
this particular theme. Among Orthodox Greeks Mary is still held most
prominent as Mother, but there the clerics have retained more control
on purity beliefs within the institutional church.

It is in these very different approaches to purity that new patterns
of the similarities and differences between two of the three related
Asian monotheisms begin to emerge. While both Islam and Christianity define women as in need of control, they do so for different reasons. Islamic purity law creates a view of the moral community in
which women lack control but carry a highly valued sexuality. Christian purity beliefs, not now formally encoded in a separate text, create
a view of a moral community in which women must be controlled by
men because they are themselves impure. Women can only achieve
purity through virginity, and that possibility is denied those who value
motherhood. Christian sexuality (like other bodily functions), is thereby
deeply immersed in dirt and guilt and, one suspects, blackness. Con-
fession prescribes a remedy for sin but not for pollution. In both cases,
of course, a gendered moral world results, in which men are in control
of women.

However, lacking the symbolic and doctrinal basis for a sexual division of space, Christian males are in a rather difficult position. Bogged
down in Christian assertions of the equality of all believers without the
Islamic gendered qualification, they seek to control the access to space
and the mobility of women by other means. The sexual division of
labour that characterises Euro-American capitalism is one result of
this process. Even more important though, is the successful appropriation of all space to a univeral, male, Christian moral community.
Christian women lack a female domain, lack female ground-space and
are unable to make inroads into those spatial domains in which male
power is located. The significance of this can be seen in Australian
universities, for example, where women academics are currently losing
the little access they won to what was, until the 1960s, cloistered
male space. Their minimal access, never legitimised, is now retreating
through the reimposition of structural constraints upon women through
a rhetoric of equality. Privileged Turkish women who left the female
domain to enter the educational institutions and industrialising
workforce set up by Atatürk in the thirties did not encounter the same
sexual division of labour. Once into male space, there was not a
gendered ranking of jobs. As a result, in that first Republican generation, the percentage of women academics, and the number of

women employed as chemical and civil engineers and in other 'male' professions, far exceeded those found among their Australian and American counterparts. These differences cannot be explained through labour shortages, as similar labour markets in, say, Australia, did not have the same result. Indeed, rather than desegregate labour forces, Australian employers and governments preferred to import male labour.

The differences in purity beliefs and the differences in the allocation of space lead to different methods of control and therefore have very important implications for understanding differences between women. These arguments apply also to Judaism, although I have not begun to work out the parameters of difference there. However, Islamic purity law appears to be a simplification of Judaic law and remains very close to it.

If one were to seek a further speculative generalisation which would encompass all three religions, the argument I would make is this: that within the earlier Asiatic religions of the eastern Mediterranean there were always at least two logical and distinct cultural possibilities. The first of these concentrates on purity and pollution of the body, and links it into an explicit gender hierarchy and an explicitly stated gendered division of space. Judaism and Islam have formally worked through this option. The second is the option taken up through formal Christianity which focuses on the sinful body and its gender hierarchy. It explicitly denies its attempt to control women's access to space through rhetorically egalitarian doctrines and dogmas which are then refracted through heterosexist racialisation onto 'other' peoples. Each of these three share the same major historical set of religious beliefs and practices—the egalitarian doctrines associated with the universal moral community which come into view at pilgrimage shrines. Women of differing religious affiliations, in particular, have always been able to share the shrines, even in deteriorating political conditions.

While much of the symbolism and ritual activity of each religion reflects the common heritage, the differing approaches to purity and gender are, I believe, immensely important. By clarifying them, the parameters of broad cultural differences begin to shift. I am not, of course, arguing that one or other is better for women. But it is clear to me, as it has been to those other travellers in their orient, that to replace a sexual division of space with one which offers no place to women, to remove concepts of purity and pollution only to replace them with those of sin and guilt, is substitution rather than improvement. Neither does secularisation offer a solution to women's oppressions. The 'western' experience of transferring beliefs about the body away from the church and into the bosom of an overwhelmingly masculinist, heterosexist medicine, psychology, psychiatry or science has led to new and appalling abuses of women, their bodies and minds.

The body of 'western' knowledge

One approach to the body has laid great stress on the importance for women of recapturing the body, and of breaking through the limits placed upon women's understandings of the body by patriarchies, in order both to develop control and to exploit what is perceived as women's 'physicality, our bond with the natural order, the corporeal ground of our intelligence' (Rich 1977: 39).

Rich (1977: 40) considers that much actual female power is inherent in female biology and that through reclaiming the body women will gain access to that power. If it is true, as she asserted over a decade ago, that 'Women are controlled by lashing [them] to their bodies' (1977: 13), then remarkably little progress has been made in untying the ropes. One of the reasons for this is that a feminist analysis of women, the body and menstruation has been too ethnocentric and too universal in its claims to provide the basis for the more subtle analyses that might help. Rich's discussion of menstruation, for example, is heavily weighted with concern about the origins of a menstrual taboo which she sees as nigh on universal. In her view, the menstrual taboo signifies '. . . the fear of woman and the mystery of her motherhood'. She argues that menstrual seclusion can be interpreted as a ritual of withdrawal which adds to women's powers, rather than as one of exclusion from a daily life which is essentially male, an insight which can be supported by more recent anthropological data. Rich (1977: 105) very clearly describes current American (Christian and Judaic) attitudes to menstruation, male fears of contamination and semen loss, and the ambivalences produced in women by notions of menstrual impurity. What she cannot explain, except by recourse to the ancient past and Jungian psychology, is why it should be so, and whether menstrual taboos and female impurity are a cause or an effect of a gender hierarchy.[118] Her interesting comments on impurity do not seem to have attracted a great deal of feminist interest and have not been systematically followed up. My work seeks to draw out the implications of the body in women's subordination, to show the ways in which universalising approaches like that of Rich can be made more precise by being more specific, and by showing how the differences between women are narratively and structurally constituted.

Growing out of contemporary anthropology, my research in Izmir was set within the problematics that knowledge created and permitted. In addressing those problems, my analysis carried that form of knowledge a little further, and perhaps in directions in which it did not readily flow. While the addition of data, the defining of the contextual fields in which those data operated, and the inscription of women into the text achieved my aims, those steps did not, and could not, address the much more fundamental critiques of humanistic knowledges that were not at that time fully recognised by anthropologists. In rewriting that research for publication, I have shown how one ethnography emerged from its field of knowledge, how limiting that field can be, how it failed to address the problems posed by the grand narratives of western knowledge, those of race, gender, sexuality, evolution and power and their representation, and how it might have been made to do so.

I believe that women's oppression and expression will only ever be delineated by women, not because men cannot do it, but because they will not. The silence of the major male social critics of the post-war period on feminist theory is truly deafening. Said, for example, when questioned on his work and the place of gender in it, is reported as saying:

> Now as for the question of gender, you cannot possibly look at imperialism or certainly let's say Orientalism without noting the prominent position in it of women—that is to say, prominent by virtue of their simultaneous subordination and centrality. The role of the oriental woman in the whole discourse, the whole imagination of the Orient, is absolutely central and pretty much unchanged; that is to say, it very rarely goes beyond the kinds of essential functions assigned to women—subordination, gratification for the male, all kinds of sensuality and wish fulfilment and so on—that really is to be found everywhere in the worst as well as best writers. And to that extent I wouldn't consider myself to have *suppressed* that [author's emphasis]. I really do feel that in that situation, in the relationships between the ruler and the ruled in the imperial or colonial or racial sense, race takes precedence over both class and gender. That is a theoretical question which I feel hasn't so far been much debated and discussed in feminist writing—I mean in historical terms as opposed to just theoretical terms. (Williams 1989: 274)

While the choice of political target is always difficult, particularly for those, like Said, who are directly involved in conflicts with multiple agendas, this should not be confused with the intellectual endeavour. The separation of race from gender and sexuality is, in my view, a mistake. Each is deeply implicated in the creation, closure and reproduction of a moral community, and each implies the other. Women have found over and over again that the universal interests for which the problem of a gender hierarchy is put aside in moments of political strife become gendered interests as soon as the fighting stops. There are many women who do not accept this view and who choose to make common cause with their men in the hope that in their new world women will, at last, take their place. All the evidence suggests that this will not happen while race and gender are treated separately. Again, I find Said's comments salutary.

> The other point I'd like to make is that although I believe certainly in the authenticity and concreteness of experience, I don't believe in the notion of exclusiveness of experience, that is to say that only a Black can understand black experience, only a woman can understand women

etc. I find that a problematic notion, the problem of insider versus
outsider as the sociologists have it. So, I think that in those respects
I have tried to deal with some aspects of gender but I have always felt
that the problem of emphasis and relative importance took precedence
over the need to establish one's feminist credentials. (Williams 1989: 278)

Race and gender are the two faces of the same hierarchising coin. We
live at present in an encultured world, a world in which the distinction
between nature and culture is known to be a creation of culture, a
world in which we know simultaneously that a natural body exists but
that we can never know it, except through culture. We also know, as
I have stressed continually, that culture and knowledges, their classifications and categories, are held in place by relations of power.

Both structural and post-structural forms of analysis are attempts to
expose the lines of power through which the fundamental structuring
structures of culture are enforced. It is interesting to note that Adrienne
Rich's work on the feminisation of the oppressed preceded Edward
Said's, but unlike his, hers was never taken up outside a rather narrow
circle of women. I have used them both, yet I think that Rich's placing
of the female body at the centre of a gender hierarchy is precisely the
element missing from Said's extensive, and absolutely correct, delin-
eations of sexuality and gender in the feminising of the western 'oriental'. It is to Rich, and those who come after her, to Spivak (1985),
Strathern (1985) and Morris (1988) that we must go if we seek the
synthesis of the oppressions of race and gender, and for a political
agenda which seeks an end to both.

However, to focus as she does, on women's biology, is to miss the
point. There is no 'natural' biology of advantage or disadvantage upon
which women's subordination can be built. The anatomy of the human
body provides an impoverished base for gender differentiation, so that
the magnitude of bodily difference must be continually manufactured
and enlarged. Men must eat more to grow bigger and women must
have bodily hair removed in order to be femininely smooth-skinned.
What men seek is total control. They must control the production of
knowledge, for it is through knowledge that culture and persons are
constituted, and they seek control of the one thing they cannot yet do,
procreation. Their fascination with reproductive technology and their
indifference to the women's bodies involved in their experiments can
be explained in no other way.

While my work indicates the difficulty of deconstructing gender
hierarchies, it also indicates one area on which political action aiming
at liberating women would need to focus; and why it is that every
material advance toward freedom seems so easily to slip back into the
familiar dimensions of hierarchy. It shows why the task is so difficult.

Endnotes

Chapter 1

1 Durrell's 'Alexandria Quartet' comprising *Justine, Balthazar, Mountolive,* and *Clea,* was completed in 1960.

2 The recent re-publishing of nineteenth century travellers' tales, women's and men's alike, signals a taste for nostalgia that must not be allowed to go unquestioned.

Chapter 2

3 Fall of Constantinople, 1453; Bosnia, 1463; Moldavia, 1504; Mohacs (Hungary) 1526; Transylvania, 1541; Croatia, 1528. Turkish expansion was not halted till rather later. If one accepts that the Renaissance originated in Florence and spun outwards through Europe, then Shakespeare's poem 'Lucrece' (1594) and the plays with classical themes like *Julius Caesar* can be seen in this context.

4

Turks	14 000
Greeks	8 000
Armenians	400
Jews	15 000
Foreigners	200
Total	37 600

Source: Ülker 1974

5 The Black Sea Ottoman Greeks have their own history which differs from that sketched out here.

6 *Population of Izmir, circa 1894*

Ottoman Subjects

Muslims	89 000
Greek Orthodox	52 000
Armenians	5 628
Jews	16 000
	162 628

175

Foreigners

Greeks	25 000
Italians	6 400
Austro-Hungarians	1 800
French	1 000
English	980
German	512
Dutch	300
Persians	200
Others	117
	36 309

Source: *Izmir Il Yilligi* 1965: 92

7   The concept of 'desacralization' is itself a foundation stone of a western knowledge which identifies secularisation with either a specific historical period or a specific, transitional, stage on an evolutionary time scale. It is a critically important method of locking other cultures and other people into an inferior position within the narratives of the evolution of western moral supremacy.

8   The literature on Schliemann and his Troy is vast. For his own work in English see Schliemann (1972 [1884]); for the continuing controversy see Traill (1984) or Wood (1985).

9   Hasluck (1929) reports his discovery of Thecla's cult in the early part of this century. Brown (1988) discusses Thecla in late antiquity.

10   The importance of Greek and Latin nomenclature in science and medicine, two of the most powerful of disciplines, should also be noted in this context.

11   While the connection with St Timothy appears to have been lost, that with John survives in connection with the Marian cycle of legends currently active at the site.

12   Dustin Hoffman

Chapter 3

13   For example, Hogarth's title, *The Penetration of Arabia* (1922).

14   While the school of painters referred to as the orientalists is usually limited to a discrete group, orientalist imagery is important in advertising, in film, video rock clips etc.

15   In this context the detail which I refer to here, and its relation to representation and power, is that discussed by Shor (1987).

16   The realism of nineteenth century orientalist painters was assisted by the camera. Gérome, for example, is said to have taken a camera with him to Cairo (Verrier 1979). See also Alloula (1987); Graham-Brown (1988).

17   Each of these portraits is illustrated in Searight (1969). E.W. Lane was an orientalist who lived some time in Cairo and is remembered for his widely read book *The Manners and Customs of the Modern Egyptians* (1836).

18   For example, Frederick Leighton's Damascene hall in his Kensington house in the 1870s and the photograph of his Arab hall, Holland Park, shown in Searight (1969: 59 & 175).

19   Palgrave (1826–1888); Doughty (1843–1926). A photograph of Bertram

Thomas painted in Arab dress by Walter Russel is the frontispiece of his *The Arabs* (1937) and Thomas photographed with his party of Arabs is in his *Arabia Felix* (1938).

20 Kabbani's (1986) work on assumed names and identities is enlightening.

21 Dickson was seven years in Kuwait as British Political Agent. He was certainly not alone in trying to live out the dream. John Frederick Lewis' painting titled *The Halt of the Duke of Northumberland in the Sinai Desert* (1856), shows the Duke in full Arab regalia, reclining on cushions and smoking the long Turkish pipe. This painting is reproduced in Jullian (1977).

22 Men like A.J. Munby (Hudson 1974). Munby's claim to be carrying out research and his use of the photograph to detail his cases is interesting in the context of this discussion.

23 The decision to portray a subjugated 'other' in such warts and all detail is often linked to humanistic notions of 'balance' being achieved outside the context of power, so that the balanced description and acknowledged detail become assimilated to structures of power.

24 He had an Arab wet-nurse; the importance of the milk-line is established in the Kuran and culturally recognised in a number of Middle Eastern regions.

25 V. Dickson's *Forty Years in Kuwait* (1971) contains remarkably little data and concentrates on the sociable aspects of her life as an official wife.

26 The role of 'pure' Arab bloodstock in producing metonymic race relations is probably important here. The great value placed by the English (in particular) on pure Arab bloodstock in the horse parallels and interacts with this theme. Many of the nineteenth century travellers, women and men alike, were fascinated by equine bloodlines, kinship and affinities and mapped an equine world over the human tribal one they detailed. The European concern with the sexuality of the stallion and the imaginary oriental 'pasha' offered powerful metaphorical possibilities; the male fascination with the supposed importance of the size of the donkey penis and its interest for women is reflected in the appearance of sexual relations between women and quadrupeds in pornography. The focus on the bestial size of the oriental penis is clearly shown in the engraving *Harem* attributed to Rowlandson, drawn some time after 1812.

27 In its Freudian formulation, obsessive voyeurism comes from 'watching, in an active controlling sense, an objectified other' (Mulvey 1989: 17).

28 Compare the romantic representation of the female slave with Lady Mary Wortley Montagu's description of those she saw in Istanbul in *circa* 1717 as 'such miserable, awkward, porr [sic] wretches, you would not think any of 'em worthy to be your house-maid' (Melville n.d.: 154).

29 For example, *The White Slave* by Jean-Jules-Antoine Lecomte de Nouy.

30 For example, Preziosi's *Interior of a Harem* (1851).

31 There are parallels here with the female landscape and its endless wildness in Australian literature.

32 'Each colonized people is defined by its conqueror as weak, feminine, incapable of self-government, ignorant, uncultured, effete, irrational, in need of civilizing. On the other hand it may also be savored as mystical, physical, in deep contact with the earth—all attributes of the primordial Mother. But to say that the conquered are seen in this way does not mean that they have been truly *seen*.

'To hold power over others means that the powerful is permitted a kind of short-cut through the complexity of human personality. He does not have to enter intuitively into the souls of the powerless, or to hear what they are saying in their many languages, including the language of silence. Colonialism exists by virtue of this short-cut—how else could so few live among so many and understand so little? . . .

'Because the powerful can always depend on the short-cut of authority to effect his will, he has no apparent need for such insights, and, in fact, it can be dangerous for him to explore too closely into the mind of the powerless'. Rich (1977: 65).

33   There is however a mention of sex and orientalism under the heading of Flaubert (Said, 1978: 356), which indicates its importance to his argument.

34   'In addition to their general cultural attitudes, Nerval and Flaubert brought to the Orient a personal mythology whose concerns, and even structure, required the Orient' (Said 1978: 180).

35   'Their Orient was not so much grasped, appropriated, reduced, or codified as lived in, exploited aesthetically and imaginatively as a roomy place full of possibility. What mattered to them was the structure of their work as an independent, aesthetic, and personal fact, and not the ways by which, if one wanted to, one could effectively dominate or set down the Orient graphically. Their egos never absorbed the Orient, nor totally identified the Orient with documentary and textual knowledge of it (with official Orientalism, in short)'. (Said 1978:181).

36   In using the term 'appropriation' I refer to a cultural movement within its relations of power. The term is not, in this formulation, reversible and the expression 'reverse appropriation' makes no sense. In a reversible form, the imputed dual movement serves to mask precisely the relation of domination which is essential to the concept.

37   Szyliowicz (1988) gives a good account of his work and a Freudian analysis of the text. Loti's portrait in Turkish garb is in the Musée Basque, Bayonne.

38   Tsigakou's *The Rediscovery of Greece* (1981) is interesting in this context and for illustrating the ways in which the Morea and the Balkans moved from the orient to the occident at a specific stage in the modern era.

39   'I will have such difficulties becoming English again: here I am Arab in habits, and slip in talking from English to French and Arabic unnoticing . . .' Cited in Tabachnick & Matheson (1988: 16)

Chapter 4

40   V. Sackville-West. This passage occurs in Massingham & Massingham (1962: 202) but they cite it incorrectly as coming from the letters of Gertrude Bell.

41   The label *lesbian* is deployed as a witchcraft accusation to divide women and is widely used to control their behaviour; it punishes those who do not, or cannot, conform to male-enforced images of 'natural' heterosexuality. The nineteenth century emphasis on sexuality and its use in creating roles and norms referring to good, bad and mad women provided, Foucault would argue, a new sexualised gender context which created strong stresses for women. While some of these women may

well have loved women rather than men, it is difficult to say whether they all did. Many women found and find that a failure to enter into heterosexuality leads them to celibacy rather than to the lesbian option. Sexuality was itself a problem for some women travellers. Margaret Fountaine's (1980) sexual exploits and her long-standing relationship with a Christian Lebanese man (who sometimes travelled with her as her servant) illustrates the ramifications of active heterosexuality for Victorian women who would be free and would exercise control and power within their own lives and those of others.

42 Her action is usually interpreted as one of literary vandalism.

43 With considerable over-writing by her husband.

44 See the discussion of the trope of disrobing in ethnographic texts in Pratt (1986: 37).

45 Her regal claims caused much discussion at the time and since, and Katherine Sim provides a most unfriendly portrait of both Lady Hester and this incident, writing of the way in which palms were well greased in order to achieve the coronation (Sim 1969: 126).

46 It is not clear whether Digby knew of the Albanian custom which offered unmarried women a male role (Wheelwright 1989: 115–116).

47 There is no indication in the literature that Eberhardt took female lovers. This may be due to a discreet silence, or to the ways in which, in a hierarchically gendered world, some women are driven into heterosexuality to retain a sense of themselves as essentially female despite their supposedly 'masculine' behaviour.

48 There are the books of Selma Ekrem (1942 & 1947), the account published under the name of Melek Hanum (1842), the *Memoirs* of Halide Edib (1926), and those of Tugay (1963).

49 Outer cloak and face covering.

50 I here follow Rich when she looks to feminism as a liberating force, although I do not share her notion of a specifically female consciousness which, in her work, appears as a natural characteristic rather than as a socially constructed one. However her sentiment and meaning I find entirely acceptable. 'Masculine intellectual systems are inadequate because they lack the wholeness that female consciousness, excluded from contributing to them, could provide . . . Truly to liberate women, then, means to change thinking itself . . .' (Rich 1977: 80–1).

Chapter 5

51 I refer to the Penguin translation of the Kuran by Dawood (1974), and to that of George Sale (many editions), which sometimes provides a closer rendering of the Arabic. Where possible I prefer to retain the Turkish spelling of Kuran, rather than the Anglicised Koran or the Arabic Quran. Similarly, for the verses of the Kuran, sometimes rendered from the Arabic as *sura* or *surah*, I retain the Turkish *sure*.

52 Hodgson (1974) gives a clear exposition of the development of the Hadith and their relation to law and the politics of the early centuries.

53 'If men strive, and hurt a woman with child, so that her fruit depart from her, and yet no mischief follow: he shall be surely punished, according as the woman's husband will lay upon him; and he shall pay as the judges determine'.

> 'And if any mischief follow, then thou shalt give life for life,
> Eye for eye, tooth for tooth, hand for hand, foot for foot,
> Burning for burning, wound for wound, stripe for stripe.'
>
> *Exodus* 21: 22–5

54 Hodgson (1974) gives an excellent discussion of the religion and the history of the Islamic Middle East which is basically that of male Islam. Levy (1971) does the same. Both deal with women within the context of family law and have little to say of purity law.

55 The material I present here may be familiar to many readers, but I want to stress that it refers only to Turkey. My research was carried out in a large city and so there is nothing here about village beliefs or those of pastoralists. There is also nothing about the differences in belief or practice between the Aegean littoral and the Anatolian plateau or the eastern plains.

56 Hanefi Islam is one of the four recognised non-Shia schools of law, and was developed into an imperial form by the Ottomans. The Turkish men I knew were mainly of the middle classes, traders and manufacturers in Izmir's central market, government officials and administrators, shop owners, bank officials, people of some education who favoured tertiary education in some form, who educated daughters as well as sons if it were possible, people who were relatively well-off but not among the very wealthy. Most of these men were Sunni Muslims of the Hanefi school, that is, they participated in the most widely accepted school of Islamic law in Turkey. A few Izmirlis were Alevi Turks but their religious beliefs are quite different, and need a separate analysis.

57 There are also six fundamental beliefs: Belief in God, in His Angels, His Book, His Prophets, the Last Day and Predestination (Davis 1968: 361).

58 The other major feasts of the Islamic calendar are Şeker Bayrami (Festival of Sweets which follows the fast) and Kurban (the Feast of Sacrifice).

59 While there are many women in Mecca for the pilgrimage rites, they remain a minority. Women are less likely to achieve the economic ability to make the pilgrimage and must have a male companion with whom to travel.

60 For a discussion of purity and gender relations in Bangladesh, see Rozario (1991).

61 For example, *Kolay Namaz Hocasi* (1982) (*Easy Prayer Instructor*) by Hafiz Yusuf Tavasli contains simple instructions and clear diagrams to indicate the required actions.

62 For example, see Siegel (1969: 109) for the situation in Aceh. The insistence of missionaries and fundamentalists on the central importance of prayer also testifies to the significance of prayer to 'being' a Muslim.

63 Women are held to be capable of losing sexual fluids during the night, just as men are.

64 In nineteenth century Istanbul, Garnett (1904: 70) remarked that even slaves working indoors who needed to tuck their skirts up and show the legs, never left the hair uncovered.

65 Evliya Effendi Çelebi (I [2]: 214) gives the origin of the shaving of the head:

> 'There are a great many Koreishites who allow their hair to grow, near Mecca; the same is the case with many Dervishes, and with a

great number of Abyssinian nations. I saw on my travels also, many other people, who let their hair grow. The Prophet having conquered Mecca, and his principal antagonists having embraced Islam, he ordered his disciple Selman Pak, the very same day, to shave his head. He became therefore the patron of all barbers, and was girded by Ali'.

Chapter 6

66　By property, Dengler means real property, land and buildings.

67　The development of women as consumers in late nineteenth century capitalism led also to the discovery of the consuming woman's disease, kleptomania (Abelson 1989). Perhaps anorexia nervosa, the woman who will not consume to excess, should be set against this background?

68　It is the move toward food crops for export markets that sets in train the ecological disasters now faced by core and peripheral economies alike.

69　The Muslim women of Delhi described by Jeffery (1979) are an example of this type of seclusion.

70　I cite one textual example, but the subject is a part of the discourse of daily life that takes place between Turks and foreigners. It was in this context that it first came to my attention. I am not aware of the precise significance of a debate on the origins of veiling among Turks when they are not speaking to foreigners, although it is of crucial importance in local debates on 'modernisation', debates of critical political importance.

71　Davis (1968) gives no details of the nature of the offences of which the women were accused.

72　There are three terms used to describe women's space which must be carefully distinguished:

　　i)　gender separation, which refers to the symbolic level
　　ii)　gender segregation, which refers to the pattern of ground-space that rests upon a symbolic model of separation
　　iii)　seclusion, the pattern gender segregation in which the boundary of the female domain is drawn at the household.

Neither gender segregation nor seclusion refer directly to the mobility of women.

73　The importance of commerce to the first Muslims is reflected in the Kuran (*Sures* 2: 198 & 4: 29). There is a great deal of information on correct commercial practice (*Sures* 3: 130, 5: 8, 2: 80 etc) and believers are constantly exhorted to give fair measure and just weight (*Sures* 11: 85, 5: 8). In addition to practical injunctions, the Kuran often uses a commercial turn of phrase or metaphor (*Sure* 57: 11) to describe the actions or intentions of God. Souls will be weighed in the balance (*Sure* 21: 48), God keeps an account book in which all good and bad deeds will be entered (*Sure* 69: 18) and so forth. In these verses of the Kuran, God addressed the people of Mecca, through Muhammed, on subjects which were important to them, using the language of daily life.

Chapter 7

74　See however, Graham-Brown (1988: 82, photo 16) for the suggestion that the introduction of rail networks offered women greater opportunities for travel.

75   Themes often treated in Turkish films, e.g. *Yol*.
76   Adrienne Rich (1977: 16) has pointed to problems with this style of conceptualisation:

> ... I soon began to sense a fundamental perceptual difficulty among male scholars (and some female ones) for which 'sexism' is too facile a term. It is really an intellectual defect, which might be named 'patrivincialism' or 'patriochialism': the assumption that women are a subgroup, that 'man's world' is the 'real' world, that patriarchy is equivalent to culture and culture to patriarchy ... History as written and perceived up to now, is the history of a minority, who may well turn out to be the 'sub-group'.

It is not necessary to accept Rich's notion and use of patriarchy or the linkage of patriarchy to concepts of 'sub-society' to accept the validity of her point that there are problems in conceptualising women's society as 'sub' anything.

77   The absence of women and of funeral laments at the graveside contrasts with funerary practice in Iran and with that of Alevi Turks and Anatolian Greeks.
78   The *Mevlidi Serif* is by Suleyman Çelebi. An English translation is provided by MacCallum (1943) 1973. While verses describing the death of the Prophet are said to exist (MacCallum 1943) I have never heard them.
79   The *mevlüt* is also used to commemorate other rites of passage and is not restricted to death. Yet its role in death rites signals its importance for the models I developed here. Its use on other occasions supports rather than invalidates its significance.
80   Village cemeteries may sometimes be much bleaker places with the dead seemingly forgotten and neglected; the range of practice is great.
81   Emine is the Turkish rendering of the Arabic Aminah.
82   The *Fatiha*:

> Praise be to God, the Lord of all creatures; The most merciful, the King of the day of judgement. Thee do we worship, and of thee do we beg assistance. Direct us in the right way, in the way of those to whom thou hast been gracious; not of these against whom thou art incensed, nor of those who go astray.

> (Sale translation)

83   *Encyclopedia of Islam* [2nd Edition]: Kaaba
84   I use the Turkish spelling with an English plural separated by the hyphen. The more familiar English spelling is 'dervish' and 'dervishes'. The circling *zikr* (ritual) of the Mevlevi order, an order which is entirely Anatolian in origin and support, is intimately connected with death and transcendence.
85   The method of slaughtering animals for food allows all the blood to drain from the carcass, as is also the case in Judaic law. Animals which are defined as having blood but which cannot be dealt with in such a way as to drain the blood out are anomalous. Thus the mixed feelings and practice over crustacea. These definitions stand in stark contrast to those of some central Asian cultures in which a beast must be killed in such a way as to keep the blood within the body.

86 'Thirsty Grandfather', *dede* being used to indicate a male forebear and often being applied to a saintly or pious character.

87 I rely largely on the work of Turner & Turner (1978) for definitions of pilgrimage and pilgrim sites.

88 There are many women at the shrine who regard all the *hoca*s as ignorant charlatans and frauds and therefore avoid their services. The *hoca*s at Susuz Dede are very poor and not well-schooled. The male *hoca*s actually regard the women pilgrims as superstitious and ignorant and the female *hoca*s as a legal impossibility and total aberration. However, both groups provide necessary functions and at times of extremity, their services can be useful. They are the precise structural equivalents of the quick-fix therapists used by so many desperate and deluded Australians and Americans and their methods have about the same degree of success.

89 The women *hoca*s, being very poor, often collect the spools and rewind as much of the cotton as possible.

90 *Dua* is free prayer. It stands in contrast to the formal prayers of obligation which I discussed in an earlier chapter.

91 Mehmed Birgevi, 'a subtle theologian who had carried on controversies with Ebu-s-sü'üd' (Hodgson 1974: (3) 123).

Chapter 8

92 For Kuwait see Bibby (1970: 220, 227 & plate 24) and Dickson (1949) for a map on an unnumbered page at the back of his book; for Turkey see Hasluck (1929: 324) and Weulersse (1946) for a photograph of the Sammandag shrine near Antakya.

93 I met several people at the annual rites of the Mevlevi order in Konya who had been sent to attend by a man in a dream, the man being identified as Hizr or perhaps Celaleddin Rumi (founder of the Mevlevi order) himself.

94 John Buchan's 'gripping yarn', *Greenmantle*, set in Istanbul, draws on Hizr and Mahdist legends.

95 Note the parallels with the Judaic Moses myths.

96 For more on Moses as a disciple of Hizr see Pourjavady & Wilson (1978: 35 n. 37).

97 Cf. Corbin (1970: 47) for an account of the mystical awakening of Ibn Arabi.

98 These transformations can be traced through the iconology of Jesus of Nazareth, his celibacy, relatively feminised appearance and gentleness; Hizr often appears as a beardless youth; while the conscious use of female forms of dress and behaviour among New Age followers and the femininity of the age to come which will complete the previously divided male, exemplifies the point I am making here.

99 See also Shakespeare's *Merchant of Venice*.

100 The language of the Turkish courts tended to be Persian, Arabic and a mixture of the two. Turkish was confined to the peasantry and not highly regarded. Yunus Emre's poetry therefore marks a significant rebellion.

101 This iconology emerges quite clearly in the account of a memorial service held at one of Emre's graves (in Sariköy) given by Huri (1959). Huri was a disciple of the Turkish mystic, Kenan Rifai, but was, I believe, from a Christian background.

102 Cf. Hasluck (1929: 262) for earlier descriptions of some of these practices.
103 The founder of the important Bayrami mystical order.
104 Ishak Çelebi founded his mosque, the Ulu Cami in Manisa, in 1366.
105 The large and ornate temple knots of Japanese shrines may lie at one end of this spectrum. For England see (Adair 1978: 198–99 & plate 12); for *brandea* on St Peter's tomb, see (Brown 1981: 88).
106 Ritual knots are also important in Japan.
107 Isik's rendering of the law is basically Hanefi, reasonably strict, and intended for Christians who might harbour misconceptions about the nature of the laws of Islam.
108 My emphasis.
109 *Nur* is not only 'halo', but is sacred light. Redhouse (1968) gives also 'the spiritual light of saintliness, glory and light of the World; Nurî Alem is a name for Muhammed.
110 Kurban is the annual Feast of Sacrifice at which each family head should sacrifice a beast.
111 In Naldöken, Bademli, Narlidere etc.
112 The series of publications concerning Cretan shepherds by Michael Herzfeld (e.g. 1985) is interesting in this context.
113 Personal communication from Dr M. Bainbridge, School of Oriental and African Studies, London.

Chapter 9

114 Of poor peasant stock and almost illiterate (Deutsch 1965), she was born in Flamske, Germany. A servant and a seamstress, she entered the Augustinian convent of Dulmen at the age of 28. The convent was suppressed, Emmerich was ill, and she spent the last twelve years of her life in pain and poverty. During these unhappy years, she received the stigmata of Jesus. She had many visions which were recorded by the young poet, Clemmens Brentano (Delaney & Tobin 1962).
115 Their involvement was not as unlikely as it might at first seem. They were a congregation of missionary priests, and with the Daughters of Charity who worked beside them, were founded by St Vincent de Paul. Their original mission had been to the galley slaves of France and they had also worked among Christian captives in Algeria. They suffered badly during the French Revolution but their fortunes were assisted by the appearance of the Virgin Mary to one of their Daughters of Charity, Catherine Labouré. Labouré's visions formed the basis of the popular cult of the Miraculous Medal which led to the revival of the Vincentian orders' missionary work.
116 Although there is a time lag between Emmerich's vision and the priestly response to it, the origin of the site and its discovery by the Lazarists fits in well with the visionary origins of other nineteenth century European Marian shrines. In this case, rather than the vision occurring locally, the Lazarists acted as proxies for Catherine Anne Emmerich, a role for which their loyalties to Mary had already equipped them. Not only did they have close and established links with the cult of the Virgin, but in Izmir they were a minority group among the predominating Orthodox Christians with whom they competed for souls and status. Eugène Poulin, Superior of the Lazarist seminary in Izmir 'thought it only proper that Panaya (i.e. Meryem Ana) be in Catholic possession' (Deutsch 1965:

20). The social status of the Lazarist order in Izmir to some extent paralleled the disadvantaged social status of the individuals who would normally have the visions upon which the 'modern' Marian shrines are based.

117 Archaeologists have established that the foundations of the ruined house identified as Mary's *could* date from the first or second century AD (Foss 1979: 95, 137 & 177), which is not surprising. Like the present inhabitants of the coastal plains and ports, the ancient Ephesians fled the summer heat and pestilence of the towns for the relief of the shady hills nearby. The hills surrounding Ephesus are littered with the remains of ancient farms and summer houses. If one grants that the house is dated to roughly the period of Mary's death, could *this* house be Mary's, the house described in detail in Emmerich's visions? Emmerich saw a stone house on a hillside outside Ephesus which was covered in the beautiful wildflowers of the region, wild lavender, cyclamen, daisies, purple orchids and many others. This house meets those criteria, as would many others. But as yet neither the recreated 'Way of the Cross' that Emmerich saw Mary making, nor the cave in which she saw Mary buried, have been located. These details are of no practical relevance to the shrine, which is well-established and popular, but they are of importance in examining the ways in which cults are established and grow, and in correctly locating the place of pilgrimage within the two competing universalistic monotheisms of the Aegean coast.

118 It is here that anthropology can sometimes help, for recent interest in the subject has been considerable. There are not only studies of women and menstruation in a variety of societies (Krygier 1982; Kondos 1982; Hanson 1982), but also those of menstruating men (Hogbin 1970; G. Lewis 1980).

Bibliography

Abelson, E.S. (1989) 'The Invention of Kleptomania' *Signs* 15 (1): 123–43

Adair, J. (1978) *The Pilgrims' Way* London: Thames & Hudson

Adams, W.H.D. (1878) *Women of Fashion* London: Tinsley Brothers

Aidin, E.N. (1931) 'Recent Changes in the Outlook of Women in the Near and Middle-East' *Journal of the Royal Central Asian Society* 18 (4): 518–30

Aktepe, M. (1958) *Patrona Isyani: 1730* Istanbul: Yildiz

Ali, M.M. (1950) *The Religion of Islam* Lahore: Ahmadiyyah Anjuman Ishaat Islam

Allen, A. (1980) *Travelling Ladies* London: Jupiter

Allen, M. and Mukherjee, S.N. (eds) (1982) *Women in India and Nepal* Canberra: Australian National University Press

Alloula, M. (1987) *The Colonial Harem* Manchester: Manchester University Press

Anderson, M. (1980) *Approaches to the History of the Western Family 1500–1914* London: Macmillan

Araz, N. (1978) *Anadolu Evliyalari* (*The Saints of Anatolia*) Istanbul: Atlas Kitabevi

Arberry, A.J. (1961) *Discourses of Rumi* London: John Murray

Ardener, E. (1972) 'Belief and the Problem of Women' in J.S. La Fontaine (ed) *The Interpretation of Ritual* London: Tavistock

——(1975) 'The "Problem" Revisited' in S. Ardener (ed) *Perceiving Women* London: Malaby Press

Aswad, B. (1967) 'Key and Peripheral Roles of Noble Women in a Middle Eastern Plains Village' *Anthropological Quarterly* 40 (3): 139–52

——(1971) *Property Control and Social Strategies: Settlers on a Middle Eastern Plain* Ann Arbor: Michigan

Bates, Ü. (1978) 'Women as Patrons of Architecture in Turkey' in L. Beck and N. Keddie (eds) *Women in the Muslim World* Cambridge, Mass.: Harvard University Press

Bean, G.E. (1966) *Aegean Turkey. An Archaeological Guide* London: Ernest Benn

Beck, L. and Keddie N. (eds) (1978) *Women in the Muslim World* Cambridge, Mass.: Harvard University Press

Benedict, P. (1974) (a) *Ula. An Anatolian Town* Leiden: E.J. Brill
——(1974) (b) 'The Kabul Günü: Structural Visiting in an Anatolian Provincial Town' *Anthropological Quarterly* 47 (1): 28–47
Berger, J. (1980) *About Looking* London: Writers and Readers
Berkes, N. (1964) *The Development of Secularism in Turkey* Montreal: McGill University Press
Bernal, M. (1987) *Black Athena: The Afroasiatic Roots of Classical Civilization* London: Free Association Books
Bibby, G. (1970) *Looking for Dilmum* Harmondsworth: Penguin
Birge, J.K. (1937) *The Bektashi Order of Dervishes* London: Luzac & Co.
Blanch, L. (1954) *The Wilder Shores of Love* London: John Murray
Bloch, M. (1982) 'Death, Women and Power' in M. Bloch & J. Parry (eds) *Death and the Regeneration of Life* London: Cambridge University Press
Bloch, M. & Parry, J. (eds) (1982) *Death and the Regeneration of Life* London: Cambridge University Press
Blunt, Lady A. (1879) *Beduin Tribes of the Euphrates* London: John Murray
——(1881) *A Pilgrimage to Nejd* London: John Murray
Bourdieu, P. (1966) 'The Sentiment of Honour in Kabyle Society' in J.G. Peristiany (ed) *Honour and Shame: The Values of Mediterranean Society* Chicago: Chicago University Press
——(1977) *Outline of a Theory of Practice* Cambridge: Cambridge University Press
Brandel-Syrier, M. (1960) *The Religious Duties of Islam as Taught and Explained by Abu Bakr Effendi* Leiden: E.J. Brill
Brandes, S. (1981) 'Like Wounded Stags: Male Sexual Ideology in an Andalusian Town' in S.R. Ortner and H. Whitehead (eds) *Sexual Meanings* New York: Cambridge University Press
Braudel, F. (1972) *The Mediterranean and the Mediterranean World in the Age of Philip II* London: Collins
Brown, P. (1971) *The World of Late Antiquity* London: Thames and Hudson
——(1981) *The Cult of the Saints* Chicago: Chicago University Press
——(1988) *The Body and Society* London: Faber and Faber
Bruce, I. (1951) *The Nun of Lebanon. The Love Affair of Lady Hester Stanhope with Michael Bruce* London: Collins
Burton, I. (1876) *The Inner Life of Syria, Palestine, and the Holy Land* (2 vols) London: Henry S. King & Co.
Burton, R.F. (1898) *Personal Narrative of a Pilgrimage to Al-Madinah & Mecca* (2 vols) London: George Bell & Sons
Busbecq, Ogier G. de (1927) *The Turkish Letters of Ogier Ghiselin de Busbecq, Imperial Ambassador at Constantinople, 1554–1562.* Oxford: Clarendon Press
Cadoux, C.J. (1938) *Ancient Smyrna* Oxford: Basil Blackwell
Çelebi, Evliya (Evliya Effendi Chelebi) (1834) *Narrative of Travels in Europe, Asia and Africa in the Seventeenth Century* (2 vols) Translated by J. von Hammer London: Oriental Translation Fund
Chandler, R. (1764) *Travels in Asia Minor* London: British Museum
Chelhod, J. (1973) 'A Contribution to the Problem of the Pre-eminence of the Right, Based upon Arabic Evidence' in R. Needham (ed) *Right and Left: Essays in Dual Classification* Chicago: University of Chicago Press
Christian, W.A. (1972) *Person and God in a Spanish Valley* New York: Seminar Press

Clay, E. (1971) 'Introduction' in R. Chandler *Travels in Asia Minor* London: British Museum

Corbin, H. (1970) *Creative Imagination in the Sufism of Ibn Arabi* London: Routledge, Kegan Paul

Cosar, F.M. (1978) 'Women in Turkish Society' in L. Beck & N. Keddie (eds) *Women in the Muslim World* Cambridge, Mass.: Harvard University Press

Coulson, N.J. (1964) *A History of Islamic Law* Edinburgh: Edinburgh University Press

——(1971) *Succession in the Muslim Family* Cambridge: Cambridge University Press

Coulson, N.J. & Hinchcliffe, D. (1978) 'Women and Law Reform in Contemporary Islam' in L. Beck and N. Keddie (eds) *Women in the Muslim World* Cambridge, Mass: Harvard University Press

Croutier, A.L. (1989) *Harem. The World Behind the Veil* London: Bloomsbury

Daniel, N. (1962) *Islam and the West: The Making of an Image* Edinburgh: Edinbugh University Press

Davis, F. (1968) *Two Centuries of the Ottoman Lady* Unpublished PhD Thesis: Columbia University

Davis, R. (1970) 'English Imports from the Middle East 1580–1780' in M.A. Cook (ed) *Studies in the Economic History of the Middle East* London: Oxford University Press

Dawood, N.J. (1974) *The Koran* Harmondsworth: Penguin

Dekker, R.M. and van de Pol, L.C. (1989) *The Tradition of Female Transvestism in Early Modern Europe* London: Macmillan

Delaney, J.J. & Tobin, J.E. (1962) *Dictionary of Catholic Biography* London: Hale

Delphy, C. (1984) *Close to Home* London: Hutchinson

Dengler, I.C. (1978) 'Turkish Women in the Ottoman Empire: The Classical Age' in L. Beck and N. Keddie (eds) *Women in the Muslim World* Cambridge, Mass.: Harvard University Press

Detienne, M. (1981) 'Between Beasts and Gods' in R.L. Gordon (ed) *Myth, Religion and Society* Cambridge: Cambridge University Press

Deutsch, B.F. (1965) *Our Lady of Ephesus* Milwaukee: Bruce Publishing Company

Dickson, H.R.P. (1949) *The Arab of the Desert* London: Allen & Unwin

Dickson, V. (1971) *Forty Years in Kuwait* London: Allen & Unwin

Djaît, H. (1985) *Europe and Islam* Berkeley: University of California Press

Dobkin, M. (1967) 'Social Ranking in the Women's World of Purdah: A Turkish Example' *Anthropological Quarterly* XL (2): 65–72

Doganbey, H. (1963) *Mecca the Blessed, Medina the Radiant* London: Elek Books

Donaldson, B.A. (1973) *The Wild Rue: A Study of Muhammedan Magic and Folklore in Iran* New York: Arno Press

Doughty, C.M. (1888) *Travels in Arabia Deserta* London: Cambridge University Press

Douglas, M. (1966) *Purity and Danger* Harmondsworth: Penguin Books

Douglas, M. and MacCormack, S. (1978) *The Illustrated Golden Bough* London: Macmillan

Edib, H. (1926) *Memoirs* London: John Murray

Eflaki, S.A. (1976) *Legends of the Sufis* (Transl. J.W. Redhouse) London: Theosophical Publishing House

Ekrem, S. (1942) *Unveiled: The Autobiography of a Turkish Girl* New York: Ives Washburn

——(1947) *Turkey Old and New* New York: Charles Scribners

El Saadawi, N. (1980) *The Hidden Face of Eve* London: Zed Press

Emerson, M.E. (1925) 'The Outlook For the Women of Turkey Today' *Muslim World* 15: 269–73

Emin, A. (Yalman) (1930) *Turkey in the World War* New Haven: Yale University Press

Emmerich, A.C. (1954) *The Life of the Blessed Virgin Mary* London: Burns & Oates

Encyclopedia of Islam (2nd edition) (1960) Leiden: E.J. Brill

Enloe, C. (1989) *Bananas, Beaches and Bases* London: Pandora

Fallers, L.A. & Fallers, M. (1976) 'Sex Roles in Edremit' in J.G. Peristiany (ed) *Mediterranean Family Structures* London: Cambridge University Press

Faroqhi, S. (1984) *Towns and Townsmen of Ottoman Anatolia* Cambridge: Cambridge University Press

Fellows, C. (1852) *Travels and Researches in Asia Minor* London: John Murray

Foss, Clive (1979) *Ephesus after Antiquity: A Late Antique, Byzantine and Turkish City* Cambridge: Cambridge University Press

Foucault, M. (1978) *The History of Sexuality* Harmondsworth: Penguin Books

——(1986) *The Use of Pleasure* New York: Vintage Books

——(1988) *The Care of the Self* Harmondsworth: Penguin Books

Fountaine, M. (1980) *Love Among the Butterflies* London: Collins

Frank, K. (1986) *A Voyager Out* London: Corgi

Garnett, L.M.J. (1891) *The Women of Turkey and their Folk-Lore* London: David Nutt

——(1904) *The Turkish People* London: Methuen

——(1912) *Mysticism and Magic in Turkey* London: Sir Isaac Pitman & Sons

Garnett, L.M.J. and Stuart-Glennie, J.S.S. (1891) *The Women of Turkey and Their Folk-Lore* (2 vols) London: David Nutt

Geary, G. (1878) *Through Asiatic Turkey* London: Sampson Low, Marston etc.

Gerber, H. (1976) 'Guilds in Seventeenth Century Anatolian Bursa' *Asian and African Affairs* 11 (1): 59–86

——(1980) 'Social and Economic Position of Women in an Ottoman City, Bursa, 1600–1700' *International Journal of Middle East Studies* 12: 231–44

Goitein, S.D. (1979) 'The Sexual Mores of the Common People' in A.L. al-Sayyid-Marsot (ed) *Society and the Sexes in Medieval Islam* Malibu: Undena

Gökalp, A. (1978) 'Hizr, Ilyas, Hidrellez: Les Maitres des Temps, le Temps des Hommes' in R. Dor & M. Nicolas (eds) *Quand le Crible Etait Dans la Paille . . .* Paris: Maisonneuve & Larose

Good, M-J. Del Vecchio (1978) 'A Comparative Perspective on Women in Provincial Iran and Turkey' in L. Beck & N. Keddie (eds) *Women in the Muslim World* Cambridge, Mass.: Harvard University Press

Gould, A.G. (1976) 'Lords or Bandits? The Derebeys of Cilicia' *International Journal of Middle East Studies* 7: 485–506

Graham-Brown, S. (1988) *Images of Women. The Portrayal of Women in Photography of the Middle East 1860–1950* London: Quartet Books

Granqvist, H. (1931) *Marriage Conditions in a Palestinian Village* Helsinki: Societas Humanarum Litterarum

190   *A World of Difference*

——(1947) *Birth and Childhood among the Arabs* Helsingfors: Societas Humanarum Litterarum

——(1965) *Muslim Death and Burial: Arab Customs and Traditions in a Village in Jordan* Helsinki: Societas Humanarum Litterarum

Graves, P.G. (1976) *Lawrence of Arabia and His World* London: Thames & Hudson

Guide de Pélerin à Panaghia Capouli avec Plan de la Maison (1896) Izmir

Hamilton, A. (1975) 'Aboriginal Women: The Means of Production' in J. Mercer (ed) *The Other Half* Melbourne: Penguin Books

Hanson, F.A. (1982) 'Female Pollution in Polynesia' *Journal of the Polynesian Society* XCI (3): 335–381

Hart, U.K. (1987) *Two Ladies of Colonial Algeria* Athens, Ohio: Ohio University Press

Hasluck, F.W. (1918–19) 'The Rise of Modern Smyrna' *British School at Athens Annual* 23: 139–47

——(1929) *Christianity and Islam Under the Sultans* (2 vols) Oxford: Clarendon Press

Hawking, S. (1988) *A Brief History of Time* London: Bantam Books

Haynes, S. (1974) *Land of the Chimaera. An Archaeological Excursion in the South-West of Turkey* London: Chatto & Windus

Herodotus (1954) *The Histories* Harmondsworth: Penguin

Hertz, R. (1960) *Death and the Right Hand* London: Cohen & West

Herzfeld, M. (1985) *The Poetics of Manhood: Contest and Identity in a Cretan Mountain Village* Princeton: Princeton University Press

Hirschon, R. (1978) 'Open Body/Closed Space: the Transformation of Female Sexuality' in S. Ardener (ed) *Defining Females* London: Croom Helm

Hodgson, M.G.S. (1974) *The Venture of Islam* Chicago: University of Chicago Press

Hogarth, D.G. (1922) *The Penetration of Arabia* London: Clarendon Press

——(1925) *The Wandering Scholar* London: Oxford University Press

Hogbin, I. (1970) *The Island of Menstruating Men. Religion in Wogeo, New Guinea* Scranton: Chandler Publishing Company

Houlbrooke, R.A. (1984) *The English Family 1450–1700* London: Longman

Hudson, D. (1974) *Munby: Man of Two Worlds. The Life and Diaries of Arthur J. Munby 1828–1910* London: Abacus

Hurgronje, C. Snouck (1931) *Mekka* London: Luzac & Co

Huri, S. (1959) 'Yunus Emre: In Memoriam' *Muslim World* XLIX: 111–23

Inalcik, H. (1970) [a] 'The Rise of the Ottoman Empire' in Holt, P.M. *et al.* (eds) *The Cambridge History of Islam* Cambridge: Cambridge University Press

——(1970) [b] 'The Heyday and Decline of the Ottoman Empire' in P.M. Holt, *et al.* (eds) *The Cambridge History of Islam* Cambridge: Cambridge University Press

——(1970) [c] 'The Ottoman Economic Mind and Aspects of the Ottoman Economy' in M.A. Cook (ed) *Studies in the Economic History of the Middle East* London: Oxford University Press

——(1973) *The Ottoman Empire* London: Weidenfeld & Nicolson

Isik, H.H. (1975–81) *Endless Bliss* Istanbul: Waqf Ikhlas Publications (5 vols)

Issawi, C. (ed) (1966) *The Economic History of the Middle East 1800–1914* Chicago: Chicago University Press

Izmir Il Yilligi (1965) Izmir: Municipality of Izmir

Jarvie, I.C. (1984) *Rationality and Relativism* London: Routledge & Kegan Paul

Jeffery, P. (1979) *Frogs in a Well* London: Zed Press

Jenkins, H.D. (n.d.) *Behind Turkish Lattices* London & Glasgow: Collins

Jennings, R.C. (1975) 'Women in Early 17th Century Ottoman Judicial Records—the Sharia Court of Anatolian Kayseri' *Journal of the Economic and Social History of the Orient* 18 (1): 53–114

——(1978) 'Zimmis (non-Muslims) in Early 17th Century Ottoman Judicial Records; the Sharia Court of Anatolian Kayseri' *Journal of the Economic and Social History of the Orient* 21 (3): 225–93

Jullian, P. (1977) *The Orientalists. European Painters of Eastern Scenes* Oxford: Phaidon

Kabbani, R. (1986) *Europe's Myths of Orient* Bloomington: Indiana University Press

Kalças, E. (1977) *Breakfast in Asia and Lunch in Europe* Bornova, Turkey: Bilgehan Matbaasi

Kamal, A. (1964) *The Sacred Journey* New York: Duell, Sloan & Pierce

Kandiyoti, D. (1977) 'Sex Roles and Social Change: A Comparative Appraisal of Turkey's Women' *Signs* 3 (1): 57–73

Keddie, N. and Beck, L. (1978) 'Introduction' in L. Beck and N. Keddie (eds) *Women in the Muslim World* Cambridge, Mass.: Harvard University Press

Kingsley, M. (1897) *Travels in West Africa, Congo Français, Corsico and Cameroons* London: John Murray

——(1899) *West African Studies* London: John Murray

Kiray, M. (1975) 'Izmir: The City That Could Not Become Organized' in B. Güvenç (ed) *Social Change in Izmir* Ankara: Social Science Association of Turkey

——(1976) 'The New Role of Mothers: Changing Intra-familial Relationships in a Small Town in Turkey' in J.G. Peristiany (ed) *Mediterranean Family Structures* Cambridge: Cambridge University Press

Kobak, A. (1988) *Isabelle. The Life of Isabelle Eberhardt* London: Chatto & Windus

Kondos, V. (1982) 'The Triple Goddess and the Processual Approach to the World: the Parbatya Case' in M. Allen & S.N. Mukherjee (eds) *Women in India and Nepal* Canberra: ANU Press

Kongar, E. (1976) 'A Survey of Familial Change in Two Turkish *Gecekondu* Areas' in J.G. Peristiany (ed) *Mediterranean Family Structures* Cambridge: Cambridge University Press

Kuhn, A. (1982) *Women's Pictures. Feminism and Cinema* London: Routledge, Kegan Paul

Krygier, J. (1982) 'Caste and Female Pollution' in M. Allen & S.N. Mukherjee (eds) *Women in India and Nepal* Canberra: ANU Press

Lane, E.W. (1836) *The Manners and Customs of the Modern Egyptians* London: J.M. Dent

Lévi-Strauss, C. (1987) *Anthropology and Ritual Transvestism* Oxford: Basil Blackwell

Levy, R. (1971) *The Social Structure of Islam* Cambridge: Cambridge University Press

Lewis, G. (1980) *Day of Shining Red. An Essay on Understanding Ritual* Cambridge: Cambridge University Press

Llewellyn, B. & Newton, C. (1985) *The People and Places of Constantinople. Watercolours of Amadeo, Count Preziosi 1816–1882* London: Victoria & Albert Museum

Lott, E. (1867) *Harem Life in Egypt and Constantinople* London: Richard Bentley

MacCallum, J. (transl) (1943) *The Mevlidi Serif* London: John Murray

Machin, B. (1982) 'St George and the Virgin' Unpublished paper

Malek, A.A. (1963) 'Orientalism in Crisis' *Diogenes* 44: 107–8

Mantran, R. (1970) 'L'Empire Ottoman et le Commerce Asiatique aux 16ᵉ et 17ᵉ Siècles' in D.S. Richards (ed) *Islam and the Trade of Asia* Oxford: Cassirer

——(1977) 'The Transformation of Trade in the Ottoman Empire in the Eighteenth Century' in T. Naff and R. Owen (eds) *Studies in Eighteenth Century Islamic History* Carbondale: Southern Illinois University Press

Marcus, A. (1985) 'Men, Women and Property' *Journal of the Economic and Social History of the Orient* 36 (2): 137–63

Marcus, J. (1983) *Women and Religion in the Turkish City of Izmir.* PhD Thesis: Macquarie University, Sydney

Mardin, S. (1973) 'Centre–Periphery Relations: A Key to Turkish Politics' *Daedalus* (Winter) 169–90

——(1974) 'Super Westernization in Urban Life in the Ottoman Empire in the Last Quarter of the Nineteenth Century' in P. Benedict (ed) *Turkey: Geographic and Social Perspectives* Leiden: E.J. Brill

Massingham, H. & Massingham, P. (1962) *The Englishman Abroad* London: Phoenix House

Meeker, M.E. (1971) 'The Black Sea Turks: Some Aspects of Their Ethnic and Cultural Background' *International Journal of Middle East Studies* 2 (4): 318–45

——(1976) 'Meaning and Society in the Near East: Examples from the Black Sea Turks and the Levantine Arabs' *International Journal of Middle East Studies* 7: 243–70 (part 1) & 383–422 (part 2)

Megas, G.A. (1963) *Greek Calendar Customs* Athens: Rhodis

Melek, Hanum (1842) *Thirty Years in the Harem* New York: Harper & Bros.

Melville, L. (n.d.) *Lady Mary Wortley Montagu: Her Life and Letters (1689–1762)* London: Hutchinson

Merlin, M.D. (1984) *On the Trail of the Ancient Opium Poppy* London: Associated University Presses

Mernissi, F. (1975) *Beyond the Veil* New York: John Wiley & Sons

——(1977) 'Women, Saints and Sanctuaries' *Signs* 3 (1): 101–12

Moore, H. (1988) *Feminism and Anthropology* Cambridge: Polity Press

Morier, J. (1895) *The Adventures of Hajji Baba of Ispahan* London: Methuen

Morris, M. (1988) *The Pirate's Fiancée* London: Verso

Morton, H.V. (1936) *In the Steps of St Paul* London: Rich & Cowan

Mulvey, L. (1989) *Visual and Other Pleasures* London: Macmillan

Naff, T. and Owen, R. (eds) (1977) *Studies in Eighteenth Century Islamic History* Carbondale: Southern Illinois University Press

Needham, R. (1973) *Right and Left: Essays in Dual Symbolic Classification* Chicago: University of Chicago Press

——(1979) *Symbolic Classification* Santa Monica: Goodyear Publishing

Olson, R.W. (1974) 'The Esnaf and the Patrona Halil Rebellion of 1730: A

Realignment in Ottoman Politics?' *Journal of the Economic and Social History of the Orient* 17–23

Owen, R. (1977) 'Introduction' in T. Naff and R. Owen (eds) *Studies in Eighteenth Century Islamic History* Carbondale: Southern Illinois University Press

Pagels, E. (1979) *The Gnostic Gospels* New York: Random House

Patlagean, E. (1987) 'Byzantium in the Tenth and Eleventh Centuries' in P. Veyne (ed) *A History of Private Life. From Pagan Rome to Byzantium* Cambridge, Mass.: Harvard University Press

Peristiany, J.G. (ed) (1965) *Honor and Shame: The Values of Mediterranean Society* London: Weidenfeld and Nicolson

Pick, C. (1988) *Embassy to Constantinople. The Travels of Lady Mary Wortley Montagu* London: Century

Pococke, R. (1772) *Voyages* (6 vols) Paris: J.P. Costard

Pourjavady, N. and Wilson, P.L. (1978) *Kings of Love* Teheran: Imperial Iranian Academy of Philosophy

Pratt, M.L. (1986) 'Fieldwork in Common Places' in J. Clifford & G.E. Marcus (eds) *Writing Culture* Berkeley: University of California Press

Pribham, E.D. (1988) *Female Spectators. Looking at Film and Television* London: Verso

Price, A.W. (1985) *The Ladies of Castlebrae* London: Headline

Quinn, N. (1977) 'Anthropological Studies on Women's Status' *Annual Reviews in Anthropology* 6: 181–225

Rabinow, P. (1977) *Reflections on Fieldwork in Morocco* Berkeley & Los Angeles: University of California Press

Ralli, A. (1909) *Christians at Mecca* London: William Heinemann

Ramsay, W.M. (1895/97) *The Cities and Bishoprics of Phrygia* Oxford: Clarendon Press

Ramsay, Mrs. W.M. (1897) *Impressions of Turkey* London: Hodder & Stoughton

Redhouse Yeni Türkre-Ingilizcc Sözluk (1968) Istanbul: Redhouse Yayinevi

Repp, R. (1977) 'The Altered Nature and Role of the Ulema' in T. Naff and R. Owen (eds) *Studies in Eighteenth Century Islamic History* Carbondale: Southern Illinois University Press

Reuther, R.R. (1979) *Mary, the Feminine Face of the Church* Guildford: SCM Press

Rich, A. (1977) *Of Woman Born: Motherhood as Experience and Institution* London

Rich, B.R. (1986) 'Feminism and Sexuality in the 1980s' *Feminist Studies* 12 (3): 525–61

Rodinson, M. (1974) 'The Western Image and Western Studies of Islam' in J. Schacht & C.E. Bosworth (eds) *The Legacy of Islam* Oxford: Clarendon Press

Rogers, S.C. (1978) 'Woman's Place: A Critical Review of Anthropological Theory' *Comparative Studies in Society and History* 20 (1): 123–62

Rozario, S. (1991) *Purity and Communal Boundaries: Women and Social Change in a Bangladeshi Region* Sydney: Allen and Unwin

Runciman, S. (1954) *A History of the Crusades* London: Penguin Books

——(1975) *Byzantine Civilization* London: Methuen

Said, E.W. (1978) *Orientalism* London: Routledge & Kegan Paul

——(1981) *Covering Islam* London: Routledge & Kegan Paul

——(1983) *The World, the Text and the Critic* London: Faber & Faber

——(1985) 'Orientalism Reconsidered' *Race and Class* 27 (2): 1–16

Sale, G. (n.d.) *The Koran* London: Frederick Warne & Co.

Schimmel, A-M. (1975) *Mystical Dimensions of Islam* Chapel Hill: University of North Carolina Press

Schliemann, H. (1972 [1884]) *Troja: Results of the Latest Researches and Discoveries on the Site of Homer's Troy* Chicheley: Paul P.B. Minet

Schneider, J. and Schneider, P. (1976) *Culture and Political Economy in Western Sicily* New York: Academic Press

Searight, S. (1969) *The British in the Middle East* London: Weidenfeld and Nicolson

Segalen, M. (1983) *Love and Power in the Peasant Family* Oxford: Basil Blackwell

Senior (n.d.) *Ephesus or Jerusalem? The Tomb of the Virgin Mary* Izmir

Senior, N.W. (1859) *Journal Kept in Turkey and Greece in the Autumn of 1857 and the Beginning of 1858* London: Longman & Co.

Shaw, S.J. and Shaw, E.K. (1976) *History of the Ottoman Empire and Modern Turkey* (2 vols) Cambridge: Cambridge University Press

Shor, N. (1987) *Reading in Detail. Aesthetics and the Feminine* London: Methuen

Shorter Encyclopedia of Islam (1964) Leiden: E.J. Brill

Siegel, J.T. (1969) *The Rope of God* Berkeley: University of California Press

Sim, K. (1969) *Desert Traveller. The Life of Jean Louis Burckhardt* London: Victor Gollancz

Spivak, G.C. (1985) 'Three Women's Texts and a Critique of Imperialism' *Critical Inquiry* 12 (1): 17–34

Stark, F. (1954) *Ionia. A Quest* London: John Murray

Starr, J. (1978) *Dispute and Settlement in Rural Turkey: An Ethnography of Law* Leiden: E.J. Brill

Starr, J. & Pool, J. (1974) 'The Impact of a Legal Revolution in Rural Turkey' *Law and Society Review* 8 (4): 533–60

Steensgaard, N. (1973) *The Asian Trade Revolution of the Seventeenth Century* Chicago: University of Chicago Press

Steiner, F. (1956) *Taboo* London: Penguin Books

Stirling, P. (1965) *Turkish Village* New York: John Wiley & Sons

Stoneman, R. (1987) *Land of Lost Gods. The Search for Classical Greece* London: Hutchinson

Strabo (1928) *The Geography of Strabo* London

Strathern, M. (1985) 'Dislodging a World-View: Challenge and Counter-Challenge in the Relationship between Feminism and Anthropology' *Australian Feminist Studies* 1: 1–26

Sümer, F. *et al.* (eds) (1972) *The Book of Dede Korkut* Austin: University of Texas Press

Sutton, C., S. Makiesky, D. Dwyer & L. Klein (1975) 'Women, Knowledge and Power' in: R. Rohrlick-Leavitt (ed) *Women Cross-culturally: Change and Challenge* The Hague: Mouton

Szyliowicz, I. (1988) *Pierre Loti and the Oriental Woman* London: Macmillan

Szyliowicz, J.S. (1966) *Political Change in Rural Turkey. Erdemli* The Hague: Mouton & Co.

Tabachnick, S. (1981) *Charles Doughty* Boston: Twayne

Tabachnick, S. and Matheson, C. (1988) *Images of Lawrence* London: Jonathan Cape

Tapper, N. (1983) 'Gender and Religion in a Turkish Town: A Comparison of Two Types of Formal Women's Gatherings' in P. Holden (ed) *Women's Religious Experience* London: Croom Helm
——(1978) 'The Women's Subsociety among the Shahsevan Nomads of Iran' in L.B. & N. Keddie (eds) *Women in the Muslim World* Cambridge, Mass.: Harvard University Press
Taskiran, T. (1976) *Women in Turkey* Istanbul: Redhouse
Tavasli, Hafiz Yusuf (1982) *Kolay Namaz Hocasi* Istanbul
Thierry, E.R. (1979) *Le Mystère de la Maison de la Viège* Izmir
Thomas, B. (1937) *The Arabs* London: Thornton Butterworth
——(1938) *Arabia Felix: Across the Empty Quarter of Arabia* London: Jonathan Cape
Tidrick, K. (1981) *Heart-beguiling Araby* Cambridge: Cambridge University Press
Tiffany, S.W. (1978) 'Models and the Social Anthropology of Women: A Preliminary Assessment' *Man* (n.s.) 53: 34–51
Tilly, L.A. and Scott, J.W. (1978) *Women, Work and Family* New York: Holt, Reinhardt and Winston
Traill, D.A. (1984) 'Schliemann's Discovery of Priam's Treasure: A Re-examination of the Evidence' *Journal of Hellenic Studies* 104: 96–115
Trinh, Minh-ha T. (1989) *Woman, Native, Other* Bloomington: Indiana University Press
Tsigakou, F.M. (1981) *The Rediscovery of Greece* London: Murray
Tugay, E.F. (1963) *Three Centuries* London: Oxford University Press
Turner, B.S. (1978) *Marx and the End of Orientalism* London: George Allen & Unwin
Turner, V.W. (1969) *The Ritual Process* Harmondsworth: Penguin Books
Turner, V.W, & Turner, E. (1978) *Image and Pilgrimage in Christian Culture* New York: Columbia University Press
Ülker, N. (1974) *The Rise of Izmir 1688–1740* PhD Diss: University of Michigan
Urry, J. (1985) 'Social Relations, Space and Time' in D. Gregory and J. Urry (eds) (1985) *Social Relations and Spatial Structures* London: Macmillan.
Vambéry, A. (1865) *Travels in Central Asia* London: John Murray
Veinstein, G. (1976) '"Ayan" de la Région d'Izmir et Commerce du Levant (deuxième moitié du XVIIIᵉ siècle)' *Etudes Balkaniques* 3: 71–83
Vernant, J-P. (1982) *The Origins of Greek Thought* London: Methuen
Verrier, M. (1979) *The Orientalists* London: Academy Editions
Vryonis, S. (1971) *The Decline of Medieval Hellenism in Asia Minor* Berkeley: University of California Press
Wallerstein, I. (1974) *The Modern World-system: Capitalist Agriculture and the Origins of the European World-economy in the Sixteenth Century* New York: Academic Press
——(1984) *The Politics of the World-economy* Cambridge: Cambridge University Press
Warner, M. (1978) *Alone of All Her Sex. The Myth and the Cult of the Virgin Mary* London: Quartet
Wazan, Emily de (1911) *My Life Story* London: Edward Arnold
Westermarck, E. (1933) *Pagan Survivals in Muhammedan Civilizations* London: Macmillan
Weulersse, J. (1946) *Paysan de Syrie et du Proche-Orient* Paris: Gallimard

Wheelwright, J. (1989) *Amazons and Military Maids. Women Who Dressed as Men in the Pursuit of Life, Love and Happiness* London: Pandora

Wikan, U. (1980) *Life among the Poor in Cairo* London: Tavistock

Williams, R. (1989) *The Politics of Modernism. Against the New Conformists* London: Verso

Winstone, H.V.F. (1978) *Gertrude Bell* London: Jonathan Cape

Wood, M. (1985) *In Search of the Trojan War* London: Duckworth

Zilfi, M.C. (1985) 'Elite Circulation in the Ottoman Empire: Great Mollas of the Eighteenth Century' *Journal of the Economic and Social History of the Orient* 36 (3): 318–64

Zwemmer, S.M. (1939) *Studies in Popular Islam* London: Sheldon Press

Index

Purity and Communal Boundaries
Women and social change in a Bangladeshi village
Santi Rozario

Purity and Communal Boundaries explores the rich complexities of a central Bangladeshi village, populated by Muslims, Hindus and Christians.

Through a carefully constructed theoretical framework Santi Rozario demonstrates the ways in which class and communal domination reinforce gender inequality. The position of women is analysed in terms of linkages between religious values, sexuality, economics and politics. Rozario also examines the divergence between the demands of the economy and the system of values in Bengali society.

By linking gender, communal and class domination, *Purity and Communal Boundaries* raises questions regarding the complex position of women in Bangladesh as well as in other cultures. It also offers a valuable contribution to the sociology and ethnography of South Asian village life, and the sociology of religion.

As a Bangladeshi women, Santi Rozario is in a unique position to explore this subject. She has overcome the constraints on mobility that would normally bar local women from conducting the kind of extensive anthropological fieldwork represented here. The result is an unusual achievement—the scholarly perspective of a Bangladeshi woman on her own society.

Santi Rozario is a lecturer in sociology at the University of Newcastle. Her teaching and research interests include women's studies, the sociology of religion, and community and development studies.